Clematis for Small Spaces

Clematis for Small Spaces

Raymond J. Evison

Timber Press

Published in 2007 by
Timber Press, Inc.
The Haseltine Building
133 S.W. Second Avenue, Suite 450
Portland, Oregon 97204-3527, USA
www.timberpress.com
For contact information regarding editorial,
marketing, sales, and distribution in the United
Kingdom, see www.timberpress.co.uk.

Designed by Dick Malt
Printed in China

Library of Congress Cataloging-in-Publication Data
Evison, Raymond J.
  Clematis for small spaces / Raymond J. Evison.
      p. cm.
  Includes bibliographical references and index.
  ISBN-13: 978-0-88192-851-8 (alk. paper)
  1. Clematis. I. Title.
  SB413.C6E948 2007
  635.9'3334--dc22
                                        2007019026

A catalogue record for this book is also available from
the British Library.

Contents

Acknowledgements

Many thanks are due to Diana Rowland for her tremendous work in the preparation of this text; without her help the book would still remain unwritten. I also wish to thank Tim Henderson for his great help in reviewing the original text and for his advice. I am grateful to Charis Ward and to the Royal Horticultural Society for allowing me to use their gardens at Abbey Dore Court, Herefordshire, and Wisley, Surrey, respectively, for photographic purposes. Finally, thanks are due to Erica Gordon-Mallin of Timber Press for her editorial work.

How to Use This Book

The aim of the book is to provide practical advice, guiding you through 'easy gardening' with clematis and helping you to select the most rewarding species or cultivars to suit your individual needs.

There are several different ways to approach the process of choosing a clematis. You may have a particular niche in which you would like to plant a clematis—for instance, the front of a herbaceous border, a hanging basket or a balcony. If this is the case, simply turn to the appropriate chapter to read about the best clematis for your chosen garden location.

On the other hand, you may already have spotted a species or cultivar that appeals to you. Whether you have seen it in another garden, in the media or even by searching the internet, you will need to know where it can be planted and how it should be cared for. You can use this book to gather practical information about a clematis that has caught your eye.

Personally, I approach the process of choosing a clematis rather differently: I select them based on their flowering season. First I identify a host plant or host support that would benefit from the presence of a clematis growing with it, or on it, and in doing so establish the period in which I would like the clematis to bloom.

With this in mind, I have divided the plant descriptions into three chapters according to their flowering season. Together, Chapters 10 through 12 form a directory of the best-performing clematis for today's gardens—so if you are seeking a clematis for a certain flowering period, you can turn to the appropriate directory chapter to browse a range of high-performance plants until you discover the clematis that is right for you.

The Three Flowering Seasons and Their Characteristics

Clematis are generally thought of as belonging to three different Pruning Groups, and these correspond to the periods in which they flower. The way in which clematis produce their flowers, the way they grow, how they can be grown, and with which types of host plant, all relate to their pruning requirements. Moreover, early-season-flowering clematis all flower on old wood, while midseason-flowering clematis flower on both old and new wood and late-season-flowering clematis flower on new wood only.

Early-Season-Flowering Clematis
- flowering period early winter to mid spring
- flowers on old wood
- Pruning Group One

Midseason-Flowering Clematis
- flowering period late spring to early summer
- flowers on old and new wood
- Pruning Group Two

Late-Season-Flowering clematis
- flowering period midsummer to late autumn
- flowers on new wood
- Pruning Group Three

Seasons

Throughout the book the time of year is given as a season to make the reference applicable to readers all over the world. In the northern hemisphere the seasons may be translated into months as follows:

Early Season
Early winter	December
Midwinter	January
Late winter	February
Early spring	March
Mid spring	April, May

Late Season
Midsummer	July
Late summer	August
Early autumn	September
Mid autumn	October
Late autumn	November

Midseason
Late spring	May
Early summer	June

Awards

Many of the clematis plants described in this book have gained awards. The Award of Garden Merit, denoted by the symbol ♛, is given by the Royal Horticultural Society to recognize plants of outstanding excellence for garden use, whether grown in the open or under glass. It is of practical value to gardeners in that it highlights exceptional plants among the tens of thousands currently offered in the international horticultural trade. The British Clematis Society awards the Certificate of Merit to clematis cultivars that have performed outstandingly on the Society's Trial Grounds. Both awards are noted in the clematis' individual directory entries where appropriate.

Chapter 1

Introduction

Clematis 'Guernsey Cream', which produces an exceptional number of flowers in spring and early summer, was one of the first cultivars to be raised in the author's nursery.

Clematis, for me, have become a way of life; perhaps they *are* my life! Over the years clematis have given me the opportunity to travel worldwide, to meet many people and to see the genus in cultivation as well as—more thrillingly—in the wild. I cannot imagine anything more satisfying than seeing a clematis that I have developed, bred or introduced growing successfully in someone's garden, wherever that may be.

For me, the desire to acquire every newly introduced cultivated variety (cultivar) of clematis may have waned recently, perhaps because there have been so many new ones raised and named in the past few years. However, I am increasingly passionate about exploring the genus through breeding, collecting and sharing information. The thrill that I experience upon discovering a clematis species (especially one that is new to me), in the wild or in someone's collection, is as strong as ever and at present I am starting to rebuild my collection of clematis species, from 'wild collected' sources wherever possible. I am eager to plan my next expedition to China and the Far East to photograph the different species in their natural habitats and to learn more about this diverse genus that continues to astonish and inspire me.

I am often asked what ignited my interest in clematis and why, after almost half a century of involvement in the clematis world, I am still so intrigued by this genus. By the age of fifteen I was working with my father and John Treasure at Burford House Gardens in Shropshire, England. At sixteen, I met the great plantsman Percy Picton—and then my clematis bug really became a reality. Percy's stories of the days when he worked with Ernest Markham for William Robinson at Gravetye Manor, and their contact with the great clematis family of Jackmans of Woking in the early 1900s, made me feel connected to a legacy of clematis enthusiasts, cementing my eagerness to learn as much as I could about the genus. I was also lucky enough to meet the horticulturalist Christopher Lloyd, and at twenty-four I helped him with his first book on *Clematis*.

Clematis alpina flowers in early spring and goes on to produce masses of seedheads.

Soon I developed a passion for breeding my own clematis, and by the 1960s and 1970s I was competing with Walter Pennell and Jim Fisk at Flower Shows such as Chelsea. While a junior partner at Treasures of Tenbury, we won a coveted Royal Horticultural Society (RHS) Chelsea Gold Medal for the quality of the clematis we grew—an unforgettable achievement that reinforced my passion and commitment. I have continued to seek out new cultivars and forms of clematis ever since.

Clematis 'Ernest Markham', clambering over the foliage of *C. montana* 'Elizabeth'.

My Criteria

Recently the number of species and cultivars of clematis available to gardeners has increased immeasurably, mainly due to the success of the International Clematis Society, of which I was a founding member in 1984, and to all the other Clematis Societies formed around the world in more recent years. Members of these Societies can now exchange information about the genus as well as plant material, and amateur breeders around the world are encouraged to create some exciting new plants. Breeding achievements in Japan,

Poland, Latvia and Estonia have been most enlightening, as have those in the British Isles and the United States.

This explosion of new clematis has raised the issue of how to choose the best value-for-money plants when gardening with clematis in small spaces. Questions abound: are the clematis long-flowering enough? Are they free from disease problems? Are they easy to grow? I am afraid that I am rather critical of many that have recently been raised and introduced to gardens, because in my view they do not meet what I consider to be the real requirements for a good plant. However, I know that the passage of time will thin these out and only the best ones will become established as desirable garden plants. After all, the flurry of breeding activity in the mid to late nineteenth century gave the gardeners of that time five hundred cultivars to choose from by the turn of the century, of which only about fifty are still available and grown today.

In the following pages, I present a selection of clematis that I believe offer *real* garden value, when grown in garden locations where space is at a premium. I have chosen species and cultivars that are disease-resistant, with a good habit, attractive foliage, interesting flowers and a long flowering period. I am most grateful to Ruth Gooch of Thorncroft Clematis Nursery, Norfolk, England, and to Maurice Horn of Joy Creek Nurseries near Portland, Oregon, USA, who have given me great help in the selection of clematis for this book. We have set some fairly stiff criteria!

I know that in certain areas, zones or countries, particular clematis mentioned in this book may not perform as well as some of those left out of the selection. There will also be those of which we, jointly, have no first-hand experience and which therefore I have not included. But overall, the plants selected for inclusion are certainly the best for the job of growing in compact niches—containers, borders, terraces and a myriad of other small spaces.

A New Approach to Clematis

For gardeners these days, particularly those new to gardening, it seems the trend is to have smaller, more compact gardens. People have less time for gardening due to the number of other leisure activities in which they are involved or their opportunities to travel, so 'easy gardening' is the future for all but the specialist collector and real plant enthusiast. Yet I think that all of us—even those who covet 'easy gardening'—are on the lookout for something new and different.

I travel around the world a great deal, and this book was started on an airplane flying to the United States and written in New York, San Francisco and

Guernsey. It is when I talk to people on these travels that I grow to understand the trepidation with which many approach clematis. Many people who are new to gardening perceive these plants as being difficult to grow, perhaps because the pruning schemes can be confusing. Although gardeners' general lack of confidence about cultivating clematis has been apparent for a long time, the situation has worsened rapidly in recent years.

It is unfortunate that newcomers are so often put off growing clematis. I have learned that breeders needed to pay attention—and respond—to the needs and concerns of modern-day gardeners. This point was brought home to me most emphatically during the early 1990s, when I met with my joint venture partners, Mogens N. Olesen and his wife, Perenille, owners of the extremely successful Danish rose breeding company, Poulsen Roser A/S. I noticed the trends that they were experiencing with roses, and what they were aiming for in the future. I learned that people around the world were gardening in smaller spaces than in the past, as they had less time for gardening in the traditional way. Smaller gardens require small, lower-growing plants (especially in the case of clematis), but the future would require plants that were also easy to grow, with more flowers and—another new requirement—longer flowering periods.

From our first breeding programme in 1995, the aim was to create smaller-growing, longer-flowering clematis plants—not with exceptionally large flowers, but with more medium-sized flowers which were in balance, size-wise, with the new shorter-growing plants. For me it was just a matter of using my many years of experience in growing and breeding clematis and referring to my large collection of old cultivars. Many of those used as mother plants in the first years had been bred in the later part of the nineteenth century. Luck was with us: we had clearly picked the correct parent plants, and we created the new 'breed' of shorter-growing clematis from the very first year's work in 1995. However, much remains to be done.

I believe that one need not have a large garden to experience the joys of clematis. As this book shows, clematis can work well in a range of compact spots found in small town, suburban and even city gardens. The use of the new shorter-growing clematis for limited spaces is discussed in detail, and I explain how they can complement other plants.

Some of the older clematis are still extremely useful for growing up into trees or hedges, which is an excellent use of limited space. The modern clematis can be used like this, but they also lend themselves to a much wider range of planting opportunities—helping to create a living room-like space full of flower and colour outside the house, thus making the garden feel like an extension of the home. In the following pages I focus on modern gardening

Free-flowering and compact, *Clematis* PICARDY 'Evipo024' is from the new 'breed' of shorter-growing clematis.

with high-performance clematis, including species along with old and new cultivars, and I discuss the easiest ways in which to care for them.

   This book is very different from my previous books on clematis. It aims to enthuse all gardeners, to encourage keen enthusiasts and to introduce newcomers to growing clematis—all in simple, hands-on terms. I hope that you will plant the clematis I recommend in these pages, and that you find them to be great value for money, easy to grow, and enormously satisfying.

Chapter 2

History and Development of Clematis

Clematis cirrhosa var. *purpurascens* 'Freckles', developed from the species first introduced in the 16th century.

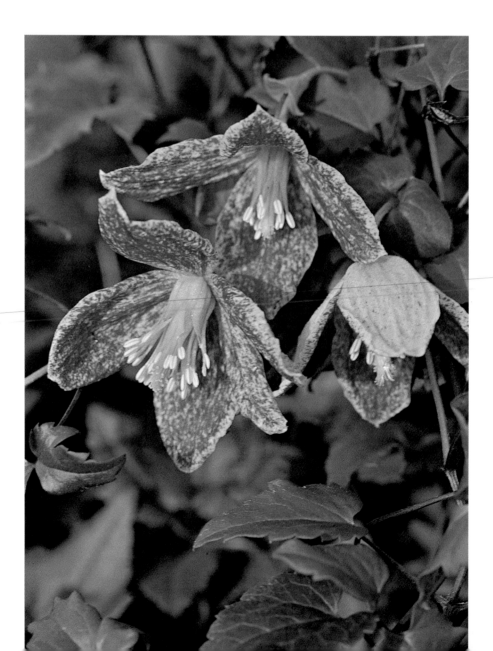

The name 'clematis' is derived from the Greek *klema* which means 'vine branch' or 'vine-like'. The word is pronounced in many ways around the world today. The pronunciation I prefer is "CLEM-a-tis" with emphasis on the first syllable and the *a* pronounced as in "around". However, many others—particularly in North America—pronounce it as "clem-A-tis", with emphasis on the second syllable and the *a* sounded as in "mat", and this is also acceptable.

Some three hundred *Clematis* species are known to exist today, and it is likely that a number of additional species remain to be discovered (particularly in China). The total number of clematis species is also subject to change when taxonomists unite several species together under one name, which may later be split again.

Breeding Clematis Through the Centuries

Early records tell us that some of the European clematis species started finding their way into Britain as early as the sixteenth century. As people travelled further afield, plants were collected and brought back to Europe—but it was not until the mid nineteenth century that many of these found their way to North America.

The only species native to the British Isles is *Clematis vitalba*, so the British gardeners of the sixteenth century must have been pleased to have had the chance to grow *C. viticella* from around 1569, when it was introduced from northern Italy. Since then it has given us so many very useful garden plants. It is believed that *C. viticella* 'Purpurea Plena' and *C. viticella* 'Purpurea Plena Elegans' were grown in European gardens in the sixteenth century. These, I believe, must have been chance seedlings from *C. viticella*—or they may have been sports, as I raised several which were almost identical from a batch of *C. viticella* seedlings some years ago. However, to have had double-flowered cultivars such as these so early in plant breeding and development must have been exciting, and these are still considered to be garden-worthy plants today.

Before the end of the sixteenth century, other European species had found their way to England. *Clematis cirrhosa* var. *cirrhosa* has since given us some very good plants such as *C. cirrhosa* var. *purpurascens* 'Freckles' and *C. cirrhosa* 'Wisley Cream', both of which do well in the milder areas of Europe and of

North America. *Clematis flammula* has a marvellous scent but is sometimes difficult to get right in cold, wet soils; fortunately, one of its offspring, *C.* ×*triternata* 'Rubromarginata', produces billows of small starry flowers with a very strong almond-vanilla scent, and is much more vigorous and a very strong-growing plant. *Clematis integrifolia* var. *integrifolia* is a fine herbaceous plant for the mixed perennial/shrub border, growing only to about 2–2.5 ft. (60–75 cm). It, too, has given us some very useful plants; the blue-flowered species now provides us with both pink- and white-flowered cultivars. Finally, *C. recta* var. *recta* is also perennial and herbaceous in habit, and like *C. cirrhosa* var. *cirrhosa*, *C. flammula* and *C. integrifolia* var. *integrifolia* it is very variable in the wild. As a cultivated plant, it produces many seeds each year. Sometimes as many as ten per cent of the seedlings it produces have purple foliage, so it is always worth trying to reproduce *C. recta* var. *recta* from seed to see its offspring.

The seventeenth century seems to have been devoid of introductions to the British Isles, but in the early part of the eighteenth century several North American species such as *Clematis crispa* and *C. viorna* were introduced. It was not until very recently that these two species gave rise to new cultivars. (I believe that *C. crispa*, with its scented flowers, should have been used more in early breeding work.) In recent years, our nursery in Guernsey has developed a range of cultivars from these species, but these have not yet been introduced into gardens.

In 1776, the introduction of *Clematis florida* into Sweden by Carl Peter Thunberg caused great interest. Sadly, though, this plant did not find its way into gardens and seems to have been lost to cultivation. When Dr. Philipp von Siebold introduced *C. florida* var. *sieboldiana* from Japan to the Leiden Botanic Garden in Holland in 1837, it almost immediately sported to produce *C. florida* 'Plena'. Both plants were then introduced into English gardens, but unfortunately these marvellous clematis proved to be almost sterile and could not be used in breeding work. More recently, plants have been raised from sports of *C. florida* var. *sieboldiana* and *C. florida* 'Plena' in Japan, England and Guernsey. These sports have both male and female flower parts and could therefore be used in breeding work. Dr. von Siebold also introduced other Japanese clematis cultivars into Europe at that time, but these now appear to be lost to cultivation. However, it was his introduction of the Chinese species *C. patens* into Europe that offered European breeders the opportunity to develop the large-flowered cultivars we grow today.

Japanese breeders have been developing forms of *Clematis patens* for perhaps three hundred years. Some of the original cultivars introduced in the nineteenth century, such as *C.* 'Amalia', 'Louisa' and 'Monstrosa', have now been lost to cultivation. When one visits Japan it is easy to find *C. patens* and

its forms in the wild, but no one is really sure if these are native to Japan or whether the plants found in the wild are just naturalized seedlings. I have been fortunate enough to find both blue and white forms as well as double and semi-double forms (which may be cultivars) growing in the wild. It really is most exciting to suddenly spot these in scrub, small shrubby bushes or grassland. It is *C. patens*—whether Chinese, Japanese or its cultivars introduced from Japan in the period 1830–1860s—that gave the European breeders the opportunity to develop the cultivars for our gardens of today.

Other important nineteenth-century introductions were *Clematis lanuginosa* in 1851, and *C.* 'Fortunei' and 'Standishii' in 1863. *Clematis lanuginosa* is thought by some experts to be a cultivar, as it was found by Robert Fortune in a churchyard near Ning-po in China. However, it was a very useful introduction as it provided the breeders of the 1850s and 1860s with the chance to create some later-flowering large-flowered cultivars by crossing it with *C. viticella* and its cultivars.

The first European breeder to gain success was from Belgium or Holland when, in 1830, *Clematis* 'Eriostemon' was raised by crossing *C. viticella* with *C. integrifolia*. This cross has since been repeated, producing similar-looking cultivars. However it is to Isaac Anderson-Henry of Edinburgh, Scotland, that we must give credit for producing the first really large-flowered cultivar, *C.* 'Reginae', which was produced when he crossed *C. lanuginosa* and *C. patens azure grandiflora* in 1855. Sadly, this plant is now lost to cultivation, though Anderson-Henry later made an enduring contribution by breeding the world-famous *C.* 'Henryi' and 'Lawsoniana'. We must equally applaud the

Clematis 'Henryi', bred by Anderson-Henry in 1870, still enjoys great popularity in North America.

famous clematis family of Jackmans of Woking, England, who also achieved a breakthrough in 1858 when they created the world-famous C. 'Jackmanii' which is still grown and sold in vast numbers today.

Beginning at this point in the mid nineteenth century, some five hundred clematis were created by breeders in Europe, some of the most noteworthy coming from Jackmans of Woking, Cripps and Son of Tunbridge Wells and Charles Noble of Sunningdale, all in England. In the same period French, German and Swiss breeders were also very active and successful. Although the main focus was on the large-flowered cultivars, double-flowered cultivars were also of great interest. The Jackmans successfully raised the new-looking tulip-shaped clematis by crossing the American species *Clematis texensis* with C. 'Star of India', raising marvellous plants such as C. *texensis* 'Duchess of Albany' and C. *texensis* 'Sir Trevor Lawrence', named after a former President of the Royal Horticultural Society. During the 1880s, most of these European clematis found their way to the United States when they were displayed at flower shows in Philadelphia and Boston. Incidentally, some breeding work was also being carried out in the United States, as well as in Canada where Dr. Frank Skinner was looking to create more winter-hardy cultivars for the Canadian gardeners.

Clematis plants fell from favour in the early 1900s in Britain due to the new problem of clematis wilt causing death to young plants. It was William Robinson and Ernest Markham at Gravetye Manor in Sussex, England, who then started to introduce good cultivars of the Viticella Group from France. I believe that these cultivars must have been less prone to clematis wilt, and the efforts of Robinson and Markham resulted in a resurgence of interest in clematis from 1914 onwards.

In the United States and Europe throughout the twentieth century, breeders introduced some fine cultivars, but also many that have not stood the test of time. During the 1980s and 1990s, a great surge of breeding work again took place in Europe and Japan, the emphasis being on early large-flowered cultivars of the patens type from Japan. But in Latvia and Estonia, more work was done with some of the later-flowering species and cultivars, bringing us some very useful new garden plants.

What the early breeders attained, especially with some of the very early-flowering, large- and small-flowered cultivars they raised, was due to some excellent selection work—and, perhaps, some good luck. Cultivars such as *Clematis* 'Jackmanii' (1858), 'Miss Bateman' (mid 1860s), 'Henryi' (1870), 'Mrs Cholmondeley' (1873), 'Mrs George Jackman' (1877), 'Daniel Deronda' (1882), 'Marie Boisselot' (1885), 'Nelly Moser' (1897), and the Viticella Group cultivars 'Étoile Violette' (1885), 'Kermesina' (1883) and the small-flowered C. ×*triternata* 'Rubromarginata' (1862) are all plants that would find their way onto the best-seller lists if they were raised today. Admittedly, however, some of these cultivars only produce what I would describe as terminal flowers—that is, they produce just one single flower per growing stem rather than flowering all along the stem. (We use this latter attribute as an important criterion in our selection work in Guernsey.)

Contemporary Breeding

Gardeners today are seeking exceptional value: they need their plants to be longer-flowering and they prefer having many flowers at one time. Disease resistance and ease of growing are also valued. Nowadays, new clematis introduced to the market have to compete in the flowering and value league with many, many other good plants. Perhaps this was not the case in the late nineteenth or early twentieth centuries—and even now, some clematis specialists do not seek particular criteria, but look only for unusual flowers. This is often a misguided approach, as the flowers that look most interesting are not necessarily from the most garden-worthy plants.

Clematis 'Étoile Violette' associates well with *C. texensis* 'Pagoda' on this rustic garden fence. Both offer a long flowering period as they flower along their growing stems.

In the selection work we do in Guernsey, as part of the breeding and development work my company carries out with its Joint Venture partner, Poulsen Roser A/S from Denmark, Mogens Olesen (its Managing Director) and our team apply very strict criteria before new clematis are placed on the market. We breed and develop plants to meet those criteria simply because we know that the contemporary gardener will buy only the most desirable cultivars. Our quest to breed short, compact, free-flowering, repeat-flowering, disease-resistant clematis means that we throw away many thousands of new clematis cultivars each year because they do not meet these standards and requirements.

It has been rewarding to bring to the market such exciting and compact plants as the Boulevard Collection of clematis from the Evison and Poulsen breeding programme. These compact, free-flowering plants provide the gardener with the chance to grow clematis in small spaces. Cultivars such as *Clematis* Picardy 'Evipo024' and *C.* Angelique 'Evipo017' produce an exceptional number of flowers, while the even smaller-growing *C.* Bijou 'Evipo030' is ideal for window boxes, planters or hanging baskets—so even someone with the tiniest garden or balcony can enjoy growing these compact new clematis. Other breeders are also producing similarly compact, free-flowering plants such as *C.* 'Piilu' raised in Estonia.

The same criteria also apply to the taller-growing garden clematis; they need to offer good value for money. The exceptional *Clematis* Rosemoor 'Evipo002', introduced as part of the Royal Horticultural Society's Bicentenary Plant Collection, produces a vast number of flowers and is long-flowering. However, it is perhaps *C.* Harlow Carr 'Evipo004', part of the same Collection, that gave us the biggest surprise: during trials in the heat of California, it flowered from mid-March until mid-November and even with temperatures of 100°F (38°C) and higher, it continued to flower with masses and masses of its velvet purple-blue flowers.

The search for exciting new clematis will continue. As a breeder, I have observed that new colours, along with clearer blues and reds, are still sought after, and more double large-flowered cultivars seem to be what people desire. Scent in the medium- to large-flowered cultivars is also a 'must', as is vibrant colour. (I expect that the first breeder to create that buttercup yellow evocative of *Caltha* will have achieved a special goal.) Yet although much remains to be done, I take my hat off to the breeders of the past for all that they achieved for us.

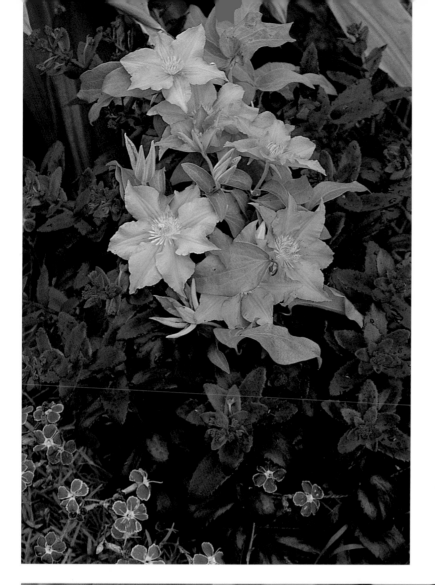

Clematis ANGELIQUE 'Evipo017', growing over a purple-foliaged sedum, produces an exceptional number of flowers over a long period.

Clematis HARLOW CARR 'Evipo004', which has been known to flower from mid March until mid November in the California heat.

Chapter 3

Habitat, Classification and Morphology

Clematis patens, flowering in the wild in
Japan, where it enjoys scrubland. Through
its offspring, this species is the predominant
parent of the new compact clematis.

The genus *Clematis* comprises around three hundred species scattered throughout the world. The ones included in this book are mainly native to the northern hemisphere, and either have great garden value in themselves or are parents of garden worthy cultivars developed for growing in containers or for the flower and shrub borders.

This book is intended to be practical and useful, rather than technical and academic; those interested in greater detail on the habitat, classification and botanical aspects of clematis can carry out their research with other reference books on the subject. Rather than going into great detail here, I will instead give a simple overview so that the plants you eventually choose to add to your garden can be understood.

Habitat

In the wild, clematis can grow in scrub (like the rampant *Clematis montana* var. *montana* from the Himalayas), on mountain tops (*C. alpina* var. *alpina* or *C.macropetala* var. *macropetala,* for instance) or in meadows (exemplified by *C. integrifolia* var. *integrifolia* or *C. tubulosa*). Some, such as *Clematis armandii* from central China, are evergreen, but most are deciduous, losing their foliage during the autumn and winter months and growing again each spring. A few are highly fragrant, like the almond-scented *C. flammula* from southern Europe and the hyacinth-scented *C. tubulosa* from the meadows of northern China.

Many flower only on the current season's new growth (for instance, *Clematis viticella* from Italy and southern Europe, or the cultivars of *C. texensis* from Texas, USA), but the majority flower from the previous season's ripened stems (like *C. alpina* var. *alpina* from the European Alps, or *C. macropetala* var. *macropetala* from China and Mongolia and *C. montana* var. *montana* from China and the Himalayas.

Clematis patens, a native of China that has also naturalized in Japan (though some suspect it to be a separate species from the Chinese form), produces its main crop of flowers in spring and early summer from the ripened previous season's stems. This species has given us the genes for the large-flowered cultivars we grow today and is the predominant parent, through its offspring, of the compact new low-growing clematis for the patio and smaller gardens.

With its vast area and wide variety of climatic conditions, China is home to about one hundred thirty-five *Clematis* species, including some that are evergreen (*Clematis armandii*) as well as many deciduous species (*C. macropetala* var. *macropetala*). The country's clematis flowers vary from small and star-shaped (*C. gracilifolia*), to flat and open (*C. hexapetala*), to pitcher-shaped (*C. lasiandra*), to tubulose (*C. rehderiana*). While China's *C. patens* and its offspring are to thank for the larger-flowered clematis we grow today, many of the species currently growing in China do not meet the criteria I have set for this book; their flowers are not dramatic enough, their flowering period is too short and generally they grow too tall.

North America has its fair share of interesting species, from the extremely vigorous *Clematis virginiana* and *C. ligusticifolia,* which are almost invasive weeds with star-like flowers, to the more interesting *C. texensis* and *C. viorna* with pitcher-shaped flowers. European species have also made a great contribution to today's good-value garden plants. Examples include *C. viticella* with its small nodding flowers, the fine herbaceous perennial *C. integrifolia* var. *integrifolia* with its nodding, somewhat open flowers, and the highly scented *C. recta* var. *recta* which produces a multitude of small star-like white flowers.

I have been fortunate enough to travel to China, Japan, South Africa, New Zealand, the European Alps, the United States and Canada to see clematis species in their native habitats. I have seen clematis plants thriving in surprising places; sometimes, seed blown from the parent plant and lodged in cracks or crevices germinates and grows without any apparent moisture. However, the best native plants have become established with their root systems beneath the shade of rocks or scree (or other plant material), giving them that all-important cool root system. This is a simple lesson we must remember when cultivating the plants in our gardens: always give added shade to the plant's root system.

Plants that have established themselves in positions where there is no support nearby simply form mounds or clumps. When they are exposed to biting winds, they can become stunted or almost dwarfed. Some scramble along on top of other low-growing plant material at ground level while others, finding good support, clamber up into large shrubs or small trees. My greatest surprise as to how plants in the wild differ from those in cultivation came in New Zealand, where I found *Clematis paniculata* growing up to 30 ft. (10 m) into large trees, while in cultivation it reaches 15 ft. (5 m) at the most (and normally is much shorter).

Generally speaking, clematis species that are similar in habit grow in similar locations around the world. The evergreen species are generally found only in southern China, New Zealand and Australia. An exception is *Clematis cirrhosa* var. *cirrhosa*, which, in its native southern Europe, actually loses its

This interspecies hybrid, the result of a natural cross between *Clematis tubulosa* and *C. brevicaudata*, was found in China in 1998.

Despite being native to the mountains *Clematis montana* var. *rubens* is perfectly at home in this lowland New Zealand garden.

foliage during the heat of the summer. It also does so when grown in other mediterranean climates, as found in parts of California—but perversely, in England and the northwestern United States, it remains evergreen and does not lose its foliage. The clematis which belong to the Atragene Group, *Clematis alpina* var. *alpina* and *C. macropetala* var. *macropetala* from Europe and China respectively, and the Japanese species *C. alpina* var. *ochotensis*, all seem to grow in mountainous areas, as do *C. montana* var. *montana*, *C. orientalis* and *C. tibetana*.

Some clematis species breed freely amongst themselves while others do not. While I was in China in 1998, northwest of Beijing, I found interspecies hybrids between *Clematis tubulosa*, a herbaceous perennial plant, and *C. brevicaudata*. *Clematis brevicaudata* is similar to the European species *C. vitalba* and the North American *C. virginiana* and *C. ligusticifolia*. (These have also been used in crosses with forms of *C. tubulosa* in cultivation.) The resultant wild Chinese seedling, as yet unnamed, was most similar to *C. ×jouiniana* 'Praecox' and would, I believe, make a useful ground cover plant. The New Zealand species also interbreed freely in the wild, and have been used more recently in producing a range of interesting cultivars, but because they lack winter-hardiness I will not profile them here.

Classification

The genus *Clematis* belongs to the family Ranunculaceae, and many clematis bear a resemblance to other members of this very large family. Some of the better-known members include *Aquilegia*, *Thalictrum*, *Delphinium*, spring-flowering *Aconitum*, and *Helleborus* which, like *Clematis*, enjoys a deep alluvial soil. Many of the clematis species I have recently discovered in China have tiny starry flowers that remind me of the flowers of the thalictrums, and the spurs on the base of the sepals of *C. koreana* look very similar to the spurs on the flowers of the aquilegias. Sadly, breeders have not yet developed large-flowered cultivars with deep yellow flowers like those of the king cup (*Caltha*), another family member, which enjoys the moisture of a wet meadow; maybe this is just a dream!

The clematis described in this book include only a limited selection of species and their cultivars. These species range from scandent trailing or climbing shrubs (like *Clematis alpina* var. *alpina*), to the sub-shrubs (for instance, *C. heracleifolia*), to the shorter-growing herbaceous perennial clematis such as *C. integrifolia* var. *integrifolia*. These clematis are not listed in a systematic classification but are described with their uses as garden plants.

Clematis highlighted in this book include:
– the evergreen species and their cultivars, which are most useful for growing into trees;
– the Alpina and Macropetala Groups and their cultivars, which make great plants on tripods in the border, or on walls and trees at the back of the border;
– the Montana Group and their cultivars, which are superb for covering large walls and fences;
– the late-spring- to early-summer-flowering large-flowered cultivars derived mainly from *Clematis patens*, which make ideal plants for the border or in pots;
– the midsummer- to autumn-flowering large-flowered cultivars which are most useful for growing in small trees or roses, or through low-growing shrubs;
– the Viticella Group; and
– the later-flowering species and their cultivars, which give great value at the back of the border on fences or walls, whether scrambling around at ground level or growing on tripods or up into large shrubs.

Clematis terniflora,
a Japanese species,
produces panicles
of highly scented
flowers.

Morphology

The leaves of clematis are either evergreen or deciduous, ranging from large leathery leaflets (*Clematis armandii*), to finely cut leaflets, to simple compound leaves of the large-flowered cultivars, which can also divide into three to five leaflets. The flowers are generally bisexual, but occasionally unisexual as with the New Zealand evergreen species. The flowers are borne singly as in the case of many large-flowered cultivars, or in panicles as with *C. terniflora* or *C. flammula*.

Unlike roses and many other flowers, clematis do not have petals and in most instances the colourful part of the clematis flower is the sepals. The number of sepals they have varies widely from four to perhaps ten or many more in the case of double-flowered cultivars. The flower shape also varies greatly from the flat open flowers of *Clematis patens* and the large-flowered cultivars, to the nodding flowers of *C. alpina* var. *alpina*, the star-like flowers of *C. flammula*, the tubular flowers of *C. tubulosa* var. *davidiana* and the bell-shaped flowers of *C. tangutica* 'Bill MacKenzie'.

The sepals are generally the most dramatic part of the flower. (An exception is *Clematis florida* var. *sieboldiana* for which violet purple petaloid stamens are the outstanding feature.) The colours also vary considerably, but it is most important to mention that the flower colour of the large-flowered cultivars, especially the early ones, may vary from year to year when they open in the springtime.

Because clematis have sepals rather than petals, the flowers need good light levels and heat to develop the flower colour properly. During a cold spring when temperatures have been low and sunshine scarce, the flowers will sometimes open with very little colour. Some will be off-white or a greenish muddy shade. As the spring weather improves the later flowers will open with the correct colour. It is perplexing when this happens, but it is just a weather-related problem. In very hot climates, such as parts of California or southern Europe, the flower colour will become more intense, and sometimes the deep reds take on blackish hues.

Some species bring especially attractive features in the garden. For instance, some of the early-flowering species and their cultivars produce most attractive seedheads once the flowers have faded. (The seedheads of the alpina and macropetala types are particularly appealing.) A considerable number of the early large-flowered cultivars have outstanding large spherical seedheads which give an added dimension to their value as garden plants. While the large-flowered cultivars are unscented, some clematis species have a marvellous scent when in full flower; *Clematis flammula* with its almond scent is amazing, as is *C. montana* 'Elizabeth' with its strong vanilla fragrance.

Chapter 4

Combining Clematis with Other Plants

Clematis texensis 'Étoile Rose' growing
next to *Onopordum* makes a lovely
contrast of colour, shape and texture.

When growing clematis, I enjoy combining them with other plants. Many gardeners today share this preference. It is certainly not a new idea—in fact, William Robinson was gardening with clematis in this way almost a century ago at Gravetye Manor in Sussex, England. I have been fortunate enough to have seen many clematis species growing and associating with surrounding plants in their native habitats of China, Japan and other countries including New Zealand. Taking inspiration from these wild plants that grow naturally together, I enjoy combining clematis with other plant material in a garden environment; it is great fun to experiment, and the results are often highly rewarding.

In this chapter, I will explore which clematis are best suited for combining with trees, shrubs, climbers and other plants. This will be a general overview; if you would like more information on any of the clematis described briefly here, please turn to the full plant descriptions in Chapters 10–12 for more detailed recommendations. I will discuss the clematis according to the seasons during which they naturally come into flower.

What To Do (And What *Not* To Do)

Clematis have a well-deserved reputation for associating marvellously with a wide range of plants. Indeed, it is particularly easy to select viable combinations, as clematis colours not only blend well together but also intermingle harmoniously with other plants. However, careful planning is required in order to create the right environment. It is vital that the clematis look natural in a cultivated garden and are at home with other plants, herbaceous perennials and trees.

When partnering clematis with other plants, you should first consider the habit of the clematis, assessing it alongside the appearance of the host support or the habit of the host plant. Ask yourself whether the flower size and shape of the clematis will be appropriate alongside its companion, or whether the combination looks too contrived. Just as there are many favourable combinations, there are also some unfavourable ones.

For instance, I would not wish to plant a semi-double or double large-flowered cultivar such as *Clematis* Josephine 'Evijohill' to grow up into an old apple or pear tree. While this clematis might be used effectively to clothe the tree's trunk, it would look wrong growing up into the branches of that type of tree; the large, fully double flowers would render it incompatible with its

host. A double large-flowered clematis is a somewhat contrived, cultivated plant, looking more at home in a formal border, or growing in a container on an elegant plant support.

An apple or pear tree growing in a border needs a smaller-flowered clematis, and certainly the double-flowered *Clematis viticella* 'Purpurea Plena Elegans', with stems dripping with glorious fully double 1- to 1.5-in. (2- to 3.5-cm) wide flowers, would be a great companion. Perhaps better still would be one of the single-flowered viticella types, especially a paler-coloured one such as *C.* CONFETTI 'Evipo036'—its tiny deep pink nodding bell flowers would contrast beautifully with an apple tree's pale green foliage.

As well as ensuring that the clematis' habit and type of flower work well with its host, one must decide whether the clematis in question is actually suitable for the host. To determine this, you will want to ask various questions. For instance: the flower shape and colour may work, but is the habit compatible? Do you need to retain the previous season's stems on the clematis to obtain those sought-after double or semi-double flowers? Or will it flower well at the correct time if it is pruned hard in the spring? Does the host plant need pruning, and if so, how much? If you need to retain the stems of the clematis to get the early double flowers, can this be done if the host needs hard pruning each spring?

Asking the right questions before embarking on planting combinations can avoid problems later on. For instance, you might be tempted to partner the marvellous semi-double and double flowers of *Clematis* 'Louise Rowe' with the deep red flowers of a rose trained on an upright. However, this would ultimately be problematic as the rose would no doubt need hard pruning from time to time, whereas the clematis needs its old stems to remain so that the early spring and summer flowers can emerge. It is therefore much better to select a clematis that not only has the right flower colour to blend with the rose, but also can be pruned hard each spring so that its pruning requirements do not conflict with those of the rose. For instance, *Clematis* Wisley 'Evipo001' would work well with *Rosa* 'Albertine' and *C.* Galore 'Evipo032' is a good match for *R.* 'American Pillar'.

Moreover, I would avoid planting an early large-flowered clematis to grow up into the base of a conifer that has grey, green or golden foliage. The clematis would need to retain its previous season's stems in order to give its display of early flowers; this could work, but I like to enjoy evergreen trees such as conifers for their natural beauty during the winter months—and I feel that leaving the stems of an early large-flowered clematis mixed in with the clean growth of a conifer all winter, especially with the clematis' brown, dead leaves hanging lifelessly, would be rather undesirable.

This particular problem can be avoided by selecting a small- or large-flowered, late-flowering clematis that requires hard pruning each year. (Yes, in theory the clematis needs its pruning to be carried out in late winter or early spring, but its main bulk of stems and old foliage can be cut away in mid to late autumn, allowing the beauty of the conifer to be enjoyed during the winter months.) Some of the new medium- to large-flowered cultivars, such as *Clematis* ROSEMOOR 'Evipo002', produce their flowers somewhat earlier than some of the older cultivars such as *C.* 'Madame Édouard André'. These new cultivars can be pruned down hard, allowing the conifer to be enjoyed during the winter months, but still giving a crop of flowers from early summer through mid autumn. The red flowers of *C.* ROSEMOOR 'Evipo002' are only 4–5 in. (10–12.5 cm) across, so they would not seem disproportional to the conifer form, shape or foliage density, and they could look outstanding against grey, green or golden foliage.

Clematis ROSEMOOR 'Evipo002', ideal for partnering with a conifer.

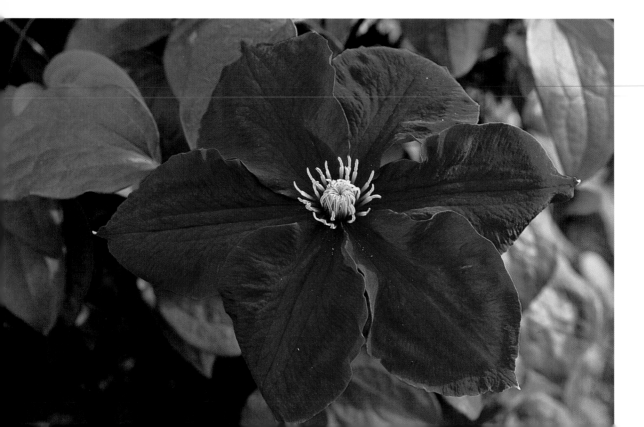

You should also pay careful attention to the placement of clematis in the garden. It would be a mistake, for instance, to plant a late large-flowered clematis like *Clematis* 'Jackmanii' to grow in a container in the hope that it would provide midsummer flowers. This marvellous old cultivar flowers only after it has produced perhaps 6 ft. (2 m) of growth, and therefore the base of the plant looks bare with no flowers. A clematis like this is much better if grown through climbing, rambler or botanical roses, where its lower stems become entwined with its host. A better clematis for planting in a container would be *C.* Cezanne 'Evipo023' in combination with a golden-leaved euonymus such as *Euonymus fortunei* 'Variegatus'.

Early-Season-Flowering Clematis

The early-season-flowering clematis bloom from winter to late spring, and belong to Pruning Group One. (For more information on the Pruning Groups, see Chapter 14). All the clematis grouped together here flower from the previous season's ripened stems, and include both evergreen and deciduous clematis.

The evergreen clematis that are included in this book, *Clematis armandii* and *C. cirrhosa* and their cultivars, are very useful plants for growing through older trees such as *Prunus* or apple trees, or for covering a wall or fence at the back of a border. Their foliage is attractive, while their flowers are small enough to give additional interest during the winter months—plus, they are in scale with small trees.

The Alpina and Macropetala Groups, which are deciduous, are wonderful for growing on very exposed fences or walls, and also work nicely on obelisks in a mixed border of perennials, where they serve as accent plants. While their habit is rather too dense for them to be grown in association with many other shrubs or climbers, they do lend themselves very well to clothing the trunks of small trees, reaching up 7–8 ft. (2.5–2.75 m) into the lower branches where their nodding flowers (followed by masses of fluffy seedheads) offer additional interest throughout the late spring, summer and autumn months. Do mix the cultivars together, as their pastel shades blend perfectly and they can create a beautiful patchwork effect.

Clematis from the deciduous Montana Group are generally vigorous and would swamp many plants, but they are outstanding for clothing large wall areas, for densely covering low or high fences, and for clambering up into pines or other large trees. The dark evergreen pines are great hosts, and their foliage contrasts well with the small white or pink flowers. The montanas can grow up to 30–40 ft. (9–12 m) into large trees, where their stems naturally

Clematis montana 'Broughton Star' would look stunning grown up into a copper-foliaged beech tree.

climb and cling onto the smaller branches of the trees without causing damage. In New Zealand I saw a stunning planting combination where the somewhat less vigorous *Clematis montana* 'Broughton Star' was grown through a copper beech tree, *Fagus sylvatica* 'Purpurea', to great effect.

Although the montanas are extremely vigorous, some can be contained in smaller areas. *Clematis montana* 'Freda' is one of the least vigorous, reaching only 15 ft. (5 m) or so. It can be grown along low fences at 3 ft. (1 m) in height—or perhaps on a low wall at an end of a border, particularly if the wall is framing a set of garden steps. When used in this way, the growth needs to be cut back perhaps twice during the summer months retaining about 6 in. (15 cm) of new growth that will ripen for flowering the following season. *Clematis montana* 'Jenny' can also be used in this way, its semi-double flowers creating much interest. In fact, if the area is large enough, say 3 × 12 ft. (1 × 4 m), these two montanas could be grown together as their flower colours would complement each other.

I find the foliage of *Clematis montana* var. *rubens* 'Tetrarose' to be particularly attractive. Its leaves are perhaps the largest of any of the montanas; they are thicker (being a tetraploid form of *C. montana* var. *rubens*) and are bronzy green in colour, especially in the heat of summer. The flowers are somewhat cup-shaped, and because I like to be able to enjoy its merits, I would plant this montana in a place where one could walk close by and appreciate it.

When positioning any of the aforementioned clematis in a garden location, it is important to keep their early flowering period in mind. Because they produce their flowers during late winter and into late spring, their host support or host plant will need to be able to support their growth through the winter months.

Midseason-Flowering Clematis

Clematis in this category produce their flowers from late spring to early summer, and many go through to early and mid autumn. Together they are classified as Pruning Group Two. The early flowers are produced from the ripened stems of the previous season, followed by flowers which are produced from the current season's stems, thus extending the flowering season. In this book I describe over fifty different cultivars that fit into this group of clematis; needless to say, their habit, flowering ability and possible position in the garden are highly variable.

Single Large-Flowered Clematis

This group consists of the earliest-flowering of the single large-flowered clematis that bloom in late spring. Examples include *Clematis* 'Dawn', *C.* 'Guernsey Cream' and *C.* 'Miss Bateman'. They do not repeat flower as well as other single, slightly later-flowering cultivars, such as *C.* ALABAST 'Poulala', *C.* ANNA LOUISE 'Evithree', *C.* 'Nelly Moser' and *C.* HYDE HALL 'Evipo009', but they are valuable garden plants because they are the first to produce the large flowers in late spring. Their full descriptions and ultimate heights can be found in Chapter 11.

For these compact early large-flowered plants, positioning in the garden is especially important. They are brilliant for growing over a low-growing evergreen shrub, such as *Ceanothus thyrsiflorus* var. *repens*, which grows to

Clematis ALABAST 'Poulala', one of the first large-flowered clematis to bloom in late spring.

Clematis 'Fujimusume' looks outstanding when it flowers at the base of a pale pink rose.

Clematis ANNA LOUISE 'Evithree', a repeat-flowering early large-flowered cultivar, blends beautifully with blue-flowered ceanothus.

6–9 ft. (2.5–3 m), or over *Cotoneaster microphyllus*. These clematis produce only about 6–12 in. (15–30 cm) of new growth before they flower, so they do not overwhelm their hosts. Due to their early flowering I feel that it is useful to place them in the front of a border where they can scramble and be enjoyed at close quarters. They also look stunning growing up into wall-trained evergreen shrubs, like taller-growing ceanothus or cotoneaster at the back of a narrow border or on a house wall.

Other cultivars fitting into this very early-flowering section include *Clematis* 'Fujimusume', *C.* 'H. F. Young' and *C.* VIVIENNE 'Beth Currie'. The first two, with their pale blue flowers, look well with silver- or golden-foliaged euonymus such as *Euonymus fortunei* 'Coloratus'. *Clematis* VIVIENNE 'Beth Currie', with its deeper-coloured flowers, needs a lighter background such as a grey-foliaged shrub to show off its flowers to best effect. If roses are grown on an obelisk in a border, their lower branches can be enhanced by these three clematis. *Clematis* 'Fujimusume', for instance, looks outstanding with pale pink roses when it is grown at the base of the rose.

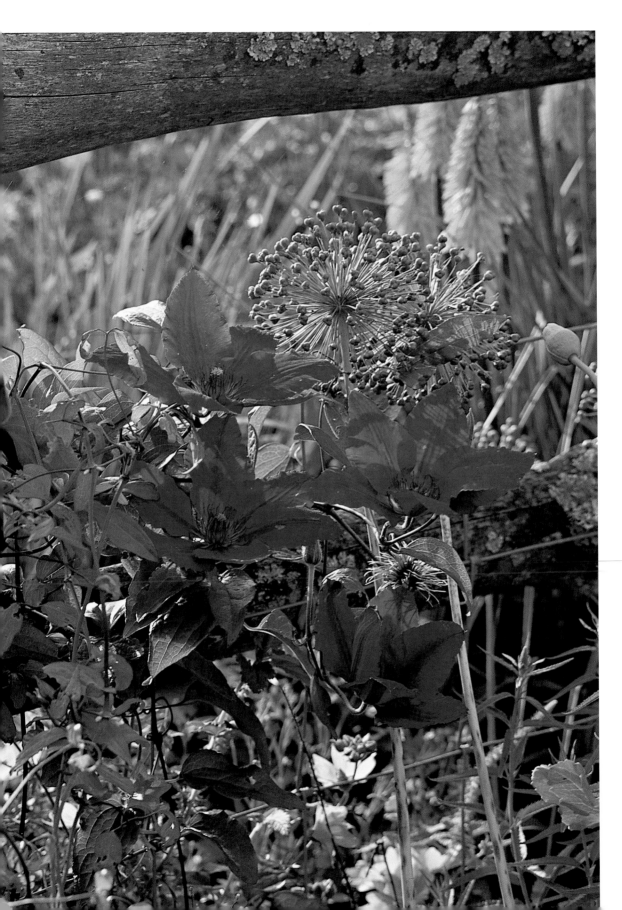

Slightly later (in late spring/early summer), large single-flowered clematis such as *Clematis* ALABAST 'Poulala', *C.* ANNA LOUISE 'Evithree' and the famous *C.* 'Nelly Moser' come into bloom. These clematis produce their early flowers on stems that are 12–24 in. (30–60 cm) long and are therefore more vigorous than their earlier-flowering counterparts. They lend themselves to enhancing any type of wall-trained shrub, whether evergreen (such as *Pyracantha* 'Orange Glow') or deciduous (like *Robinia hispida* 'Rosea'). They are most successful when grown through any free-standing evergreen or deciduous shrubs in a border or up into obelisks. However, if your garden is at all exposed to strong winds on a regular basis, you should grow these very large-flowered clematis through other wall-trained or free-standing evergreen shrubs, where their flowers are less likely to be badly damaged by wind. (In windy areas the small-flowered viticella types can be used; these will be discussed later in this chapter.)

Other options within this group include *Clematis* 'Doctor Ruppel' (with stunning rosy-mauve flowers), *C.* 'Niobe' (dark plum red) and *C.* ROYAL VELVET 'Evifour' (deep rich velvet purple). This last cultivar looks best with grey-foliaged plants, as does *C.* 'Silver Moon' with its silvery mauve flowers. Most of the above mentioned cultivars can also be grown in containers on the patio.

Shorter-Growing Clematis

A new group of early medium-flowered clematis from recent breeding carried out by Poulsen and myself, as well as by other breeders in Europe and Japan, are ideal for the smaller garden. They offer the opportunity to grow a more compact clematis that produces flowers that are only 3–5 in. (7.5–12.5 cm) wide, but are more free-flowering and also longer-flowering. Many not only have terminal flowers on each stem, as with older cultivars like *Clematis* 'Miss Bateman' or *C.* 'Nelly Moser', but also flower continuously down the stem, with each stem having as many as nine flowers. In addition to these characteristics which make for a much longer flowering period, these new clematis have the advantage of being repeat-flowering, many producing new growth as soon as one crop of flowers has almost finished, providing yet another flush of flowers.

Those belonging to the Boulevard Collection, such as *Clematis* ANGELIQUE 'Evipo017', *C.* CEZANNE 'Evipo023', *C.* CHANTILLY 'Evipo021', *C.* PARISIENNE 'Evipo019' and *C.* PICARDY 'Evipo024', perform outstandingly, as does *C.* 'Piilu', which was raised in Estonia.

This new group of free-flowering compact plants allows gardeners to grow clematis that will thrive in small gardens in towns or cities, where space is limited. They work well with more compact wall-trained shrubs or free-

Clematis ROYAL VELVET 'Evifour' adds a splash of colour when planted among mixed herbaceous perennials.

Clematis CHANTILLY 'Evipo021', a new shorter-growing, repeat-flowering clematis, needs a companion plant that complements its flower colour and shape, such as *Cotinus coggygria* 'Royal Purple'.

standing shrubs, and can thrive in containers for the patio, deck garden or even on balconies where space is very limited. They combine very favourably with many other plants to create ideal planting associations, working especially nicely with low-growing herbaceous perennial plants and ground cover plants like *Potentilla* species and *Cotoneaster microphyllus,* which are generally used at the front of a border or in narrow borders near to the house or other buildings.

Excellent combinations abound. For instance, *Acer palmatum* 'Atropurpureum' is a great host for *Clematis* CEZANNE 'Evipo023', as the pale blue flowers and pale yellow anthers of the clematis contrast perfectly with the deep purple foliage of this *Acer*. The purple, green, grey or variegated foliage of the barberry family (*Berberis* subspecies) offers many opportunities as well: *Berberis thunbergii* f. *atropurpurea* would provide an outstanding foil for the deep purple flowers of *C.* PICARDY 'Evipo024', or perhaps this clematis could be used with the foliage of *B. thunbergii* f. *atropurpurea* 'Harlequin' which is speckled purplish pink. Growing *C.* ANGELIQUE 'Evipo017', with its greyish pale blue flowers, through *Buddleja* 'Lochinch'—offsetting the soft grey foliage of the buddleja and its long panicles of lavender-blue flowers—is another natural planting opportunity.

I am certain that *Cotinus coggygria* 'Royal Purple' would offer the absolutely perfect contrast for the creamy green, slightly pink rounded flowers of *Clematis* CHANTILLY 'Evipo021', while the pale blue *C.* PARISIENNE 'Evipo019' would need the grey foliage of either *Santolina chamaecyparissus* or *Senecio* 'Sunshine', or even the Jerusalem sage (*Phlomis fruticosa*), to provide the right colour background and foliage variation to showcase it to best effect. For the delightful

C. 'Piilu', with its pale pink-mauve striped flowers, the purple-leafed sage, *Salvia officinalis* 'Purpurascens', would provide the ideal background.

These clematis are most useful plants, as they can be either pruned hard each season or left with some of the previous season's stems to bring about those early flowers. When growing in the planting combinations described above, I prune them down to within about 12 in. (30 cm) of ground level. The old stems that remain provide some early flowers, but the extra new growth revitalizes the plant, giving it a fresh new start each spring. The other great advantage with these new clematis is that they flower freely from the previous season's stems and from the current season's growth, which is a great bonus for those gardening in the colder climates of North America or northern Europe.

Very Compact Clematis

Two more new and very exciting clematis are ideal for extremely small spaces. *Clematis* BIJOU 'Evipo030', violet-mauve, and *C.* FILIGREE 'Evipo029', silvery blue, are extremely compact, growing only to about 12–18 in. (30–45 cm) tall. Flowering in late spring/early summer directly from the previous season's stems and basal buds, they can be grown in the front of a border, over very low-growing host plants, in a container, or even in hanging baskets. In late summer/early autumn they sometimes put on slightly taller flowering stems which can be pruned back after flowering. They are ground-hugging and can be grown alone—but I prefer to plant them with other low-growing shrubs such as *Corokia cotoneaster* (the wire-netting bush), *Cotoneaster dammeri* or *C. horizontalis* (the fish-bone cotoneaster) or the flat, spreading brooms such as *Cytisus ×kewensis* or *Genista lydia*.

Clematis PARISIENNE 'Evipo019' is compact, repeat-flowering and very free-flowering. Grey-foliaged plants will complement it nicely.

Gardeners with very limited space will welcome the extremely compact *Clematis* Filigree (above), which meshes well with low-growing shrubs, and the impressive, fully double-flowered *C.* 'Evipo029' Crystal Fountain 'Evipo038' (left), which is best with free-standing evergreens or wall-trained shrubs.

These 'dwarf' clematis are very adaptable and can be used with a wide selection of low-growing perennials at the front of the border; grey-foliaged plants such as *Artemisia absinthium* 'Lambrook Silver' or *A. ludoviciana* 'Silver Queen' offer wonderful contrast, as does *Anaphalis triplinervis* with its white, starry, everlasting flowers. Alternatively, they can be used as permanent bedding plants and each spring additional annual bedding plants can be introduced to associate with them. Because they are so new, the planting possibilities have not yet been fully explored; now is the time to experiment.

Semi-Double and Double-Flowered Clematis

Just when the last mentioned group of clematis are beginning their flowering season, the semi-double and double-flowered clematis are also producing their first displays. These clematis produce stems of 12–24 in. (30–60 cm) before their large flowers open. They include the older *Clematis* 'Daniel Deronda', deep purple-blue, which usually displays semi-double and single flowers at the same time; *C.* 'Mrs George Jackman', an old favourite of mine which also produces semi-double and single flowers coloured a pretty creamy white; and *C.* 'Louise Rowe', with very pale mauve single, semi-double and double flowers that all open simultaneously. The newer cultivars which have only fully double flowers include *C.* ARCTIC QUEEN 'Evitwo', white; *C.* JOSEPHINE 'Evijohill', rosy lilac pink; and *C.* CRYSTAL FOUNTAIN 'Evipo038', lilac blue.

All of these semi-double and double-flowered clematis are best grown through evergreen shrubs (either free-standing or wall-trained), especially in windy locations. Many have such large, almost top-heavy flowers, especially older cultivars such as *Clematis* 'Proteus', that they really need some protection from the elements. (Heavy rain and wind, of course, do the most damage.) Because of their free-flowering, compact habit, the double-flowered clematis described here will do very well in containers, on patios, or in other small garden areas where space is at a premium.

In my view, the placement of these semi-double or double-flowered clematis in the garden is most important; if this is not given careful consideration, they really can look out of context or their planting can look too contrived. As mentioned earlier, I do not believe that they should be grown up into, for instance, an old apple or pear tree—not only because the clematis' flowers could get blown about and damaged by wind, but also because I feel that they would look out of place in a tree. Trees are better hosts to the smaller, more free-flowering clematis such as the viticella types. In light of the rather exotic shapes of cultivars such as *Clematis* JOSEPHINE 'Evijohill' and *C.* CRYSTAL FOUNTAIN 'Evipo038', I am of the opinion that the semi-double and double clematis should be grown in a more formal part of the garden—placed close to the dwelling, or in a container on the patio or deck garden.

However, the opportunity for planting these 'exotics' in association with other plants is indeed exciting. Before I list some favourable planting combinations, it is important to remember that these clematis need to retain their previous season's stems in order to produce those early flowers. Therefore, remember that they should not be planted with hosts that need any type of serious pruning each year. (For this reason you will want to avoid some roses.)

Let us look at a selection of climbing or wall-trained plants that are well suited for hosting clematis with semi-double or double flowers. *Abeliophyllum distichum*, which blooms in early spring with bluish pink flowers, has a good open framework that would work well with *Clematis* Crystal Fountain 'Evipo038'. The cream-pink variegation on the leaves of the choice climber *Actinidia kolomikta* would also work well with this distinctive-looking clematis.

Clematis Josephine 'Evijohill' will look rather splendid growing up into the foliage and drooping panicle flowers of *Buddleja colvilei*, and its deep rose-coloured flowers which appear in June are a perfect complement. Moreover, I think that the silvery green leaves and pure white, scented flowers of *Buddleja fallowiana* var. 'Alba' would be a dream if it were planted with *Clematis* Franziska Maria 'Evipo008'. If the buddleja needed hard pruning from time to time, then this clematis would still flower well on its new growth after it, too, received the occasional hard prune.

Tempting as it may be to plant some of these clematis up into camellias if grown in a border or against a wall, I like the elegant foliage of the camellia too much to swamp it with a clematis. However, some—such as the cultivars of *Camellia sasanqua*—have a more open framework of branches which would lend themselves to hosting one of these doubles. A good choice here would be *Clematis* 'Mrs George Jackman', as its flowers are not too large and its habit is not over-vigorous.

As we continue alphabetically through the climbers and wall-trained shrubs we come to *Ceanothus*. If you are in a location where you can grow these evergreens, they make perfect hosts for the single- or double-flowered clematis. *Ceanothus* 'Autumnal Blue' and 'Burkwoodii' flower from midsummer to autumn, and require pruning at the same time as the semi-double and double-flowered clematis, which works perfectly. *Clematis* Arctic Queen 'Evitwo' would again be a marvellous companion as its creamy white double flowers would blend and contrast well with the blue flowers of these two ceanothus. Moreover, the very pale, almost off-white flowers of *Clematis* 'Louise Rowe' would be a perfect match for *Ceanothus* 'Autumnal Blue'. With its striking pinkish mauve double flowers, *Clematis* Empress 'Evipo011' would enjoy growing through *Ceanothus* 'Cascade', which has powdery blue flowers, while *Clematis* 'Royalty' with its rich purple-mauve, semi-double flowers would associate nicely with the deep, bright blue *Ceanothus* ×*veitchianus*. This

last ceanothus, and also *Ceanothus* 'Autumnal Blue', are slightly more winter-hardy than others.

If you are fortunate enough to be able to grow *Cytisus battandieri* (the Moroccan broom), then I cannot think of a more exciting combination than planting *Clematis* Franziska Maria 'Evipo008' to grow up into its branches. The silvery satin-like foliage of the broom and its small pineapple-like flowers, coupled with the dark purple-blue double flowers of the clematis, is truly a 'must'. Escallonias are also perfect wall partners for all semi-double or double-flowered clematis; with their evergreen foliage and small, pink, white or apple blossom-coloured flowers, they serve as very good hosts.

With its extra-large purple-blue flowers and yellow anthers, *Clematis* 'Daniel Deronda' needs to be partnered with something special. If you have a border along a large, south-facing wall and live in a mild climate where you can grow the yellow-flowered *Fremontodendron* 'California Glory', a brilliant association can be made.

If you live in an area where *Garrya elliptica* can be grown on a north- or east-facing location, this shrub, which produces long, silky catkins in the

Clematis Empress 'Evipo011', whose dramatic pink double flowers are complemented by powdery blue flowers. Try it with *Ceanothus* 'Cascade'.

The elegant, white double-flowered *Clematis* Arctic Queen 'Evitwo' adds summer beauty to evergreen wall-trained shrubs.

middle of winter, looks terrific but perhaps a little uninteresting during the summer. Why not give it added summer beauty by using it as a host for any of the white doubles such as *Clematis* Arctic Queen 'Evitwo' or *C.* 'Mrs George Jackman'? Other ideal wall-trained hosts for single, double or semi-double clematis include *Magnolia grandiflora* and its selected cultivars, *Pyracantha*, *Solanum crispum* 'Glasnevin', *Wisteria sinensis* and wall-trained fruit trees such as pears. Of course, the list of possible hosts for these semi-double and double-flowered clematis is almost endless, but it really does depend on your garden location and what can be grown as a useful host.

Keep in mind that many of the older double or semi-double large-flowered clematis produce only single flowers if they are killed to ground level during severe winter weather. Certain newly introduced cultivars always produce double or semi-double flowers on both the old and the new stems, and are therefore ideal for the colder climates. They include *Clematis* Arctic Queen 'Evitwo', *C.* Josephine 'Evijohill', *C.* Crystal Fountain 'Evipo038' and the recently introduced *C.* Franziska Maria 'Evipo008'.

As the season moves along into midsummer, we are fortunate to have some of the extra-large-flowered cultivars coming into bloom. Many of these will flower from this time until early to mid autumn if the weather is mild. Again, these clematis produce their first crop of flowers from the ripened previous season's stems but the majority of their flowers come from the current season's growth. They are much more vigorous in habit, reaching up to 10–12 ft. (3–3.5 m) in height, and are very useful garden plants, giving us very large flowers on a taller plant. They lend themselves perfectly to being grown into small, mature wall-trained trees such as magnolias. In areas where the large-

flowered magnolias such as *Magnolia* ×*soulangeana* 'Alba' or *M.* ×*soulangeana* 'Lennei' only occasionally have the chance to produce a good crop of flowers because of late spring frosts, these clematis are extremely useful, and cultivars such as *Clematis* 'Marie Boisselot', *C.* 'Henryi', *C.* 'General Sikorski' and *C.* 'Ramona' can add significant colour and interest to such small trees during the summer months. (Even if the magnolia has flowered well, it is always a bonus to have additional summer blooms.)

Clematis 'General Sikorski' is useful for enhancing a small tree such as a magnolia.

Late-Season-Flowering Clematis

Classified as Pruning Group Three, the late-season-flowering clematis bloom from midsummer to autumn on the current season's stems. As they are very diverse in their habit and flower shape, they are extremely valuable plants for growing in combination with trees, shrubs, ground cover and herbaceous perennial plants—some being herbaceous perennials themselves.

To explain how they can be used with other plants to best effect, I will discuss these late-season-flowering clematis according to their various habits. They are: the late large-flowered cultivars, the Viticella Group, the later-flowering species and their cultivars (many of which are herbaceous perennials).

Late Large-Flowered Cultivars

The late large-flowered cultivars have a great variety of uses in the garden. Their flowers are showy and colourful, ranging between whites, mauves, blues, purples and reds.

Combining Late Large-Flowered Clematis with Roses

When the late large-flowered clematis are teamed with roses, they take on one of their greatest roles in the garden. Climbing roses are the obvious choice, but rambling roses, species and botanical roses, and the modern hybrid shrub roses can also give excellent results. The roll-call would be enormous if I were to list all of the possible planting combinations, but I will list a selection that I am sure will work well.

Looking first to the climbing roses: the blue of *Clematis* WISLEY 'Evipo001' blends perfectly with the dark red of *Rosa* 'Étoile de Hollande'. With the clear pink climbing *R.* 'Cécile Brünner', the old *C.* 'Gipsy Queen' would give a marvellous contrast, while the companion to the pink *R.* 'Zéphirine Drouhin' should be the purple *C.* 'Jackmanii' (raised at about the same time as this *Rosa* cultivar in the 1860s). Of the yellow shades, with *R.* 'Golden Showers', which is suitable for pillars, I would use *C.* 'Błękitny Anioł' (syn. 'Blue Angel'), whose delicate pale bluish flowers would contrast well.

As for the rambling roses: the salmon pink flowers of *Rosa* 'Albertine' would give contrast to *Clematis* 'Rhapsody', as would any of the purples or blues. The combination of *C.* 'Perle d'Azur' with *R.* 'Albertine' is one of my personal favourites—and so the choices continue.

Clematis 'Gipsy Queen', one of the late large-flowered clematis that associate so well with pink climbing or rambler roses.

Partnering Late Large-Flowered Clematis with Wall-Trained Shrubs

Another important use of the late large-flowered clematis cultivars is to grow them through, or with, any type of wall-trained tree or shrub. I recommend planting *Clematis* 'Comtesse de Bouchaud' or *C.* 'Barbara Harrington' to grow up into *Solanum crispum* 'Glasnevin'; these clematis' flowers contrast extremely well with this Chilean potato tree with its clusters of rich purple-blue flowers. Due to their volume of flowers, these clematis are very dramatic if grown alone or in association with other colours from their section or other climbing plants, such as ipomoeas, on a formal steel or wooden obelisk in a border. Such plantings with (for instance) annual sweet peas on a self-made obelisk of birch branches make an ideal statement and provide vertical interest in a border. The RHS garden at Wisley makes exceptional use of this method where David Jewell, the Superintendent of the Floral/Ornamental Department, uses 6-ft (2-m) long branches of *Betula pendula,* the native British silver birch.

Cultivars such as the white *Clematis* 'John Huxtable', as well as *C.* 'Madame Édouard André', can be co-planted with climbing aconitum, *Aconitum volubile*, or perhaps the climbing *Dicentra scandens*. The greenish lilac-blue aconitum will be livened up by the slightly creamy white flowers of *C.* 'John Huxtable',

The very free-flowering *Clematis* 'Barbara Harrington' would contrast marvellously with a blue-flowered wall-trained shrub such as *Solanum crispum* 'Glasnevin'.

while the pale yellow flowers of the dicentra contrast beautifully with the deep red of *C.* 'Madame Édouard André' and blend with its yellow centre.

All of the aforementioned clematis and others that belong to the late large-flowered group are also ideal to grow with other climbers on pillars, poles or uprights on archways or pergolas. The different clematis within this group can be planted to associate with one another, too; for example, *Clematis* WISLEY 'Evipo001' looks marvellous with the purple *C.* 'Gipsy Queen'.

The Easy-to-Grow Viticella Group

The Viticella Group clematis differ from the larger-flowered cultivars within the late-flowering group, in that they have smaller flowers which they produce in greater abundance. Otherwise, they are closely related to the larger late-flowering cultivars and can be used in very similar planting combinations with roses, through other wall-trained or free-standing shrubs, and on poles, pillars or obelisks with other climbers. *Clematis* GALORE 'Evipo032' contrasts very well with *Rosa* 'American Pillar', its plum purple flowers adding interest and appeal. With its deep purple flowers, *Clematis* 'Étoile Violette' is a natural partner for *Rosa* 'New Dawn' which has very pale pink flowers.

All members of the Viticella Group make outstanding statements if grown on obelisks in the border, whether by themselves or mixed. Such bold statements of colour from these summer-flowering clematis ensure that they will mix well with all types of other perennials, adding an extra dimension to a border. Success lies in carefully planning the contrast of foliage and flower between the clematis and their companions.

Viticellas for Trees and Archways

Clematis from the Viticella Group are a 'must' for growing up into old free-standing fruit trees such apples, pears or cherries; they grow up to 10 ft. (3 m) or more. Charming cultivars, like *Clematis* CONFETTI 'Evipo036' with its nodding deep pink flowers, look so elegant as their stems trail gracefully down out of the pale green foliage of an old apple tree.

Another way to make the most of *Clematis* CONFETTI 'Evipo036', or maybe the delightful, slightly scented *C.* 'Betty Corning', is to use the clematis on archways. Very often a border will be dissected by a pathway, with perhaps one or two archways placed over it so that climbing plants such as roses can be grown—and it is delightful to be able to look up into the nodding flowers of either of these two cultivars against a blue sky. Of the two, perhaps *C.* CONFETTI 'Evipo036' is better for this purpose as its foliage is not as dense as that of *C.* 'Betty Corning'.

In her garden at Abbey Dore Court in Herefordshire, England, my mother-in-law, Charis Ward, uses such metal archways to great effect. In fact, her

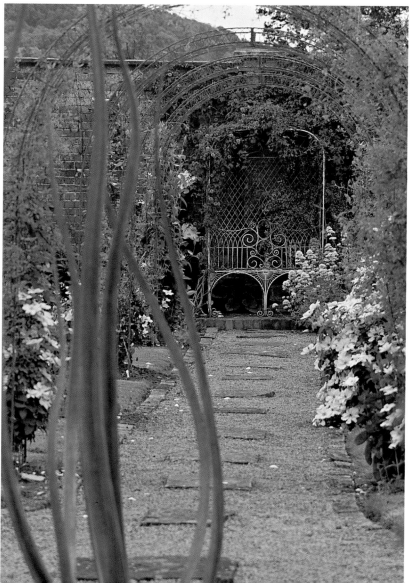

Clematis CONFETTI 'Evip0036' is ideal for growing up over an archway where its bell-shaped flowers can be admired from below.

These archways are enhanced early in the year by low-growing clematis at the base. Later in the season they are covered with late-flowering types such as *Clematis* CONFETTI 'Evip0036'.

Clematis 'Venosa Violacea' contrasts very well with golden-foliaged heathers at ground level.

pathway divides up a lawn area and four archways are used, each planted with *Clematis* Confetti 'Evipo036' on both sides. At the base of each archway she has planted either *C.* 'The Bride' or *C.* Chantilly 'Evipo021'. These compact plants grow to only 3 ft. (1 m), and at their bases *C.* Bijou 'Evipo030' and *C.* Filigree 'Evipo029' are planted and allowed to just creep at ground level. As one can imagine, this makes very good use of several types of clematis, from the tall-growing *C.* Confetti 'Evipo036' to the creeping *C.* Bijou 'Evipo030'. Here, low-growing perennials are also used, as are spring-flowering bulbs which are planted around the base of the clematis.

Viticellas and Ground Cover Plants

In addition to being grown up into trees or large shrubs with, for instance, golden, grey or variegated foliage, the Viticella Group clematis can be combined successfully with ground cover plants. Very often in gardens one is faced with a large sloping bank which must be planted with either ground cover plants or flat spreading junipers, so that the soil is held in place. Such sites, or even flatter areas where ground cover plants are used, offer perfect opportunities for planting clematis—and winter- or summer-flowering heathers, junipers such as *Juniperus sabina* 'Tamariscifolia' (Spanish juniper), *Alchemilla*, *Anaphalis*, *Artemisia* 'Powis Castle', the prostrate and low-growing cotoneasters such as *Cotoneaster dammeri*, *C. horizontalis* or *C. microphyllus*, or any of the *Potentilla* family all make ideal hosts. Low-growing grey-foliaged plants, in particular, offer a perfect background for clematis flowers; the grey-leaved salvias, the senecios or the grey santolinas, when grown en masse as ground cover plants, are perfect host plants for most of the Viticella Group clematis.

Clematis Avant-Garde 'Evipo033', whose unusual flowers are best complemented by green, grey or golden foliage.

Let us consider which Viticella Group clematis are best for using with the types of ground cover we have just mentioned. *Clematis* 'Alba Luxurians' with gappy white flowers, usually with green tips to the sepals, would look well with grey foliage or with the light greens of the winter-flowering heathers. *Clematis* 'Carmencita', raised by the late Dr. Magnus Johnson in Sweden, is very colourful and produces masses of nodding carmine flowers which have a satin texture. Due to its dark colour it really needs a light background such as the golden foliage of some of the heathers which are grown for their summer foliage colour; any of the creamy yellow-flowered potentillas such as *Potentilla fruticosa* 'Tilford Cream' or the primrose yellow *P. fruticosa* 'Elizabeth' would be ideal. With its rich, bright red flowers, *C.* 'Madame Julia Correvon' needs a similar host—as does *C.* 'Royal Velours', which has stunning deep velvety purple flowers that I believe look best with either purple-foliaged plants or, for a greater contrast, the grey foliage of *Senecio*.

The beautiful flowers of *Clematis* 'Venosa Violacea' or *C.* Palette 'Evipo034', which have purple or blue veins running through their sepals, need to be

carefully placed to make the best of their unusual colouring. The former contrasts well with golden-foliaged heathers while (in my view) the latter looks best with either grey-foliaged heathers or purple foliage. The new *C.* Avant-Garde 'Evipo033', with its strange, small, double red flowers, can associate well with any type of green, grey, golden or variegated foliage. It is a fun and unusual plant that deserves a special place in the garden where its interesting look can be displayed to best effect. For instance, it would look stunning flowering over a low-growing silver or golden variegated evergreen.

Some Viticella Group clematis are a bit too vigorous or produce too much dense foliage to be grown over other ground cover plants. These include

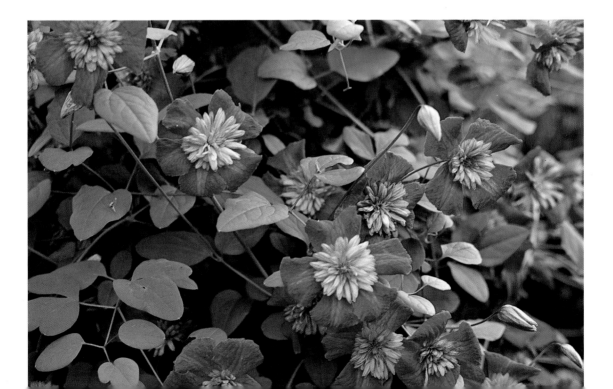

Clematis 'Étoile Violette', which looks brilliant in (for instance) a variegated holly, and *C*. 'Polish Spirit', which is best in a small tree such as a sorbus. One of my all-time favourites is *C. viticella* 'Purpurea Plena Elegans', a plant from the sixteenth century that produces dusky violet-purple nodding flowers. Its elegant double flowers do not look at their best when seen clambering about at ground level, and should instead be viewed when grown through other wall-trained shrubs or up into a small tree such as *Amelanchier lamarckii* (formerly *canadensis*). When growing these viticella types through or over low-growing or ground cover plants, it is best to allow the host plant to become established for about two years before planting the clematis to prevent the host from becoming swamped. With old established plantings, if space is not available to 'pop in' a clematis, then the odd plant can be removed at about 10 ft. (3 m) intervals and the clematis planted in its place. If possible, always plant the clematis on the shaded side of the host to give the clematis shade at its root system.

Clematis in this group rarely, if ever, suffer from clematis wilt and are reliable plants of great garden value. If grown up obelisks, into small trees or at ground level, they will never fail to produce a good crop of flowers. I strongly recommend that when they are grown with ground cover or low-growing plants, they should be pruned back hard, to about 12 in. (30 cm) from ground level, in the late autumn or very early winter so that the host plants are cleared of clematis stems and foliage over winter. This is most important when using these clematis to grow over winter-flowering heathers or other evergreen foliage plants such as junipers, as the host's flowers and foliage need to be enjoyed during the late autumn, winter and early spring months.

Later-Flowering Species and Their Cultivars

This group is diverse and very variable in terms of habit, type of flower and where the plants are best suited in the garden. Of the forty or so clematis selected in this grouping, thirty are almost entirely herbaceous perennial in habit. These thirty can be planted among other herbaceous plants or smaller-growing shrubs to help create a wonderful mixed border and will be discussed in Chapter 6. The other ten or so clematis in this grouping are of climbing habit and can be grown in a variety of garden positions, bringing extra colour and interest towards the end of the summer flowering season.

One of these climbers is *Clematis flammula*, a variable species from southern Europe which produces masses of tiny white flowers giving a delightful almond scent. It looks best when grown through a dark evergreen tree such as a Common English holly, *Ilex aquifolium,* where the very dark green leaves give the greatest contrast to the masses of white flowers. The same treatment can be used for the Japanese species, *C. terniflora,* which has white flowers similar in shape to those of *C. flammula*. Keep in mind that this species is quite invasive in some

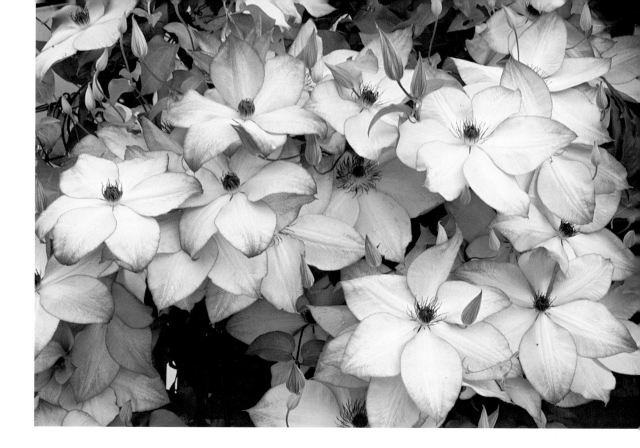

parts of the United States and Canada, and its seedlings need to be dealt with at an early stage. *Clematis terniflora* needs a sunny, hot position to flower well and therefore tends to underperform in England, except in the south. On the other hand, it is a great plant for North American gardens where it is known as the 'sweet autumn clematis'. Due to its vigorous habit in North America it needs a large evergreen tree or pergola to be seen at its best.

Clematis florida var. *sieboldiana* produces probably the most dramatic flowers of any clematis; sometimes it is thought to be a passion flower and not a clematis, due to its purple-coloured centre. All of the Florida Group cultivars that I have selected for this book need to be partnered with other evergreen wall-trained shrubs, or grown in a container for patio culture. I have found these to work best if grown through ceanothus, where their flowers can be displayed well. *Ceanothus* 'Autumnal Blue' flowers from July onwards—and its flowers combine attractively with those of the florida types. Perhaps an even better companion for the florida types would be *Ceanothus* 'Burkwoodii' which has a looser habit than *C.* 'Autumnal Blue', but also flowers throughout summer and autumn.

The floridas flower towards the end of early summer until the frosts of autumn or early winter and are always seen as elegant flowering plants. As mentioned earlier, *Clematis florida* var. *sieboldiana* has a dramatic flower with the purple petaloid stamens contrasting well with the creamy white sepals. A newer cultivar, *Clematis* Viennetta 'Evipo006', is similar in flower and habit except that its flower has a larger, bolder centre. *Clematis* Pistachio, 'Evirida', a

Clematis 'Fond Memories' would look great with a large shrub such as *Buddleja colvilei*.

plant that I raised as a sport some years ago, has creamy white sepals and a tuft of grey anthers with a green centre. As mentioned earlier, all of these flower late into the season on long flowering stems. The later they flower, the greener the sepals become, due to lower light levels—which I see as an added bonus.

The fully double-flowered *Clematis* Cassis 'Evipo020' has purple-veined flowers and contrasts well with the blue flowers of the ceanothus, but would also look charming if grown with a yellow or silver variegated wall-trained *Euonymus fortunei* cultivar, for instance. *Clematis* 'Fond Memories', a large-flowered single florida type with pink-mauve flowers, is a relative newcomer to the range and produces many more flowers than any of its aforementioned peers. Also, due to its extra vigour it needs a larger wall-trained shrub, such as the slightly tender *Buddleja colvilei,* to grow into. The deep rose-coloured flowers of the buddleja make a perfect colour combination to show off the elegant flowers of *C.* 'Fond Memories'.

The Texensis Group

Clematis in the marvellous Texensis Group could almost be considered herbaceous in habit, as they die back to near ground level each winter. The first of the five I will highlight here, *Clematis texensis* 'Pagoda', has good vigour and plentiful nodding flowers which have pinkish purple veins against a creamy background. It is best grown up into a small tree or large shrub where it is possible to view the flowers from below. It can look lovely with pink or cream roses if grown on an archway or obelisk, but probably the best host for this clematis would be *Pyrus salicifolia* 'Pendula' (the willow-leafed pear), where the clematis flower colour would blend perfectly with the grey foliage of the weeping pear.

The next three have gorgeous tulip-shaped flowers which I feel should be viewed from eye level or, even better, looked down into. One very good combination, used by the late John Treasure at Burford House Gardens, Shropshire, England, was to plant the satiny candy-pink *Clematis texensis* 'Duchess of Albany' to grow over a bed of the low-growing shrub *Caryopteris* ×*clandonensis* which has grey-green leaves and violet-blue flowers that offer a perfect foil to the flowers of the clematis. *Clematis texensis* 'Princess Diana' (syn. 'The Princess of Wales'), with its darker, luminous pink-mauve flowers, needs to be combined with fresh green foliage to show its flowers off to best advantage; the low-growing hebe, *Hebe rakaiensis* (formerly *H. subalpina*), with grass-green leaves and spiky white flowers, is ideal. The dusky purple-red flowers of *C. texensis* 'Sir Trevor Lawrence' are very dramatic and I prefer to use a grey-foliaged shrub as its host—something like *Senecio* 'Sunshine' (formerly *S. laxifolius*), which grows into quite dense mounds, is a good possibility. For a striking colour combination, choose *Cotinus coggygria* 'Royal

Purple' (the purple smoke bush) where its purple foliage would give a rather sophisticated colour blend.

My last recommended member of the Texensis Group is *Clematis texensis* 'Étoile Rose'. I almost left this out because in some locations it can be seriously prone to powdery mildew—yet in Charis Ward's garden at Abbey Dore Court, England, in 2006, this fine clematis was performing excellently without any sign of mildew, and so it creeps onto this list. Charis has it growing on an open wooden fence and up into a grey-foliaged thistle, *Onopordum acanthium*, where the contrast of the nodding scarlet to pale pink flowers of the clematis are shown off to great advantage by the foliage of the thistle. Be warned, however, that this clematis will need some protection to avoid an outbreak of powdery mildew.

The Yellow-Flowering Clematis

Later in the season, or at least from midsummer onwards, the nodding, yellow cowbell-like flowers of the tangutica clan begin to flower. *Clematis tangutica* 'Bill MacKenzie', which is extremely vigorous and can grow up to 16.5–20 ft. (5–6 m), is ideal for growing at the back of a border where it can clothe a wall or be allowed to scramble up into an old apple tree. Its nodding yellow flowers are quickly followed by most attractive seedheads and it goes on flowering into very late autumn, the seedheads lasting well into the winter and adding yet another feature to the garden. The somewhat less vigorous *C. tangutica* 'Lambton Park', which grows to 10–13 ft. (3–4 m) and has nodding buttercup-yellow flowers with a coconut-like scent, needs to be planted near to the front of a border. At the RHS Garden at Wisley it grows up through a frame of birch tree branches at only about 6 ft. (2 m) and adds colourful impact alongside perennials. Odd stems trail into nearby plants, creating a good contrast in foliage and flower form.

The much less vigorous *Clematis tangutica* 'Helios' has lantern-like yellow flowers which, as they mature, open flat, each sepal having a recurving tip. As this clematis grows to only about 5–6 ft. (1.5–2 m) it is a very useful plant for scrambling about over purple-foliaged shrubs such as *Berberis thunbergii* f. *atropurpurea* where it is not too overpowering in growth to swamp its host. The closely related *C. tibetana* var. *vernayi* (L&S 13342) has delightful greyish green finely-cut foliage and thick-sepalled yellow flowers which, like those of *C. tangutica* 'Helios', open flat to form an open bell-shaped flower as they mature. Due to its rather open habit—it can reach 10 ft. (3 m)—this clematis looks charming when grown through a bed of *Rhododendron yakushimanum* hybrids. These dwarf shrubs grow to only about 3 ft. (1 m) in height but are good hosts to the long trailing stems of this clematis. The stems of the clematis can be trimmed back in the autumn, allowing the handsome foliage of the rhododendrons to be enjoyed during the winter months.

Clematis that Enjoy the Heat of Summer

We come now to a very useful garden clematis that has been overlooked until recently: *Clematis* ×*triternata* 'Rubromarginata', raised in 1862, has strongly scented, star-like white flowers with wine-red margins to the sepals. Due to its fairly vigorous habit—it can grow up to 10–13 ft. (3–4 m)—it needs to be planted at the back of a border, preferably into a small tree where its stems can explore the branches and then tumble down, producing trailing swags of flowering stems. A most useful host tree would be the purple-foliaged *Prunus cerasifera* 'Nigra', where the tree's foliage would create an excellent colour combination for the white starry flowers of the clematis.

My last two choices of clematis to associate with other plants include the very deep-coloured *Clematis* Harlow Carr 'Evipo004' and *C.* Victor Hugo 'Evipo007'. These fairly new clematis need a very light background to show off their flowers to best effect due to their exceptional dark purple flower colour. *Clematis* Harlow Carr 'Evipo004' is proving to be an exceptional plant for providing flowers over a long period, especially in hot areas; for instance, in California it can flower from mid spring until mid to late autumn. Its uses as a garden plant can, of course, be wide-ranging; it is non-clinging but it does clamber up or over host plants, and it can grow up into climbing roses to about 6 ft. (2 m). (I find that it grows well through *Rosa* 'Félicité Perpétue' where its purple flowers combine well with the pale cream flowers of the rose.) However, it also does exceptionally well when grown through or over grey- or yellow-foliaged flat spreading junipers, like *Juniperus sabina* 'Tamariscifolia' or *Juniperus ×pfitzeriana* 'Pfitzeriana Aurea'.

Clematis VICTOR HUGO 'Evipo007' has very deep purple (almost blackish-purple) flowers which, like those of *C.* HARLOW CARR 'Evipo004', are borne in great abundance throughout the summer months. It could be grown over low-growing or ground cover shrubs, but although it also is non-clinging, I believe its 3-in. (7-cm) wide flowers are shown to best effect, when grown up into cream-, yellow- or pink-flowered climbing roses. Another stunning plant association would result from letting it clamber up into white-flowered *Carpenteria californica* or wall-trained *Fremontodendron* 'California Glory', where its deep purple flowers would contrast well with the bright golden yellow flowers of its host.

Chapter 5

Clematis for Containers

Clematis CEZANNE 'Evipo023' has a compact habit and is very free-flowering, making it ideal for a container.

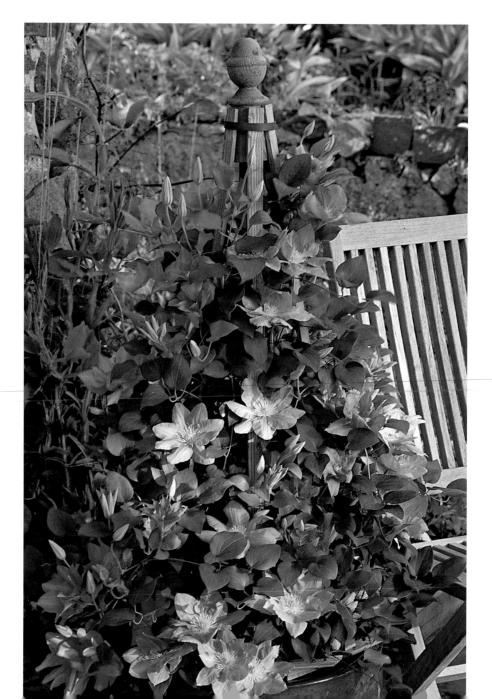

Choosing the best clematis for growing in containers is quite straightforward: it is vital to choose a species or cultivar that will provide a good crop of flowers, over the longest possible period of time. If we consider the different groups of clematis in light of their various habits and flowering periods, it is easy to identify the most suitable ones—as well as the ones that do not work as well.

Choosing Clematis for Containers

The evergreen clematis, with the exception of some of the very compact hybrids raised from New Zealand species, are too vigorous to be grown long-term in containers and their flowering period is too short.

The alpina and macropetala types can be grown successfully in containers and provide good early-flowering plants for the patio or small garden but, again, their flowering period is only about four weeks. If space is available in the garden, grow them in a 'growing' or 'nursery' area until the point of flowering and then move the containers to the desired area where they can be enjoyed during their flowering period. After they have finished flowering they can be taken back to the nursery area. All of the cultivars of *Clematis alpina* and *C. macropetala* featured in this book are suitable for container culture, and they all have attractive seedheads and occasional summer flowers.

The montana types are only suitable as container plants for about three or four years due to their very vigorous habit. They would need to be grown on a large, strong support and then planted out in a garden setting. I recommend using *Clematis montana* 'Freda' due to its more compact habit of about 15 ft. (5 m) of growth. Again, this group has only about a four-week flowering period. The pinks generally have bronze-green foliage which is of course an added bonus.

Many of the early large-flowered cultivars have an extended flowering period. These include the single, double and semi-double-flowered cultivars and clematis from the new Boulevard Evison and Poulsen Collection. All of these early large-flowered types can be grown in containers; however, some produce more flowers, and have longer flower periods than others do.

The midsummer large-flowered cultivars flower on the current season's stems, and only the more compact cultivars are suitable for container cultivation.

This is because their habit of flowering at their growing tips makes them generally too tall for successful container culture. As for the Viticella Group, the Texensis Group, the late-flowering species and their cultivars, and the herbaceous clematis, only a handful of clematis from these groups are suitable as container-grown plants due to their vigorous habit. They are much more suitable for growing with other plant material in borders or up into trees.

On the other hand, many clematis thrive in containers. I will now detail which clematis offer the best value when grown in containers, and why.

The New Compact Clematis for Smaller Gardens

A group of compact clematis has been specially bred to be longer-flowering and to produce more flowers on each stem. (As they come from the Evison and Poulsen breeding programme, you may not be surprised to learn that, in my opinion, these are the very best clematis for growing in containers.) While older cultivars generally produce one terminal flower per stem, these new clematis, comprising the Boulevard Collection, produce generally smaller flowers, with each stem having the normal terminal flower at its growing tip but also up to six additional flowers down each stem. These open starting with the terminal flower and then work back down the flowering stem.

This, of course, means that more flowers are on display at any given time, and creates a long-flowering plant. Sometimes new flowers are even produced from the side-shoots of the flowers as they die away. At the present time the colour range is limited, but in a few years a wider colour range will be available. These clematis start flowering in late spring and will continue well into the summer; in a cool summer they will continue to flower almost all the way through the summer months. New growth is produced from soil level or below, creating a second or third flush of flowers.

Presently I am experimenting by hard pruning these plants immediately after the first flush of flowers has ended in midsummer by cutting back all stems to about 12 in. (30 cm) above ground level. From such hard summer pruning the plant regenerates, sending out new growth that comes into flower some six to eight weeks afterwards. In very hot climates, re-growth is more limited, and watering and liquid feeding with rose or tomato feed are required to make sure the plant's food levels are held high enough.

These new cultivars have a great advantage over the older ones: they flower both on old stems (from the previous season) and on current growth. This is an important asset in colder areas where top growth may be killed back in cold winters. Although these flower from the previous season's stems, I believe that all top growth should be removed down to about 6–12 in. (15–30 cm) above soil level each year during late winter or early spring before new growth commences.

To date, the best of these cultivars for growing in containers are *Clematis* Cezanne 'Evipo023', pale blue with a yellow centre; *C.* Parisienne 'Evipo019', blue with a red centre; *C.* Angelique 'Evipo017', pale blue with a light brown centre; and *C.* Chantilly 'Evipo021', which is pale creamy pink with a cream centre. The slightly later-flowering *C.* Picardy 'Evipo024', with rich reddish flowers, is also a superb plant. Another outstanding cultivar, raised in Estonia, is *C.* 'Piilu' which has pink-mauve flowers with a deep pinkish bar to each sepal and a creamy yellow centre; this plant adds greatly to the selection of shorter-growing clematis. All of these cultivars grow to about 3–4 ft. (1–1.2 m) in height and can be grown on a 3-ft. (1-m) high plant support. They are therefore ideal for container culture or for growing in a border, and need not be restricted to growing only in containers.

For the garden or patio where space is even more restricted, two very compact cultivars will be suitable: *Clematis* Bijou 'Evipo030', violet-mauve, and *C.* Filigree 'Evipo029', silvery blue. These grow to only about 12 in. (30 cm) in height. They make exceptional plants for a smaller container (ideally around 12 in. [30 cm] wide), but they look even better in a slightly larger container planted up with other summer bedding plants or shallow-rooted herbaceous perennials. During the later summer months these two clematis sometimes

Clematis Angelique 'Evipo017' is rarely out of flower during the summer months.

The exceptionally compact *Clematis* Bijou 'Evipo030' is useful for very small spaces.

The eye-catching
Clematis Josephine
'Evijohill' (right)
and *C.* Crystal
Fountain 'Evipo038'
(below) add
great impact
when placed in
containers. Both
produced their fully
double flowers on
both the previous
season's and
current season's
stems over long
flowering periods.

produce odd stems that grow to about 2 ft. (60 cm), and these stems can be pruned back.

The Double and Semi-Double Cultivars

The next value-for-money clematis that are ideal for container culture are the double-flowered cultivars that form the Regal Evison and Poulsen Collection. Two of these, *Clematis* Arctic Queen 'Evitwo', white, and *C.* Franziska Maria 'Evipo008', deep blue, produce side stems that continue to flower after the terminal flower has passed its best. They therefore offer a longer flowering period (from early summer until early autumn) and can be grown on 5- to 6-ft. (1.5- to 2-m) supports, either singly, or together for maximum effect.

Two other cultivars from this Collection, *Clematis* Josephine 'Evijohill' and *C.* Crystal Fountain 'Evipo038', also offer marvellous value and have long flowering periods. *Clematis* Josephine 'Evijohill' will flower from early summer until early autumn, even in areas with hot climates such as parts of southern California. It always produces fully double flowers coloured deep pinkish mauve, and even after the outer sepals have fallen away, its pom-pom centre continues to flower, each bloom lasting at least three weeks.

Clematis Crystal Fountain 'Evipo038' has the most extraordinary flowers: the blue outer sepals surround a mass of bluish white petaloid stamens, which are sometimes suffused with pale blue. This plant is very compact, growing to only about 4–5 ft. (1.2–1.75 m), and its flowers emerge in great profusion in early summer, making it an exceptional container plant. It will produce occasional later summer flowers but they do not appear in such abundance. *Clematis* Empress 'Evipo011', a sport from *C.* Josephine 'Evijohill', is similar to *C.* Crystal Fountain 'Evipo038' but has exotic pinkish mauve flowers. Its main flowering period is in early summer when its flowers are produced from the previous season's stems.

Other extremely good double or semi-double cultivars that can be used highly successfully in containers include the very large-flowered *Clematis* 'Daniel Deronda', which produces single and semi-double flowers in early summer, followed by single flowers in late summer. Due to its exceptionally large (7–8-in. [18–20-cm] wide) spring flowers, it is best placed in a sheltered area where the likelihood of flower damage is reduced. Its flower colour is fun: the flowers open and then fade slowly from a deep purplish blue with plum highlights to a purple-blue. The sepal colour contrasts marvellously with the creamy yellow anthers.

An all-time favourite of mine is *Clematis* 'Mrs George Jackman' which has medium-sized creamy white flowers with a light brown centre. In early summer the flowers are semi-double and single, followed in late summer by single flowers. It flowers well up its stems and because its flowers are not oversized,

it is ideal for a more windy position than *C.* 'Daniel Deronda'. Another good double white that performs well in a container is *C.* 'Denny's Double'.

Clematis 'Louise Rowe' is extremely charming; in early summer it produces single, semi-double and fully double flowers, all at the same time. The sepal colour varies somewhat with the light levels and ranges from a delicate pale mauve to off-white. During mid to late summer a second crop of pale, nearly white, flowers are produced. I imagine it would work well to plant *C.* 'Louise Rowe' and *C.* 'Royalty' in the same container; in early summer, 'Royalty' produces rich purple-mauve semi-double flowers which would look striking alongside the paler blooms of 'Louise Rowe'. *Clematis* 'Royalty' also produces a good crop of later single summer flowers which are only about 3 in. (7.5 cm) wide, and these would combine well with the paler, end-of-season flowers of 'Louise Rowe'.

With its extra-large flowers, *Clematis* 'Daniel Deronda' looks striking when container-grown. Here it is flowering with a wall-trained tree of *Robinia* 'Kelseyi'.

Another pale-flowered double worth considering is *Clematis* 'Veronica's Choice'. It too produces single flowers later in the season. The outer sepals have blunt tips; they overlap and also have crimpled edges, giving the flower a frilly appearance. The sepals are coloured a pretty pale lavender-mauve, sometimes with rose pink highlights. Coupled with all this, the flowers have a slight primrose scent (though to a rose grower, they probably have no scent at all!).

The Single-Flowered Cultivars

Let us now look at some of the single-flowered older cultivars, plus a few newer ones that lend themselves to container culture due to their free-flowering, compact habit. *Clematis* ANNA LOUISE 'Evithree', named after my second daughter, has violet flowers with a good contrasting reddish purple central bar to each sepal and reddish brown anthers. Although I have always considered it to be compact, I had a great surprise earlier this year when I found it growing and flowering at about 15 ft. (5 m) up into a pyracantha on an old Guernsey house belonging to David and Jane Russell, where Jane (a locally renowned gardener) has developed a fascinating valley garden. I do not believe that this plant had been pruned in recent years and it had obviously found something rather nice to get its roots system into!

Clematis 'Dawn', a charming plant I was fortunate enough to introduce many years ago, is extremely compact and flowers very freely in early summer. It has very attractive bronze foliage in the spring, its white sepals are suffused with creamy pink, and the flowers have a dark red centre. Its late summer crop of flowers is limited, but it performs so well in the early summer that it is still very worthwhile to grow.

Clematis 'Doctor Ruppel' is an exceptional plant for growing in a container due to its free-flowering habit, and its dramatic flower colour makes it one of the best of the older clematis to grow in this way. The 6-in. (15-cm) wide flowers have deep rose pink sepals, each having a much deeper central bar, and it flowers from late spring/early summer to late summer/early autumn. The first clematis I ever raised, *C.* 'Edith' (named after my mother), produces

Clematis 'Doctor Ruppel' with the late-flowering *C.* 'Gipsy Queen', in an east-facing position in late summer.

a fine crop of white flowers with a contrasting red centre. Its main flush of flowers comes in late spring and early summer, but it does have a few late summer flowers and is very compact, growing less than 6 ft. (2 m) in height. *Clematis* 'Fujimusume', a marvellous 'blue' from Japan, is a very compact and bushy plant. Its creamy yellow centre gives a good contrast to the blue sepals. It grows to only about 5 ft. (1.5 m).

One of the first clematis cultivars that I raised in Guernsey was *Clematis* 'Guernsey Cream'; its cream-coloured sepals form a rounded flower and it has creamy yellow anthers. It is best in semi-shade as it needs good sunlight to bring out its best colour, but it can fade in full sun. However, if grown in heavy shade in a north-facing position this clematis will produce green flowers, especially in late spring. Unfortunately it does not display a good second crop of flowers, but it is an extremely reliable spring-flowering plant.

Clematis 'H. F. Young' is a highly useful container-grown plant. It is compact and very free-flowering in late spring and early summer; it will produce its rounded blue flowers later in the season but its spring flush of flowers is outstanding. The wedgwood-blue flowers of *Clematis* 'Lady Northcliffe' come out slightly later in early summer and they, too, have a contrasting yellow centre. The flowers are only 4.5 in. (12 cm) across but they are produced freely on a compact plant that grows to just 6 ft. (2 m) in height.

One of the earliest to flower each year is *Clematis* 'Miss Bateman', an old cultivar from the 1860s with white flowers which have a dark red centre. The fully rounded, 5- to 6-in. (12- to 15-cm) wide flowers are produced on short new growth from the previous season's ripened stems, making it rather compact in habit, reaching only about 6 ft. (2 m). *Clematis* 'Mrs N. Thompson' is of a similar habit and has very colourful flowers. The bluish purple flowers have a deep petunia bar to each sepal, and red anthers. The age-old favourite *C.* 'Nelly Moser' has cartwheel-like flowers that are 6–7 in. (15–18 cm) wide. Each flower has six to eight sepals which have pointed tips and are pale mauve with a deeper lilac central bar. These clematis, like many others belonging to this early large-flowered section, have rather attractive spherical seedheads which follow the flowers. The flowers are borne from late spring/early summer and again later in the summer. However, a point worth remembering is that paler clematis such as 'Nelly Moser' can fade prematurely in strong sunshine; therefore this old favourite is best grown in some shade, a north-facing location on a patio being ideal.

If the patio or growing area is rather sunny, a deep-red-flowered clematis such as *Clematis* 'Niobe' is the best bet; its deep red 6-in. (15-cm) wide flowers have very good contrasting yellow anthers. It also has a long flowering period lasting from late spring until early autumn. Another deep-coloured clematis for a sunny location is *C.* ROYAL VELVET 'Evifour', which has velvet purple sepals and a dark red centre. I have grown this in a container with *Helichrysum petiolare* to shade its roots; the helichrysum then grew up into the top growth of the clematis, its rounded grey leaves making for a great colour combination.

A useful plant for a darker corner is *Clematis* 'Silver Moon' whose silvery mauve, rounded flowers are produced most freely in the late spring/early summer. The 6-in. (15-cm) wide flowers have a creamy centre and it needs an under-planting of purple foliage or flowers so that they contrast with this unusually coloured clematis. Due to its compact habit this clematis also makes an ideal container plant, growing to only 6 ft. (2 m).

One of a few newer cultivars worth mentioning is the silvery blue *Clematis* CLAIR DE LUNE 'Evirin', which has wavy edges to the overlapping sepals. Each sepal has a base colour of white which is suffused with pale lilac, becoming darker at its edges. Its early flowers in late spring/early summer are very dramatic due to the wavy edges of the sepals, but it should be grown in some shade to avoid premature fading in strong sunlight. The same applies to *C.* ICE BLUE 'Evipo003', which was launched at the 2006 Chelsea Flower Show. Its very full early flowers have a base colour of off-white suffused with very

pale blue. This new clematis is very early to flower but it also flowers late into the autumn months. Like the new Boulevard Collection clematis, it has the advantage of flowering down its stems from the terminal flower—but it is taller-growing, with larger flowers.

Another outstanding new cultivar, *Clematis* Kingfisher 'Evipo037', launched at the 2007 Chelsea Flower Show, has almost kingfisher-blue flowers with creamy yellow centres. The 6- to 7-in. (15- to 17-cm) wide flowers are produced in great numbers—this cultivar displays a succession of flowers, as many are produced on each stem. It also has the advantage of flowering from late spring to late autumn. Its great attraction is that it holds its colour well and can be grown in a sunny location.

To conclude this section, I must mention *Clematis* Rosemoor 'Evipo002', a plant introduced as part of the Royal Horticultural Society's Bicentenary Plant Collection. This is a very free-flowering deep-red-flowered clematis with contrasting yellow anthers, producing a lot of flowers at one time and also over a long period from early summer to late autumn. It is a full plant with good foliage which performs well either in a container or growing in the garden—a potentially classic clematis.

The Later-Flowering Cultivars

As I mentioned earlier in this chapter, only a few of the later-flowering clematis that flower on the current season's stems make good container plants due to their taller-growing habit. It is, however, helpful to have a selection of these to grow on the patio or deck garden to produce that later batch of colour and interest with flowers of different shapes.

Of the midsummer- to autumn-flowering clematis, I have found certain ones to be especially suitable for containers and other small spaces. A plant that originated in 1892, *Clematis* 'Madame Édouard André', grows to only about 8 ft. (2.5 m) and can be grown on a 6-ft. (2-m) high support. The dusky red medium-sized flowers are cup-shaped and have yellow centres. It flowers quite freely from mid to late summer, and therefore has merit as a container plant. *Clematis* 'Rhapsody' has a somewhat taller habit but is still reasonably compact. Its flowers are slightly nodding and are of a stunning sapphire blue, deepening as they age. Of the newer cultivars, *C.* Bonanza 'Evipo031' is outstanding in the quantity of flowers it produces. The 3-in. (7-cm) flowers are coloured mauve-blue and are produced from early summer to late summer, but it grows to only 6 ft. (2 m) in height, making it ideal for a small patio or town garden.

The Smaller-Flowered Clematis

Of the smaller-flowered clematis of almost herbaceous habit, *Clematis* 'Arabella' can be grown very successfully in a container where it flowers for

Clematis Chinook 'Evipoo13', growing rather well in a container on a patio and flowering on a birch branch obelisk.

two to three months from late spring/early summer onwards. It can sometimes have a problem with mildew, so make sure it receives plenty of water in dry weather. Its 2- to 3 in. (7- to 8 cm) wide, rounded rosy purple flowers are great fun, especially if planted with grey-foliaged plant material or perhaps some pink-flowered shallow-rooted perennials.

In 2006 David Jewell at the RHS Garden at Wisley in Surrey, England, grew some clematis from the fairly new Festoon Evison and Poulsen Collection in containers for use in the patio or deck garden. The two most successful were *Clematis* Gazelle 'Evipoo14', white, and *C.* Chinook 'Evipoo13', purple-blue. These were planted in 2-ft. (60-cm) wide containers and grown on an obelisk made from 6-ft. (2-m) lengths of birch branches. The branches were bent over at the top, making a 4-ft. (1.2-m) high obelisk. About six small plants were put in each container. I was astonished by the number of flowers that these plants produced—and they also flowered for well over two months, proving themselves to be unusual container plants of very good value.

Clematis belonging to the Florida Group are exceptionally good for growing in containers. I particularly recommend the creamy white *Clematis* Pistachio 'Evirida', as well as *C. florida* var. *sieboldiana* and the newer *C.* Viennetta 'Evipoo06', both of which have creamy white flowers with large, dramatic purple centres. *Clematis* Cassis 'Evipoo20', with its purple-veined double flowers, is also good value. All of these clematis need a good hard prune each spring, as they can otherwise get rather leggy at their base. Their elegant flowers are to be much desired and all associate well with summer bedding plants grown at their base, giving added interest as well as that all-important shade to their root system.

For anyone wanting something different to grow in containers alongside the traditional large-flowered cultivars, I suggest trying some of the nodding pitcher-shaped species and their cultivars. They certainly offer interest, perhaps not for their volume of flowers, but because they provide a contrast to the large-flowered types. *Clematis fusca* var. *fusca* and *C. fusca* var. *violacea,* with their almost furry sepals in brown and purple, always cause fascination

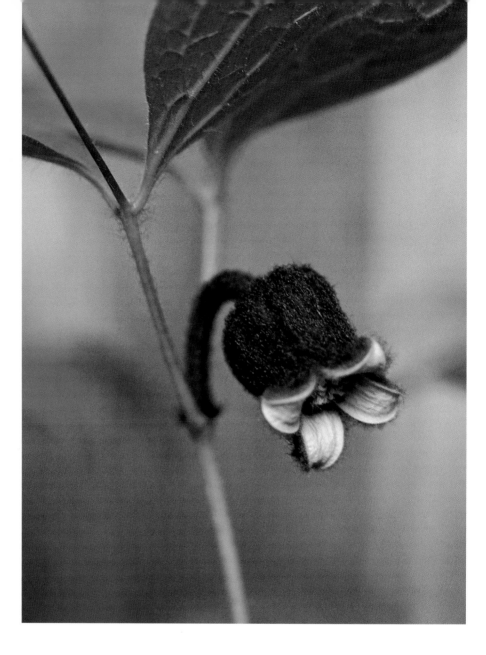

Clematis fusca var. *fusca*, an unusual-looking species, adds interest and charm to any garden.

to the visitor who does not realize that they are, in fact, clematis. *Clematis fusca* var. *fusca* will grow to under 6 ft. (2 m), sometimes to only 3 ft. (1 m), while *C. fusca* var. *violacea* will grow to 6 ft. (2 m). Its semi-nodding to nodding bell-shaped flowers are purple-brown and are followed by large, very attractive seedheads which turn from green to orange before they ripen fully, which is a point of particular interest.

Though I enjoy all of the American pitcher-shaped clematis species, I am particularly fond of *Clematis viorna*; a good form will have a creamy red-coloured flower and the flowers are followed by attractive, large, spiky seedheads. Of the newer cultivars with pitcher-shaped flowers, *C.* 'Jan Fopma', with purple-red, nodding bell-shaped flowers, and *C.* 'Buckland Beauty', with purple-red, nodding urn-shaped flowers, are most worthy plants for the container.

Caring for Container-Grown Clematis

Watering and feeding are extremely important since plants growing in containers will need more attention than those growing in the garden. The ideal container for growing clematis, as well as the method of planting and the aftercare, will be discussed in detail on pages 222–4. In the following sections, we will focus on other issues surrounding clematis in containers: over-wintering container-grown clematis, selecting plant supports, and choosing plants to add interest and provide shade to the root systems of clematis grown in containers.

Over-Wintering

In locations where winters are mild, clematis grown in containers can stay in their summer flowering positions. However, in areas where the frost will penetrate the soil in the container and freeze it solid for more than two or three days at a time, the container will need to be moved into the shelter of a shed, garage or outbuilding where it will remain frost-free over winter. This will stop the root system from being frozen for any length of time and will also protect the ripened previous season's top growth. With many of the older cultivars such as *Clematis* 'Nelly Moser', it is important to retain the old growth as it produces the late spring or early summer flowers from the ripened previous season's stems. If it is killed down to soil level, the plant can only produce flowers on new growth, which will be two months or so later in the season. Again, the Boulevard Collection clematis flower both on old and new growth, but their new growth regenerates faster and will flower earlier than that of the older cultivars.

In cold areas, the container should be taken into its winter home as soon as the frost turns the leaves of the clematis brown. Any excess top growth can be removed if desired, but the annual pruning must wait until the end of winter/early spring. (To prune these clematis in the autumn, as they are taken indoors, would encourage them to start their spring re-growth far too early and this would weaken the plant.)

The soil in the container should be kept moist but not wet over winter, allowing the plant to go into a natural dormancy. When the end of winter approaches and the worst of the winter frosts have passed, the new growth will soon begin and the clematis can be moved back outside to its summer flowering position.

At that time, carry out the spring pruning as advised in Chapter 14. Tie in all remaining stems and new growth as it appears. The top 2–3 in. (5–7 cm) of soil in the container should be removed and replaced with fresh potting soil. Make sure that the container is kept well watered, and if you are using a liquid fertilizer continue to feed as advised on the packaging. Spring or summer bedding plants (subject to season) can be planted in the container at this time to give visual impact and to provide the necessary shade for the root system of the clematis.

With plants left out over winter, it is important to keep the base of the container off the patio surface by raising it on two bricks. This helps with drainage of the container over winter; remember that clematis do not like cold, wet feet at any time. When the worst of the winter frosts have passed, spring prune, refresh, feed and under-plant as described above.

Supports

Garden centres now offer a broad range of different supports, varying from elaborate metal supports, coated in plastic or plated, to rusty metal ones. Alternatively, wooden supports come in all forms: formal obelisks, painted or unpainted, willow or hazelnut tripods or wigwam shapes. I have even used 1-in. (2.5-cm) wide mesh chicken wire made up as columns, or just simple bamboo canes.

The type of support that you choose is a matter of personal taste. However, I believe that a more formal-looking support frame of metal looks best with ceramic containers, and willow or hazelnut wigwams go well with either wooden half-barrels or terracotta pots. The height of the support will need to be 5–6 ft. (1.5–2 m) for the older taller-growing cultivars and most of the double-flowered clematis, while the newer dwarf types such as *Clematis* Cezanne 'Evipo023' or *C.* Picardy 'Evipo024' can grow happily on a 3- to 4-ft. (1- to 1.2-m) support. Wooden supports will need to be replaced more frequently and if you use the birch branch method employed at the RHS Garden, Wisley, the supports will be replaced annually.

Additional Plants for Shading Root Systems and Adding Interest

When choosing plants to give shade to the root systems of clematis in containers, one must decide whether to opt for permanent planting of low-growing shrubs such as heathers or shallow-rooted perennial plants, or to use both summer and winter bedding plants. My preference is to use summer and winter bedding plants as this gives the opportunity to create a new planting scheme each spring and winter. This also has the advantage of refreshing the topsoil in the container at the time of replanting. Yet if it is difficult to find time to do this annual work, then permanent planting of shallow-rooted perennials or shallow-rooted small shrubs also works perfectly well.

Tempting as it may be, I will not list the range of summer-flowering annuals as these may vary from country to country. It is easy to make good choices because the colours of most clematis blend perfectly with most annuals; pale blue, pale pink, grey foliage and even the hot colours are all quite possible. Winter bedding plants are more limited, but there is still a choice. Spring-flowering bulbs give that added splash of colour when it is most needed at the end of winter, so they should be used whenever possible.

The range of more permanent planting material is also vast, and it really is a matter of personal taste as to whether the colour of clematis flowers should be blended with the flower or the foliage of the additional plants. As long as these plants have a shallow-rooted habit and do not over-compete for food from the soil they will go well with the clematis. I feel that it looks rather pleasant if the additional plant material, whether annual or permanent, hangs down over the edge of the container, as it softens the container outline.

Of the perennial plants that can accompany the container-grown clematis, I recommend: *Acaena microphylla*, which develops into a carpet-like plant; *Ajuga,* for its attractive foliage and flowers; *Alchemilla mollis,* with its fresh pale green foliage and flowers; *Anaphalis triplinervis*, which has grey foliage and flowers that will blend perfectly; and the grey-foliaged *Artemisia* (either *A. absinthium* 'Lambrook Silver' or *A. ludoviciana* 'Silver Queen'). Also, the various shades of *Aubrieta* give masses of colour and the large-leaved *Bergenia* certainly offers added foliage interest throughout the year. Many of the *Dianthus* would provide plenty of summer colour, as would *Helianthemum, Heuchera, Lamium*—and so the list goes on.

Of the more woody plants, there are many suitable winter- or summer-flowering heathers, and the grey- and golden-foliaged types are particularly useful. Today gardeners can choose from increased range of hebes, in green and variegated forms. The list of possibilities continues, and I will leave you to experiment with different perennials and woody plants.

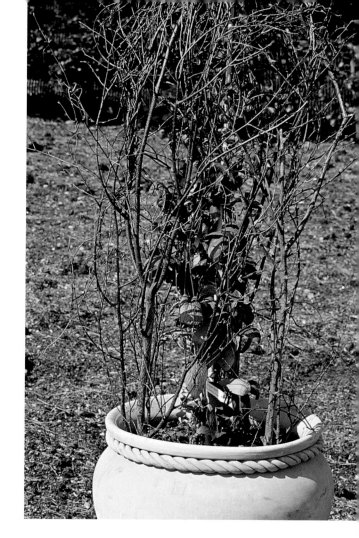

A terracotta container with a birch branch obelisk offers perfect support for a Boulevard Collection cultivar.

Chapter 6   # Clematis for Borders

Clematis 'Jackmanii', growing on an
obelisk in a mixed border of shrubs
and herbaceous perennials.

Borders come in many shapes and sizes; there are long ones, broad ones and slim ones. They can be backed by walls, by fences, by deciduous or evergreen plants or by well-established trees, perhaps old apples, pears or plums that have passed their best with regard to producing a good crop of fruit. While a border's length is not all that important, its width is critical. Let us consider a mixed border of shrubs, perennials and annuals that is at least 20–25 ft. (6.5–8 m) wide. Such a border offers many opportunities for various plant associations. I believe the best way to convey my thoughts on how clematis can add colour, interest and form to such a border is to divide the border into three areas: the back of the border, the central section, and the front 3–4 ft. (1–1.2 m) of the border.

Back of a Border

The back of a typical border might have a background fence or wall that is solid or open, but planted with wall-trained shrubs, climbers or wall-trained trees, either evergreen or deciduous. Alternatively, the background may be a formal clipped evergreen hedge such as yew (*Taxus baccata*), which is extremely dense in habit, a deciduous beech hedge (*Fagus sylvatica*), or horn-beam (*Carpinus betulus*), which do hang onto their leaves well into the winter. The background may even be the fruit trees mentioned earlier, small trees, such as magnolias, flowering cherries or *Sorbus* species, which provide an open framework of branches. We will consider the best types of clematis for adding colour and interest to such a background.

  With these types of hedges, wall-trained shrubs or climbers, evergreen or deciduous hedging, or the more open framework of an old fruit tree, I rec-ommend using only clematis that flower on the current season's stems. The late-season-flowering clematis (flowering from midsummer to autumn) fulfil this requirement. The reason for their compatibility is simple: the host will need to be pruned, trimmed, clipped or thinned out at some point, and it is much more convenient if the clematis to be grown with it is one that requires annual hard pruning.

  The various plants trained on walls or fences, especially climbing roses, would probably need pruning in late winter or early spring. Therefore, a hard-pruned clematis ties in with this requirement. An evergreen yew would

Clematis 'Étoile Violette', flowering with a yellow *Lonicera* cultivar on a fence at the back of a border.

require late summer clipping, as would beech or hornbeam. If this could be left until very early autumn, then the late-flowering clematis such as the viticella types would have almost finished flowering and their main top growth could be removed. The fruit trees would need to be pruned or tipped back in late summer but their main pruning work, if needed, would be carried out during the winter months. Ornamental trees such as magnolias would require very little pruning.

I do not believe that an elegant, clipped yew hedge should be covered with clematis; such hedges have their own character and give form to the back of a border and to a garden. On the other hand, if coniferous hedges are used as a screen at the back of a border and not trimmed annually then their free form certainly can be graced with some of the Viticella Group clematis, or perhaps the later-flowering species such as *Clematis flammula*.

Clematis 'Błękitny Anioł', gracing an archway on the edge of a small patio area at Abbey Dore Court Gardens, England.

Let us consider which clematis should be used on this type of background planting. Good choices for growing with other wall-trained plants either on a wall or on a fence include the pale blue *Clematis* 'Błękitny Anioł' (syn. 'Blue Angel'), pinkish red *C.* 'Barbara Harrington', pinkish mauve *C.* 'Comtesse de Bouchaud', deep purple *C.* 'Gipsy Queen', white *C.* 'John Huxtable', azure blue *C.* 'Perle d'Azur' and the blue *C.* WISLEY 'Evipo001'. These are, in my view, the best of the late large-flowered clematis for this purpose. Some members of the Viticella Group, namely *C.* 'Alba Luxurians' (white), *C.* 'Carmencita' (carmine), *C.* 'Étoile Violette' (purple), *C.* 'Madame Julia Correvon' (bright red), *C.* 'Royal Velours' (deep velvety purple) and *C.* GALORE 'Evipo032' (deep purple-mauve) would also work well, as would *C.* CONFETTI 'Evipo036' with nodding pink flowers, and the elegant PALETTE 'Evipo034' with blue-veined cream flowers. The best of the species and the late small-flowered cultivars for this purpose include the white *C. flammula* and *C. terniflora* (the latter underperforms in Britain but flowers well in North America), and the purple-edged white *C.* ×*triternata* 'Rubromarginata'—all three of which are scented.

On a wall or fence with very few other plants growing on it, mixing together the blues, pinks, mauves and white of the Alpina or Macropetala Groups would be fun and provide colour during early to mid spring. Similarly, on a large strongly supported fence, any of the montanas could be planted to give a great splash of white or pink during mid to late spring. For useful colour in midsummer to mid autumn, the yellow-flowered *Clematis tangutica* 'Bill MacKenzie' and *C. tangutica* 'Lambton Park' would give interest and form with their yellow nodding flowers and those gorgeous seedheads that they produce lasting well into the winter months.

In milder areas where the evergreen *Clematis armandii* and *C. cirrhosa* var. *cirrhosa* can be grown, they too can be used on walls or solid fences to give

colour and interest during late winter and early spring and, with *C. cirrhosa purpurascens* 'Freckles', during the mid to late autumn and early winter. All of these would look charming growing up into old apple trees, exploring the open framework of the trees. Do remember that *C. armandii* can look rather unsightly after five or six years when the lower 4–5 ft. (1.2–1.75 m) of its stems will look bare and possibly have dead leaves.

The most suitable clematis for adding colour to hedges at the back of a border include members of the Viticella Group and some of the later-flowering species. As mentioned earlier, I do not feel that clematis should be grown on formal evergreen hedges such as clipped yew because the clematis could spoil the hedge. However, some of the more delicate, finer-foliaged viticellas, such as *Clematis* Confetti 'Evipo036' with its delightful, nodding pink flowers, would look most attractive and would do no more harm to the hedge than the red *Tropaeolum speciosum* (flame creeper) that is used worldwide with yew. Coniferous hedges that are not trimmed annually, like *Thuja plicata*, make ideal hosts for most of the Viticella Group. The best of these include *Clematis* 'Betty Corning', *C.* 'Carmencita', *C.* 'Madame Julia Correvon', *C.* 'Venosa Violacea', *C.* Confetti 'Evipo036' and *C.* Palette 'Evipo034'. Of the later-flowering species, *C. flammula* and *C. ×triternata* 'Rubromarginata' both add interest, colour and scent.

Clematis 'Polish Spirit', flowering with a mountain ash at the back of a border in a more informal setting.

On hedges like beech or hornbeam, I would use the earlier of the late-season-flowering clematis, as the hedge would need to be trimmed in very late summer or early autumn and so the flowering period of the clematis would be restricted. Because a light colour would work best, I would recommend choosing *Clematis* 'Comtesse de Bouchaud', *C.* 'John Huxtable', *C.* 'Pink Fantasy'

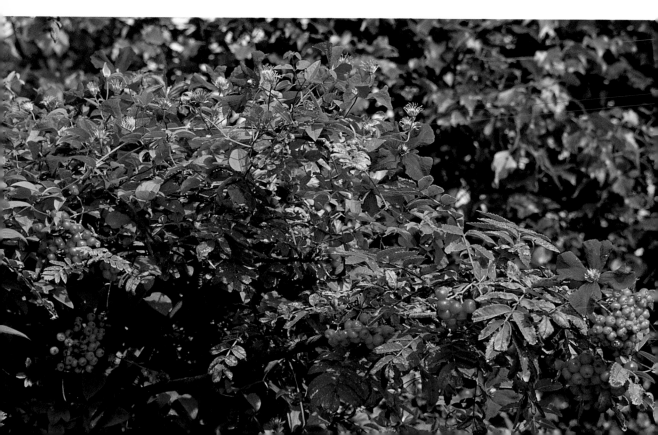

or the new *C.* BONANZA 'Evipoo31' which flowers in midsummer and grows to only about 5 ft. (1.75 m) tall.

On a background of small trees like magnolias, flowering cherries or *Sorbus* species, it is possible to grow some of the older clematis cultivars, which include *Clematis* 'Henryi' and *C.* 'Marie Boisselot' (both large white) or the pale blue 'General Sikorski'. These three flower both from the old, previous season's stems towards the end of early summer, and on new growth from midsummer onwards. They do not produce a mass of flowers at any one time but they do display colour earlier in the season than do the viticella types, and they look particularly good in magnolias. On the other hand, any of the viticella types look attractive with *Sorbus* (mountain ash), flowering cherries such as *Prunus* 'Kanzan' or *P.* 'Taihaku', or the flowering crab-apple, *Malus* 'John Downie'.

Middle Border Planting

In the middle section of the border, at about 5–12 ft. (1.5–3.5 m) from its front, the choice of clematis to give flower throughout the seasons can include the alpina and macropetala types, the large-flowered cultivars, the Viticella and Texensis Groups, and the herbaceous perennial clematis. These clematis can

Clematis 'M. Koster', flowering well on a metal obelisk in the middle of a border, where it adds height and form.

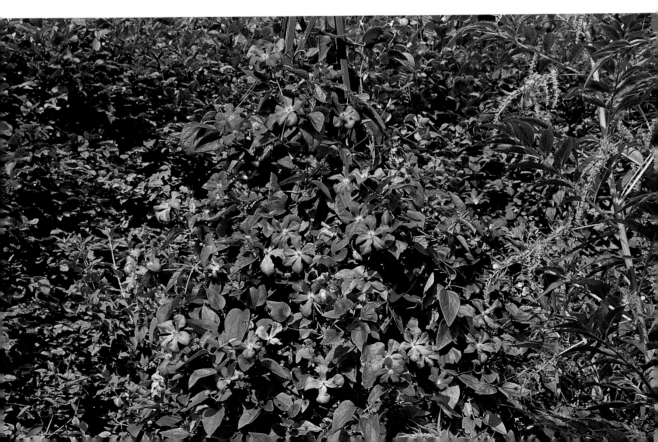

be grown with medium-sized shrubs; over and through herbaceous perennials; or on obelisks made from birch branch, metal or wood. The choices and
opportunities for exciting planting combinations are endless.

You can add vertical statements and a sense of dimension to a border by
placing metal, wooden or birch branch obelisks within it. Their height and
distance from one another really depends upon the background height and the
full depth of the border; a useful height would be 6–8 ft. (2–2.75 m), and they
should be no closer than 15 ft. (4.5 m) apart. Of course, if the obelisks are tall,
slim, wooden or metal they can be lined up more closely together but that will
give a more formal effect to the border—it really is a matter of taste. The birch
tree branches used by David Jewell at the RHS Garden at Wisley to make their
informal obelisks are about 6 ft. (2 m) high and these make bold statements in
the long borders when planted with clematis and other climbing plants.

Clematis that look good on the birch branches as well as more formal obelisks include a rather large selection of species and cultivars. The alpina and
macropetala types, including *Clematis chiisanensis* 'Lemon Bells', are really best
used on metal or strong wooden obelisks, as their previous season's stems need
to be retained from year to year whereas the birch branches will be replaced
annually. The early large-flowered clematis with medium-sized flowers are
also best used with more permanent obelisks as some of the previous season's
stems need to be retained each year; these include *C.* 'Doctor Ruppel' (deep
rose pink with darker bar), 'Fuyu-no-tabi' (creamy white), 'General Sikorski'
(blue-mauve), 'Guernsey Cream' (creamy yellow, and best in some shade),
'Hanaguruma' (cerise pink with creamy yellow anthers), 'Henryi' (white),
'Julka' (bright violet sepals with red bar), 'Kalina' (deep rosy mauve), 'Lady
Northcliffe' (wedgwood blue), 'Marie Boisselot' (white), 'Niobe' (deep red),
'Omoshiro' (creamy pink with purple margins), 'Rooran' (deep pink), 'Rüütel'
(crimson sepals and dark brown anthers), 'The Bride' (creamy white), 'Toki'
(white), 'Twilight' (deep mauve-pink), 'Warszawski Nike' (syn. 'Warsaw
Nike') (deep purple), and 'Warszawska Olga' (dusky rose-pink sepals with
deeper coloured margins), as well as *C.* Anna Louise 'Evithree' (violet with
reddish purple central bar to each sepal). Of the newer cultivars, *C.* Bourbon
'Evipo018' has a most striking deep red flower with a yellow centre.

The birch branches that are bent over to form rather bushy, round-topped
obelisks are superb hosts for the late-season-flowering clematis, which flower
on the current season's stems. These include the late large-flowered cultivars
such as pale blue *Clematis* 'Błękitny Anioł' (syn. 'Blue Angel'), pinkish red
'Barbara Harrington', pinkish mauve 'Comtesse de Bouchaud', deep velvet
red 'Gipsy Queen', blue-purple 'Jackmanii', white 'John Huxtable', dusky red
'Madame Édouard André', azure blue 'Perle d'Azur' and pink 'Pink Fantasy'. Of the newer ones, *C.* Rosemoor 'Evipo002', *C.* Harlow Carr 'Evipo004',

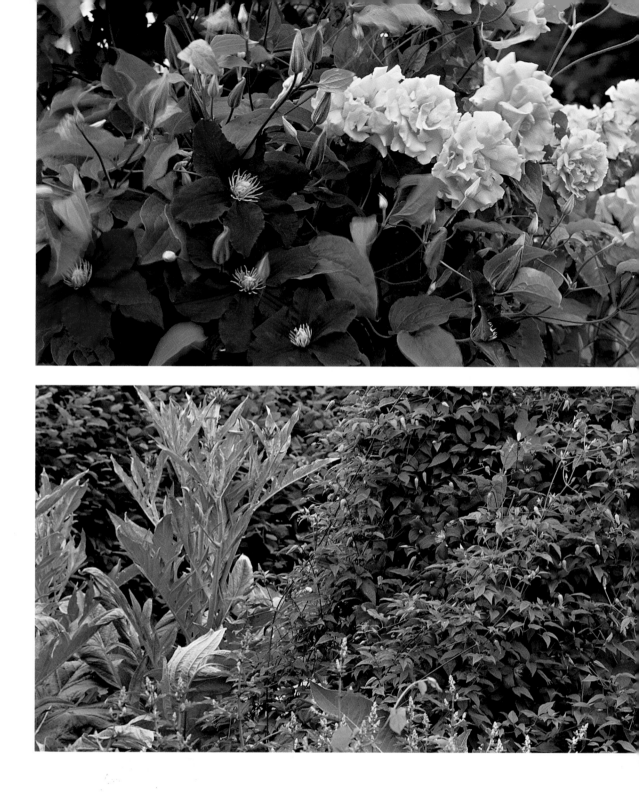

C. Victor Hugo 'Evipo007' and *C.* Wisley 'Evipo001' offer extremely good value and are very free-flowering over a long period.

Also outstanding on the birch branches are the clematis from the Viticella Group. They produce small to medium-sized flowers over a long period from midsummer to early or mid autumn, which extends the flowering season beautifully with bold blocks of colour. I have mentioned the viticellas by name earlier in this chapter and all of these would perform well. Perhaps the most desirable are *Clematis* 'Étoile Violette', *C.* 'Madame Julia Correvon', *C.* 'Polish Spirit', *C.* GALORE 'Evipo032' and *C.* 'Alba Luxurians'.

Of the late-flowering species and their cultivars, I recommend the blue-flowered *Clematis* ×*durandii* and the nodding blue-purple-flowered *C.* 'Eriostemon'. If you wish to grow a Texensis Group clematis on a support to enjoy its long period of flower (from midsummer onwards), the deep satiny pink *C. texensis* 'Duchess of Albany' is perhaps the best performing plant for this purpose. *Clematis tibetana* var. *vernaya* (*L&S 13342*) with its nodding yellow flowers and grey-green foliage, and *C. tangutica* 'Helios' (which has more open flowers) both offer added flower form and a good block of colour from midsummer onwards. Their flowers are followed by most attractive seedheads which last well into the winter months. For additional interest, *C. viorna*—creamy red pitcher-shaped flowers followed by spiky seedheads— is charming and, if not planted too far back in the border, is a 'must' for anyone wanting something a bit different.

Of course, there is nothing to stop combination planting on obelisks where annual climbers—or perhaps climbing perennials which die down during the winter such as *Ipomoea* species, *Dicentra scandens* or the climbing aconitums—can be used with clematis. For another strong combination on more formal metal or wooden obelisks, you can plant climbing roses to add contrast and interest to the clematis. In this case I would use only late-season-flowering clematis so that when the roses are pruned, the clematis can be cut back easily and the old stems removed.

As well as making bold statements of colour on obelisks, all of the foregoing clematis that I have described as being ideal for obelisks can also be grown very successfully on medium-sized deciduous or evergreen shrubs. My preference is to refrain from growing early- or midseason-flowering clematis on evergreen shrubs because I like to enjoy the foliage and form of the evergreen during the winter months (as I have mentioned many times before). It follows, then, that summer-flowering clematis are best for this purpose. Using these guidelines allows you to really appreciate the evergreen shrubs during the winter months, when the remainder of the border is rather uninteresting in its winter dress.

The type of deciduous and evergreen shrubs that I have in mind for the middle section of the border, all of which lend themselves to being hosts for the above-mentioned clematis, include *Berberis darwinii*, *B. julianae* and *B.* ×*stenophylla*. These go especially well with pale blue *Clematis* 'Błękitny Anioł' (syn. 'Blue Angel'), deep purple *C.* HARLOW CARR 'Evipo004', dusky purple *C.* VICTOR HUGO 'Evipo007', mid blue *C.* WISLEY 'Evipo001', or the reds of *C.* 'Barbara Harrington' and *C.* ROSEMOOR 'Evipo002'.

Buddleja alternifolia works well with white *Clematis* 'John Huxtable', while *B.* 'Pink Delight' looks good with the blue of *C.* 'Perle d'Azur' and *B. globosa* combines beautifully with mauve-pink *C.* BONANZA 'Evipo031' or purple *C.* GALORE 'Evipo032'. *Cornus alba* 'Spaethii', with its golden variegated leaves, would find a good companion in *Clematis* 'Niobe' or *C.* ROSEMOOR 'Evipo002', both red. Other delightful combinations include *Cotinus coggygria* with *Clematis* 'Carmencita' (carmine); the purple-leaved *Cotinus coggygria* 'Royal Purple' with purple *Clematis* 'Royal Velours' or *Clematis* CONFETTI 'Evipo036' with its nodding pink flowers; or *Cotoneaster franchetii* with purple-veined *Clematis* PALETTE 'Evipo034'.

In milder areas, where *Cytisus battandieri* (the Moroccan broom) can be grown, it looks outstanding with the large purple flowers of *Clematis* 'Gipsy Queen' or the slightly scented blue flowers of *Clematis* 'Rhapsody'. *Elaeagnus* is a very useful mid-border evergreen shrub, and it makes an ideal host for the later-flowering clematis. A combination of the *Elaeagnus* ×*ebbingei* cultivars 'Gilt Edge' and 'Limelight', with their golden variegated leaves, would lend a marvellous contrast to the rich red flowers of *Clematis* 'Madame Julia Correvon' or the mauve *C.* GALORE 'Evipo032'. The taller-growing

Clematis WISLEY 'Evipo001' providing extra colour and interest on its host, a golden-foliaged hop.

Clematis
'Alionushka',
mingling with the
purple foliage of
Atroplex in a border
of mixed plants.

Philadelphus 'Beauclerk' and 'Virginal', with their scented white flowers which are best towards the end of early summer to midsummer, can be enhanced with purple-, blue- or red-flowered clematis such as the small double red *C.* Avant-Garde 'Evipo033' or the deep purple *C.* 'Black Prince'. The planting associations are endless, and it really is a matter of going out into your garden throughout the season—you will see what is flowering, what has passed its flowering phase and what can be done to give added interest and colour to liven up that middle part of the border.

Front of a Border

Now to the really fun part of the border—the front 3–4 ft. (1–1.2 m). Here we consider using clematis with low-growing shrubs, on flat spreading junipers, through other perennial plants, on ground cover plants or just by themselves. The clematis best for this purpose are the late-season-flowering ones, including the herbaceous perennial clematis that flower from midsummer to autumn. (Keep in mind that these ideas can be used for the narrow border as well.)

Clematis ×durandii,
flowering at
ground level
with Tropaeolum
polyphyllum,
creating an
attractive colour
contrast.

Until this point I have written very little about the herbaceous perennial clematis. These offer very good value, with different and interesting flowers and—in some cases—scent. The simplest way to consider them is to go through the list in alphabetical order.

Clematis 'Alionushka', a deep mauve pink with nodding flowers, looks well either growing up into a small 3- to 4-ft. (1- to 1.2-m) birch branch obelisk, or flopping around on grey-foliaged shrubs where its flowers are shown to great advantage. *Clematis* 'Arabella' can be grown in the same way, but if it can be associated with some white-flowered herbaceous perennials where it can creep up into its host, it will blend in a most delightful way—for this purpose, white *Agapanthus* or white *Aquilegia*, white *Digitalis* (foxglove), *Crambe cordifolia* or *Gypsophila* would be perfect. *Clematis* ×*aromatica,* with its purple-white flowers which have creamy yellow centres, can be grown on birch branches placed in the soil and bent over like little hoops attached to one another at the very front of the border. If these are under-planted with *Anaphalis triplinervis,* for instance, with the clematis flowers dangling down from the low hoops, it will create an outstanding association.

Clematis ×*durandii*, deep blue, can be used in a similar way but it looks particularly dramatic when grown at the front of a border through *Tropaeolum polyphyllum,* its flowers contrasting well with the grey foliage and the yellow flowers of the tropaeolum. *Clematis fusca* var. *fusca*, with its nodding brown flowers, grows to only about 3 ft. (1 m), so it needs to be planted at the forefront. If it could be planted to grow into a *Phlomis fruticosa* (Jerusalem sage),

as the grey foliage and yellow flowers of the host plant would be a great foil for this unusual clematis.

Clematis tubulosa var. *davidiana* and *C. tubulosa* 'Wyevale' are useful plants for the front of the border. Their large, coarse leaves add interest and their pale blue, slightly scented, hyacinth-like flowers are a great attraction to butterflies. They grow to only about 3–4 ft. (1–1.2 m), depending on soil conditions, and are almost self-supporting (although using a few pea-sticks [nut twigs] or herbaceous perennial plant supports would be an advantage in windy locations). If they are grown close to, say, red bush roses, they weave their way between the rose stems creating a good colour combination and supporting themselves.

We come now to the most useful of the herbaceous clematis: the Integrifolia Group, with nodding or bell-shaped flowers. These come in pale blue, pink and white, the European species being the blue *Clematis integrifolia* var. *integrifolia,* 'Rosea' being its pink form and 'Alba' the white form. Good selections include deep pink *C. integrifolia* 'Pangbourne Pink', white *C. integrifolia* 'Hakuree', and rosy pink *C. integrifolia* 'Hanajina'. These all do best when grown up into the support of pea-sticks or herbaceous perennial supports, or allowed to intermingle with other herbaceous perennials. Grey foliage is, unsurprisingly, one of my top choices for growing near to them. They are also brilliant with bush roses, such as the white *Rosa* 'Iceberg' or any number of the pink or red bush roses.

The taller-growing cultivars from the Prairie Evison and Poulsen Collection, which have integrifolia genes in their make-up, are very useful mixed border plants. These grow to about 5–6 ft. (1.75–2 m) and therefore are best planted to grow up into other herbaceous perennials or shrubs towards the back of the front of a border. They can, of course, be grown to associate with other clematis on birch branches tied into an obelisk shape, or simply allowed to scramble around at ground level on (or through) other very low-growing ground cover plants.

Purple-blue *Clematis* Chinook 'Evipoo13', white *C.* Gazelle 'Evipoo14', pink *C.* Medley 'Evipoo12' and deep pink *C.* Savannah 'Evipoo15' are extremely vigorous and very long- and free-flowering as they produce bell-shaped, nodding flowers all along their stems. *Clematis* Gazelle 'Evipoo14' has the added bonus of being slightly scented. They can be associated with other clematis on birch branches; *Clematis* Gazelle 'Evipoo14' looks dramatic with the purple flowers of *C.* Victor Hugo 'Evipoo07' and *C.* Medley 'Evipoo12' looks marvellous with *C.* Galore 'Evipoo32' as the purple and pink flowers blend perfectly, while *C.* Chinook 'Evipoo13', with its purple-blue flowers, looks most elegant with the carmine flowers of *C.* 'Carmencita'.

Clematis 'Edward Prichard' has been around for some time but it is now

becoming much more popular, and deservedly so. Growing to about 2.5 ft. (0.75 m), it is somewhat upright and almost self-supporting, but it is best to use some pea-sticks or herbaceous perennial plant supports to help keep the growth upright. Its large coarse leaves present a bold contrast to the small pale bluish white flowers and it should be planted near to the front of the border to be appreciated. The foliage of *C.* Petit Faucon 'Evisix', which starts off bronzy green in the springtime, is a good foil to its deep purple-blue flowers. The flowers have four sepals and are open-bell–shaped and nodding at first, opening almost flat, but as they mature they reveal bright golden yellow anthers. It can be grown on birch branches or allowed to grow through green- or purple-foliaged hosts, and it looks especially appealing with *Berberis* or the deep purple foliage of *Atroplex*. It also looks charming when grown alongside yellow herbaceous perennials such as *Achillea* 'Moonshine' or some of the other taller-growing achilleas. An alternative is to use the evening primrose, *Oenothera* 'Fireworks', with its clear yellow flowers, or any of the yellow-flowered low-growing shrubby potentillas.

Clematis ×jouiniana 'Praecox' is almost a ground cover plant in its own right and blankets the ground with large coarse leaves which are a good background for its small, bluish white flowers. Because this plant is quite vigorous, it needs an area of about 4–8 ft. (1.2–2.4 m) to spread itself around, and it will scramble up into nearby plants. It looks good with grey foliage and interesting with *Artemisia* 'Powis Castle' or even *A. arborescens*. John Ravenscroft displays this great planting combination in his garden at Hodnet in Shropshire, England.

Clematis Gazelle 'Evipo014', flowering at the base of an archway with *Clematis* Confetti 'Evipo036'.

For splashes or clouds of white in a border, one of the best plants to use is *Clematis recta* var. *recta* or its purple-foliaged form, *C. recta* var. *purpurea*. Both plants can be very variable in height and are best supported by birch branches or strong pea-sticks. They can grow to 5–6 ft. (1.75–2 m) if support-ed but I have also grown them by letting them find their own way around at ground level. However, when they become established plants they are really too lax and heavy to do this. The purple-foliaged form is marvellous in the early summer but later its foliage returns to a greenish purple. In some forms the flower stems are also purple—a good foil for the tiny white flowers which are produced in great numbers and are heavily scented in most forms. As both plants are very often raised from seed, it really is best to purchase them in flower so you can carefully select the best available. I have recently seen *C. recta* flowering in a herb garden with a backdrop of a variegated privet (*Ligustrum*)—it was most dramatic! Both forms are followed by delightful seedheads, so be careful not to miss this added bonus by cutting your plants back too early.

Clematis recta var. *recta*, producing a cloud of scented white flowers at the end of a mixed border.

The Texensis Group clematis are naturally tall-growing plants that can, if supported, reach 6–8 ft. (2–2.75 m). However, as I have stated earlier, I prefer to grow these delightful clematis at ground level where I can look down into their miniature tulip-shaped flowers. The *Clematis texensis* cultivars 'Étoile Rose' and 'Pagoda' have nodding flowers so they should be grown as already described, on supports or through host plants. However, *C. texensis* 'Duchess of Albany', satiny pink, 'Princess Diana' (syn. 'The Princess of Wales'), pink with vibrant pink bar, and 'Sir Trevor Lawrence', dusky purple, can be grown over low-growing shrubs or through perennial plants where they can be viewed from above at the front of the border. Low-growing shrubs such as species of *Cotoneaster*, *Caryopteris*, *Potentilla*, or flat spreading junipers, are ideal hosts.

Other ground cover plants at the front of a border, like winter- or summer-flowering heather, also make perfect hosts for the tulip-shaped flowers of the Texensis Group clematis, as they do for most members of the Viticella Group. *Clematis* 'Venosa Violacea' with its purple-veined flowers is set off delightfully on golden-foliaged heather, for instance. However, some (such as *C.* 'Polish Spirit') are really too robust for growing on heather. Where these clematis are chosen to grow on heather and other low-growing or ground cover plants, their stems need to be 'pegged in' with pieces of wire in the late spring as new growth develops. This will help prevent them from being blown around on the host during windy weather. The clematis' top growth can be removed in mid autumn by pruning it down to about 12 in. (30 cm) from ground level so that the host plants can be enjoyed during the winter months.

Earlier in the section, when discussing the selection of clematis to grow with other plants for the front of the border, I mentioned that other mid-

The elegant nodding flowers of *Clematis texensis* 'Pagoda' contrast well with *Stipa gigantea*.

Clematis viticella 'Purpurea Plena Elegans', growing on a birch tree branch obelisk in a border of trees, shrubs and herbaceous perennials.

season-flowering clematis could be grown in this location. I do not intend to list any of these here, but I suggest that you might use a selection of these towards the front of the border by referring to the recommendations made for combining clematis with other plants in Chapter 4. However, I do not recommend using clematis with very large flowers, or the double-flowered cultivars, in the front of the border as these may get damaged by rain or slugs and then look unsightly. On the other hand, the medium- or smaller-flowered clematis produce more flowers, and these seem to be less prone to damage; what's more, if these flowers are damaged, they are replaced by new ones because of the free-flowering habit of these plants. Also, the large single, semi-double and double flowers are so big that their flowers look out of proportion with the delicate flowers or foliage of the associated perennials that would be grown at the front of the border.

For anyone wanting an early-flowering clematis that resembles the early large-flowered cultivars but has a smaller flower size, two rather special cultivars have recently been developed: blue-mauve *Clematis* Bijou 'Evipo030' and pinkish mauve *C.* Filigree 'Evipo029'. These delightful low-growing clematis, which reach only about 12 in. (30 cm) in height, are ideal for growing at the front of a border. They can be grown by themselves or planted in association with very low-growing shrubby plants or herbaceous perennials. Their colours blend with white, grey, blue and mauve flowers or foliage, flowering during early summer to midsummer and again in the late summer/early autumn months. They are mound-forming, requiring no supports, and flower from both old and new stems. Each spring, you should simply clip back their top growth, leaving 3–6 in. (7–15 cm) of old stems, which will then produce the first crop of flowers in late spring or early summer.

Growing clematis in borders with other trees, shrubs, climbing plants and perennials is, in my view, a very natural way in which to grow them. The other plants give them the support that they need; the clematis can climb up through their companions, or clamber over them. The foliage and flowers of other plants also provide that essential added shade to the clematis' root systems. Growing in perfect harmony, they give a pleasing effect and great satisfaction to those who have planned, planted and cared for them.

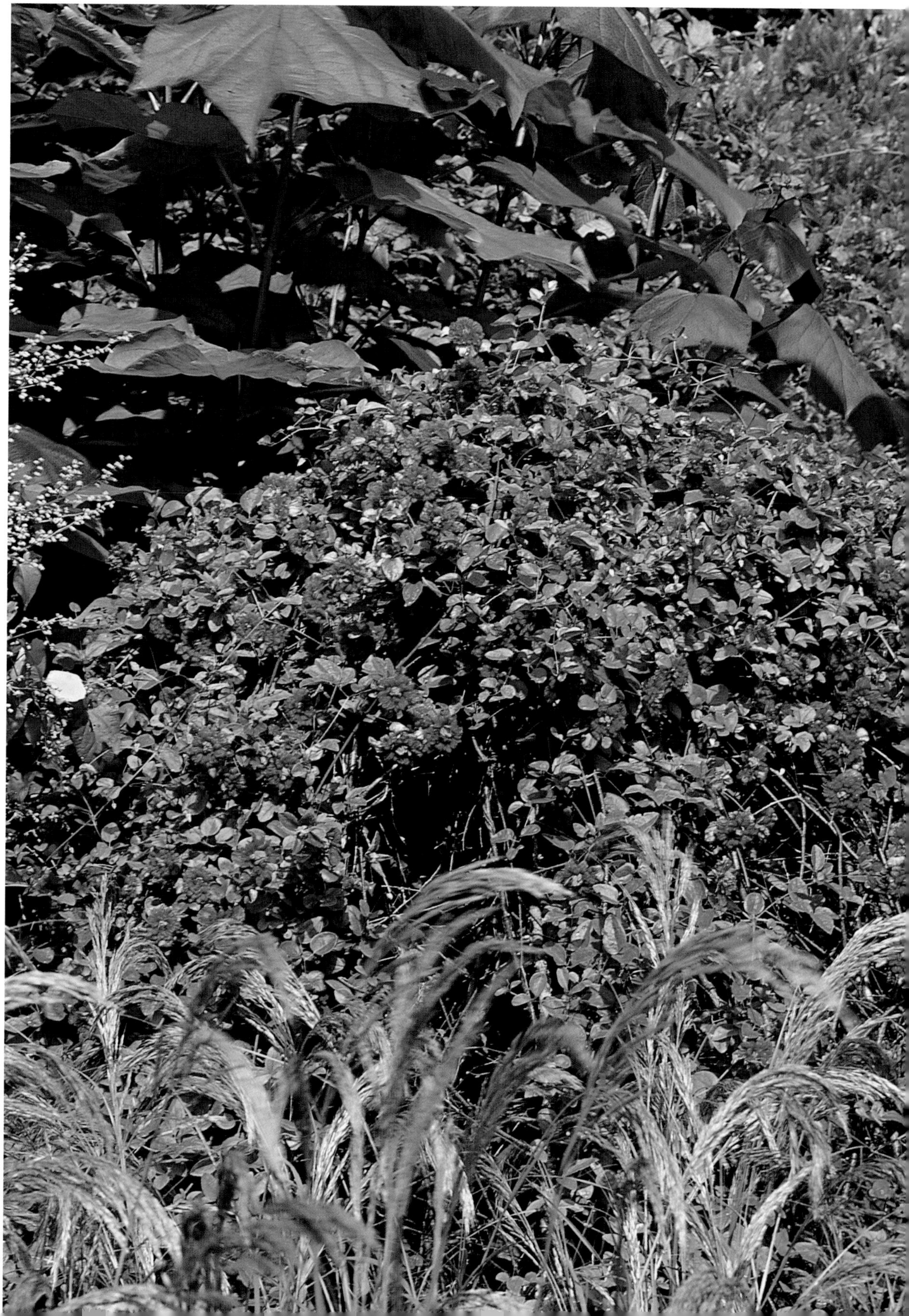

Chapter 7

Clematis for Small Gardens

Clematis Anna Louise 'Evithree', flowering
in a small wooden barrel, creates an
interesting colour statement.

Until recently it has been rather difficult to grow and flower clematis in the compact gardens found in towns, suburban areas and cities, due to the plants' tall-growing habit. Historically, clematis have needed plenty of space to grow and develop before becoming established enough to produce a good crop of flower over a long period of time. Now, fortunately, due to the work of various clematis breeders, gardeners can choose smaller-growing clematis which display a good crop of flowers over several months. I will divide this chapter into three sections, each addressing different situations commonly found in smaller gardens, and then discuss which clematis can be grown successfully in each of these compact spots.

In this chapter, I will envision a compact garden surrounding a small modern home, perhaps built on a housing estate or development, where the garden is quite small, measuring perhaps 25 ft. wide by 40 ft. long (7.5 × 12 m). Some gardens will be much smaller, of course, but they will almost certainly all have boundary walls or fences.

First, I will explore which clematis are best for adorning these walls and fences (as well as archways). I will then discuss which clematis are ideal for the patio or deck garden, which may adjoin a conservatory or garden room, and where the space will be used as an outdoor living area. Finally, I will recommend clematis for growing on balconies, in plant containers or in hanging baskets.

Clematis for Boundary Walls and Fences

Let us picture a garden surrounded by walls or fences, with one wall formed by the back of the house, and three other walls or fences, each around 6 ft. (2 m) high, which serve as the property boundaries. I imagine that there will be wall areas that have a flower border at their base, narrow or wide, where plants can be grown in the garden soil. Maybe there will be a small lawn in the central area, possibly with an archway or pergola to give height and interest. Perhaps there will be a patio or deck area where clematis can be displayed in containers.

On the house wall it will be possible to grow clematis quite high, through other plant material. If a narrow border of soil has been left at the base of the house wall, then life is made easier; if not, plants will need to be grown in a

Clematis Ice Blue 'Evipo003', flowering in a shady spot where its full colour is not bleached by strong sunshine.

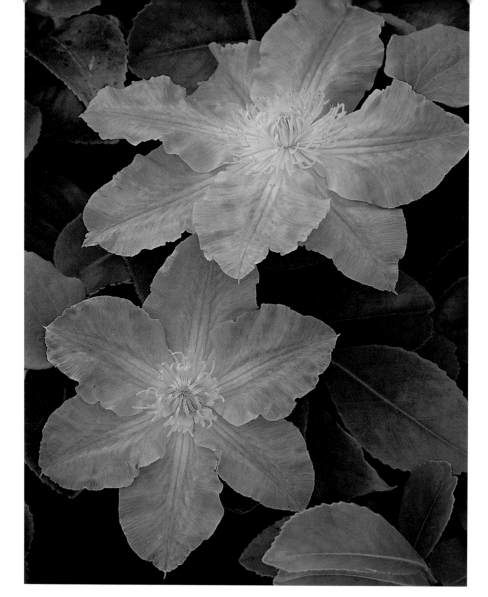

planter or container placed at the base of the wall. It is crucial to take note of which direction the house wall is facing, as this has a great impact on which plants can be grown there.

Let us look at a south-facing wall first and assume that there is a narrow 12- to 18-in. (30- to 45-cm) wide border at the base of the wall and that the soil is at least 12 in. (30 cm) deep. If the soil is of good quality and not full of builders' rubbish, it can be prepared for planting as described in Chapter 13. Otherwise the whole border may need its soil replaced with good topsoil or compost from a garden centre.

Which plants to choose? On a south-facing wall it would be good to have an evergreen shrub such as *Ceanothus* 'Autumnal Blue' or 'Burkwoodii', where a clematis could display its flowers against the dark green foliage of the ceanothus and its flowers, which bloom from midsummer onwards. A good complement to the ceanothus would be *Clematis* Anna Louise 'Evithree', which has violet flowers with a reddish purple central band to each sepal, the red *C.* 'Niobe', or the longer-flowering *C.* ROSEMOOR 'Evipooo2', coloured deep red with a yellow centre. Alternatively, *C.* JOSEPHINE 'Evijohill', with its pinkish mauve fully double flowers, would be very attractive. With yellow, pink or red climbing roses, the pale blue *Clematis* WISLEY 'Evipooo1' or the purple-flowered *C.* 'Gipsy Queen' would contrast well.

When working with a narrow border at the base of the house, remember that plants must be positioned as far as possible out from the base of the wall, so that your host and clematis receive as much natural rainwater as possible. Also, do remember to plant some shallow-rooted shrubs (such as heather) or herbaceous perennials to give that added shade to the root system of the clematis. In a small garden I would want as much flower colour as possible, so perhaps it would be best to plant some grey-foliaged summer annuals with other colourful annuals. These can, of course, be replaced in the autumn with winter-flowering pansies or primulas, or with some spring-flowering bulbs such as daffodils or tulips, again giving maximum effect of colour. If you do not have the time to do this, then simply use some herbaceous perennials or shallow-rooted low-growing shrubs.

If there is no border at the base of the house wall and the odd paving-slab cannot be removed to allow preparation of a small planting hole, it will be necessary to use a planter or large container. These need to be as large as possible, to accommodate a host plant, a clematis and some low-growing plants to shade the clematis root. Ideally, a container that is at least 2 ft. (60 cm) deep and wide should be used. Prepare it as described on page 223. If using a container of this size is feasible, then a ceanothus and clematis plus the shallow-rooted perennials or annual bedding plants can be grown together successfully as long as watering is attended to regularly and the normal feeding is carried out during the growing season.

If the house wall is north-facing, rather than south-facing, then the same requirements regarding soil or container apply. On a north-facing location it is vital to remember that you should place something (I suggest house bricks) under a container, so that it can drain properly. This is especially important during the winter months when it could become saturated with rain or snow and remain cold and wet inside its base, which is not ideal for the clematis' root system.

As far as host plants for a north wall are concerned, *Pyracantha* would be ideal, giving flowers, evergreen foliage and, of course, berries during the autumn and winter months. It is best to choose a light-coloured clematis that will show up against the evergreen foliage of a plant like a pyracantha. Pink-mauve *Clematis* 'Nelly Moser', blue *C.* 'General Sikorski' and the very pale blue *C.* ICE BLUE 'Evipooo3' would all be excellent choices.

On east- or west-facing house walls the same requirements regarding soil or containers would again apply, but the selection of a host plant and clematis to grow through it would change. A useful host plant for an east-facing location would be *Garrya elliptica,* with greyish green evergreen foliage, and long catkins during the winter months. Some excellent clematis for partnering with this charming shrub include *Clematis* 'Guernsey Cream' and *C.* ALABAST 'Poulala' (both creamy yellow), *C.* CLAIR DE LUNE 'EVIRIN' (very pale blue with red centre), or *C.* 'Pink Champagne' (syn. 'Kakio') with deep pinkish mauve flowers.

For a west-facing location, it is possible to use climbing hydrangeas or climbing roses as hosts. *Hydrangea petiolaris* is self-clinging and has flat heads of white flowers that make a great foil for virtually any type of clematis. Perhaps it would be useful to use a late-season-flowering clematis that flowers on new growth in midsummer when the hydrangea is also flowering. Any coloured clematis will blend well, but perhaps it is the pale blue of *Clematis* 'Błękitny Anioł' (syn. 'Blue Angel'), the pink/mauve of *C.* 'Comtesse de Bouchaud', the white of *C.* 'John Huxtable', the pale blue of *C.* WISLEY 'Evipo001' or the nodding pink flowers of *C.* CONFETTI 'Evipo036' that would add optimum interest and colour.

On the boundary walls and fences I believe it is best to grow clematis through other wall-trained or evergreen shrubs. If these walls or fences are only around 6 ft. (2 m) tall, I recommend growing plants that reach perhaps 7–8 ft. (2.3–2.75 m); if they happen to grow just higher than the wall or fence, they break the outline of the top, creating a more interesting background line. Of

Clematis WISLEY 'Evipo001' is an ideal late-flowering clematis for partnering with roses. Here it grows with *Rosa* 'New Dawn' on a north-facing wall.

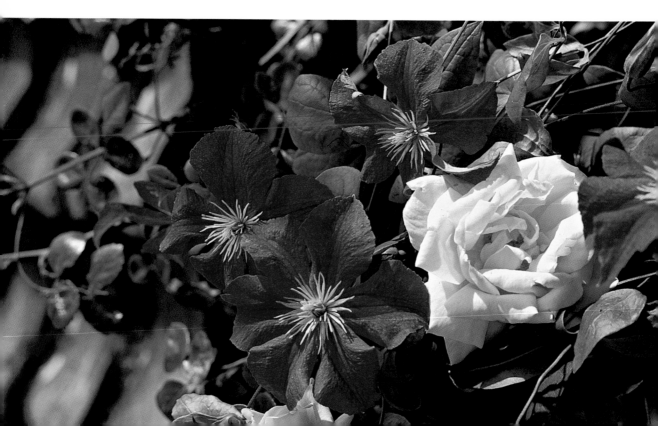

course, it may be possible to grow a climber which is not self-supporting only just over the height of the wall or fence.

In this situation, you should select climbing roses that are both colourful and amenable to a good range of different coloured clematis. The clematis you choose should in turn be late-flowering, and blend with the roses chosen. Suitable red and vermilion roses for this purpose include *Rosa* 'Danse de Feu', 'Étoile de Hollande' and 'Guinée'; of the pink shades, I enjoy the climbing *R.* 'Cécile Brünner', 'Pink Perpétue' and 'Zéphirine Drouhin' (which is thornless). Yellow climbing roses offer good contrast for the blue and purple clematis; the yellow *R. banksiae* 'Lutea' is charming, 'Gloire de Dijon' is a great favourite, and *R.* 'Mermaid'—as well as the white *R.* 'Iceberg' and *R.* 'Madame Alfred Carrière'—are all good choices.

Some of the rambler roses would also be very appropriate. Examples include *Rosa* 'Albertine', rich salmon pink; *R.* 'American Pillar', with large clusters of deep pink single flowers; *R.* 'Félicité Perpétue', with small pale cream flowers in large clusters; and *R.* 'New Dawn', shell pink with glossy green leaves. Any of these pink roses would make a great host plant for *Clematis* Harlow Carr 'Evipo004' or *C.* Wisley 'Evipo001', contrasting with the blue clematis flowers from the end of early summer until early autumn.

Other wall-trained shrubs or climbers ideal for the boundary walls or fences include abelias, *Abeliophyllum distichum*, the upright-growing *Ceanothus* 'Cascade', *C. impressus* and *C.* ×*veitchianus*, which are all best on south or west walls, as well as *Actinidia kolomikta* and *Buddleja fallowiana* var. 'Alba' which both need full sun. Camellias are suitable for north or east walls but not in very exposed, windy sites. Flowering quinces (*Chaenomeles*) are very good for exposed north- or east-facing locations and look extremely good in such positions with the nodding flowers of the *Clematis alpina* and *C. macropetala* cultivars. Also ideal are the less vigorous escallonias, such as red-flowered *Escallonia* 'C. F. Ball', rosy pink *E.* 'Edinensis', white *E.* 'Iveyi', and *E.* 'Slieve Donard' which boasts apple-blossom–pink flowers on long arching stems. *Hedera* (ivy), particularly the variegated forms like *H. canariensis* 'Variegata', makes a useful backdrop for clematis such as *C.* 'Henryi' or *C.* 'Marie Boisselot'.

The winter jasmine, *Jasminum nudiflorum*, may be a bit rampant, but it can be controlled. Its yellow winter flowers are a great bonus and it would be a useful host for a late-flowering clematis such as *Clematis* 'Venosa Violacea'. The jasmine can be pruned after flowering and before the clematis comes into growth. *Kerria japonica* 'Pleniflora' has lovely winter stems and would also be best planted with a late-flowering clematis that is pruned back before winter.

Some of the flowering honeysuckles are far too vigorous for the type of wall we are talking about, but others—such as *Lonicera* ×*brownii* 'Dropmore Scarlet', which has tubular scarlet flowers from midsummer to mid autumn—

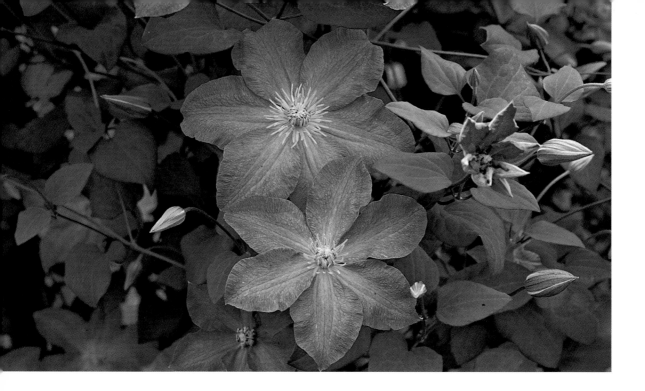

Being compact and very free-flowering, *Clematis* Bonanza 'Evipo031' is an extremely useful viticella type for small gardens.

would look marvellous with the mauve-couloured *Clematis* Bonanza 'Evipo031'. (This clematis would not swamp the honeysuckle, as it grows to just under 5 ft. [1.75 m].) *Lonicera japonica* 'Aureoreticulata' with variegated foliage would make a great background for *C.*Palette 'Evipo034' whose nodding, veined flowers would look very elegant with this honeysuckle. *Lonicera periclymenum* 'Graham Thomas' is fairly vigorous but would be a good host for the deep purple *C.*Victor Hugo 'Evipo007'.

Pyracanthas are always a favourite of mine because of their flowers, their vigour, their evergreen foliage, and their very attractive berries during autumn and early winter. *Pyracantha* 'Mohave', *P.* 'Orange Glow', *P. rogersiana* and its red-fruited cultivar *P. rogersiana* 'Flava', and the yellow-berried *P. rogersiana* 'Teton' are some of the ones I know and have grown successfully. Even if they become too tall for the wall or fence, they can be controlled easily. They make ideal hosts for either the early double or single large-flowered clematis, or the midsummer to autumn large- and small-flowered cultivars. Another useful wall-trained climber is the highly scented *Trachelospermum jasminoides,* which also has a variegated form. Both plants are evergreen but need south- or west-facing aspects. Using either with *Clematis* Confetti 'Evipo036', with dainty pink flowers, would offer added interest.

We have considered just a handful of useful wall-trained evergreen shrubs, deciduous shrubs and climbers that can be grown on walls or fences surrounding a small garden. If the border at the base of the wall or fence is 3 ft. (1 m) wide, the planting ideas explained in Chapter 5 will give you additional food for thought with regard to plant associations using clematis with other low-growing shrubs or perennials which would be suitable for a small garden. Also, it is worth considering the clematis comprising the Boulevard

Collection—all of which grow to only 3–4 ft. (1–1.2 m). These can be grown in containers for the patio, but they are equally good for growing in narrow borders at the base of a wall or fence in a small garden where space is very limited. Members of this Collection—all of which can grow up into the base of any of the wall-trained plants mentioned in this chapter—include: *Clematis* Angelique 'Evipoo17' (dusky pale blue), *C.* Cezanne 'Evipoo23' (pale blue), *C.* Chantilly 'Evipoo21' (creamy pink), *C.* Parisienne 'Evipoo19' (blue with a red centre) and *C.* Picardy 'Evipoo24' (deep purple). These clematis flower on both old and new growth, and I find that it is best to hard prune them in the late winter/early spring so that they regenerate themselves, flowering throughout the following summer months.

You should not neglect the possibility of using herbaceous clematis in the smaller garden. Plants such as *Clematis integrifolia* and its cultivars, for instance, are worth considering. Clematis of the Prairie Evison and Poulsen Collection, which grow to 4–5 ft. (1.2–1.75 m), are outstanding when grown up into the base of other wall-trained shrubs or climbers and look marvellous making their way up into climbing or rambler roses. All four cultivars, *C.* Chinook 'Evipoo13' (purple-blue), *C.* Gazelle 'Evipoo14' (white), *C.* Medley 'Evipoo12' (pink) and *C.* Savannah 'Evipoo15' (deep pink), offer additional interest due to their flower shape and the length of flowering (from two to three months during the summer). Another outstanding choice for clambering up into roses is *C.* Petit Faucon 'Evisix', with its deep purple, semi-nodding flowers, which also blooms for two to three months.

Moving away from the borders surrounding a small garden: if space permits, two or three archways can be placed over a pathway to give a different form to the garden. Archways with a central point of, say, 7–8 ft. (1.5–1.75 m)

Clematis 'Błękitny Anioł', gracing an archway on a small patio area in morning light—a perfect place to enjoy breakfast.

above the ground level offer the opportunity to plant more clematis. In this situation I would prefer to grow clematis with other climbers such as roses or some evergreens; clematis most certainly can clothe archways by themselves, but other plants add that extra-special bonus. Ideal clematis for clothing archways include the late-flowering (midsummer to autumn) large-flowered cultivars and the Viticella Group. Pale blue *Clematis* 'Błękitny Anioł' (syn. 'Blue Angel') does this exceedingly well in Charis Ward's garden at Abbey Dore Court in Herefordshire, England, as does pale pink *C.* CONFETTI 'Evipo036', where it is a delight to look up into the flowers against a clear blue sky. Although Abbey Dore Court is a large garden, this planting idea applies equally well to a smaller garden.

Clematis for Patios and Deck Gardens

Some houses or apartments will have a very limited garden area. Small patio areas are great fun and require little work—only watering and tending to the needs of plants which are mostly growing in containers. I assume such small garden areas are fairly well shaded as they will be used very much as extensions of the house, for relaxing or for taking meals during the spring, summer or early autumn months.

When planning the plants for a patio or deck garden near to the house the new, shorter-growing clematis are a real asset. If there is wall space where clematis can be grown in the soil with other wall-trained shrubs or climbers, this is ideal. Most of the host plants mentioned earlier in this chapter can be used, and the Boulevard Collection clematis can then be grown through them. Another very useful compact free-flowering plant is *Clematis* 'Piilu', with its pink-mauve striped flowers that have yellow centres. It fades a little in direct sun, and so is best in a shady position. However, if planting in garden soil is not an option, these clematis can be planted into a large container to be trained up a wall. A container that is 2 ft. (60 cm) wide and deep would also provide enough space for a host plant, such as a compact wall-trained shrub. On the other hand, you may wish to simply grow the clematis by itself or plant two of these compact clematis together. A combination of pale blue *C.* ANGELIQUE 'Evipo017' and deep purple *C.* PICARDY 'Evipo024' would look splendid. If they are under-planted with grey-foliaged plants and/or blue-, white- or pale-mauve–flowered herbaceous perennials to give shade to the root system of the clematis, this can make for an outstanding plant association.

On the open patio or deck itself, any of these compact clematis could be planted in a free-standing container. (Full instructions on how to plant up a container are given in Chapter 13 and refer to the Boulevard Collection

cultivars.) On a small patio it is important to use these more compact types, including *Clematis* 'Piilu', as they produce more flowers over a longer period of time. In such areas, each pot or container should provide the maximum amount of flower, foliage or interest for as long as possible, because space counts and every square foot (or metre) should be giving its best.

The new compact free-flowering clematis belonging to the Boulevard Collection have been designed for just this purpose. It is important to use the correct containers, with adequate drainage holes, and to select the right type of potting soil; these details are fully explained in Chapter 13. In addition to selecting which clematis to grow in containers in a small patio area, I believe it is equally important to give careful thought to the choice of additional plant material for under-planting the clematis. Attention should be paid to colour blending, the aim being to select the most interesting additional plant material that will perform over the longest possible period.

In this situation I feel that summer and winter bedding plant material should be chosen over permanent planting of perennials or shallow-rooted plant material, because colour (in either the foliage or the flowers of the additional plants) is needed to give maximum impact. You can also encourage additional growth and more flowers by regularly deadheading the clematis and their companion plants, and the usual watering and feeding tasks will also help the plants to perform well. Of course, even with the smallest of patio or deck areas, it is always best to plant into the garden soil rather than plant in a container whenever possible, as this reduces the time spent watering the plants. Moreover, if you can organize drip-irrigation directly to each container or flowerbed, this will be a tremendous advantage.

Clematis 'Piilu', a very compact free-flowering plant for the smaller garden, is best in a shady site as it can get bleached in full sun.

Though my aim is to make clematis growing 'easy gardening', I am aware that this must all seem an incredible amount of work! Yet it is not nearly as difficult as it sounds, and once your clematis are flowering with the other associated plants you will appreciate the results of the hours spent planning, planting, watering and feeding. All of this really does add pleasure to life, especially if family meals can be taken surrounded by the plants that you have cared for personally.

Growing Clematis on Balconies

Thanks to the new compact clematis mentioned above, the growing of flowering clematis on balconies has now become much simpler and more feasible. Due to their compactness these clematis are easier to train, and less vigorous, than the older cultivars. They produce their flowers on shorter stems and have more flowers on each stem; as all of these clematis have smaller flowers, their flowers do not become damaged by wind and rain so readily, and if they do become damaged in severe weather, they have so many more flower buds following behind that they are soon replaced.

Of course, on a balcony it will not usually be possible to grow these clematis through other shrubby plant material or climbers, so they will need to grow by themselves up onto some type of support. The support, placed against any side wall or the side of the apartment, can be in the form of a trellis made of either metal, plastic or wood. Wood is the obvious choice as it will not become too hot in the summer months. Please follow the guidelines in Chapter 13 for the selection of containers, drainage, potting soil et cetera.

As in the case of the small patio or deck garden, it is important to take time to select the appropriate additional plant material, so that you achieve your aims of colour, impact, good combination planting and long flowering period. If automatic drip watering/feeding lines can be installed, this will really help with the task of watering.

In my view, the best cultivars for this purpose are *Clematis* 'Piilu' (pink-mauve striped), *C.* ANGELIQUE 'Evipoo17' (dusky blue), *C.* PICARDY 'Evipoo24' (purple) and *C.* PARISIENNE 'Evipoo19' (deep blue), all of which which give flower for two to three months once established if care is taken with watering, feeding and deadheading. For very sunny balconies, *C.* ANGELIQUE 'Evipoo17', *C.* PICARDY 'Evipoo24' and *C.* PARISIENNE 'Evipoo19' are all good choices, while pale blue *C.* CEZANNE 'Evipoo23', pale creamy pink *C.* CHANTILLY 'Evipoo21' and *C.* 'Piilu' are excellent clematis for north-facing locations. In particularly windy locations, blue-mauve *C.* BIJOU 'Evipoo30' and dusky pink *C.* FILIGREE 'Evipoo29' work well; they reach only about 12 in. (30 cm)

Clematis Bɪᴊᴏᴜ 'Evipo030' performs brilliantly with other plants in hanging baskets or wall baskets.

in height, flower for two months, and can be planted to bloom with summer-flowering annuals or permanent perennials.

Clematis for Baskets

In addition to performing well in windy spots, *Clematis* Bɪᴊᴏᴜ 'Evipo030' and *C.* Fɪʟɪɢʀᴇᴇ 'Evipo029' are ideal for growing in hanging baskets or wall baskets. They are both compact and will send out stems that will cascade down from the baskets. I recommend using other plant material with these clematis to give added interest—grey foliage with pink, blue or mauve flowers would be, in my opinion, the best possible complement. During the late summer months these clematis will all flower again, and they are likely to put on some trailing stems, perhaps up to 18 in. (45 cm) long, which I would leave. When the plants flower the following season, flowers will be produced directly from these stems, creating a great effect. However, if they are growing in small containers or baskets at floor level, I generally trim them back to keep the plants more bushy in habit so that they form a mound of flowers.

Before the advent of these two cultivars, people have tried to grow many of the more compact flowering cultivars, such as *Clematis* 'H. F. Young', in baskets. Yet I believe that *C.* Bɪᴊᴏᴜ 'Evipo030' and *C.* Fɪʟɪɢʀᴇᴇ 'Evipo029' are better plants for this purpose due to their very, very compact natural habit.

Because they are quite new, we still need to learn how to get the best from them. As with growing any plants in hanging baskets, watering and feeding is most important. We know that if clematis are fed while they are in bloom, their flowering period is reduced—so I recommend feeding these two clematis well, before they come into flower. Once the buds are pea-sized, feeding should cease until the flowering begins to slow down. When the first flush of flowers slows down, you should remove the old flowerheads and then begin feeding the plants again in order to generate new growth and flowers.

Chapter 8 # Clematis for Indoors

Clematis CEZANNE 'Evipo023' can
thrive either outside, or in a
conservatory or garden room.

The concept of growing clematis indoors is not new. During the Victorian peri-od, clematis were grown in pots outside and then brought indoors at the point of flowering. I believe these were the early large-flowered cultivars, and most probably the double or semi-double large-flowered cultivars such as the com-pact free-flowering *Clematis* 'Mrs George Jackman' and *C.* 'Louise Rowe'.

Today, these same cultivars can be grown and brought into the house, con-servatory or garden room. However, we now have a range of newer cultivars from the Boulevard and Flora Collections that are even more suitable for growing indoors, due to the clematis' free-flowering and compact habit—and better still are the members of the Garland Collection, which can be grown on hoops.

New Collections for Indoors

Let us first consider some of the new cultivars that are especially suitable for growing indoors, and discuss the best place for them, as well as their cultiva-tion and aftercare, potting on and pruning. The Boulevard Collection culti-vars of *Clematis* Angelique 'Evipo017', *C.* Cezanne 'Evipo023', *C.* Chantilly 'Evipo021', *C.* Parisienne 'Evipo019' and *C.* Picardy 'Evipo024' are ideal for growing in a conservatory or garden room. These can be grown outside in a container and moved into the conservatory or garden room just at the point of flowering in late spring. Alternatively, they can be moved indoors in late win-ter just as they start to come into growth. If the latter way is chosen then these clematis will come into flower during mid to late spring. In cold locations in northern America or northern Europe the clematis can be left inside most of the year, but they will need a six-to-eight-week dormancy period during the autumn/early winter and should be placed in a cold greenhouse (glasshouse) or other frost-free location to achieve this. If the temperature does drop to 32°F (0°C) this will not harm the plants but it will ensure that they do go into dormancy.

Once again, the very compact *Clematis* Bijou 'Evipo030' and *C.* Filigree 'Evipo029', are ideal as potted plants, growing to only 12 in. (30 cm) in height. These can be treated in the same way as the Boulevard Collection and brought into the 'indoor' location whenever desired.

The clematis that make up the Garland Collection work exceptionally well indoors. These belong to the Florida Group, and because of their flowering habit they will flower in the house, conservatory or garden room for six to eight weeks without stopping. (However, although they can be flowered throughout the year, they will require a rest period at some point.) Clematis from this Collection include *Clematis* Pistachio 'Evirida' (creamy white with a green centre), *C.* Viennetta 'Evipo006' (creamy white with a large purple centre), *C.* Cassis 'Evipo020' (purple-veined double) and *C.* Peppermint 'Evipo005' (greenish white double).

The Garland Collection clematis can be grown and flowered entirely in a normal well-lit living room, kitchen or dining room. Although they can also be grown outside in the garden once their use as houseplants has ended, these cultivars are truly houseplant clematis which have been specially bred to grow and flower on hoops or obelisks as an indoor plant for the house or conservatory. They flower for several weeks at a time; once flowering has finished, you should prune them back to encourage further blooms three to four months later.

Cultivation and Aftercare

Once you purchase your clematis, the way in which you cultivate and care for it will make all the difference. The Boulevard and Flora Collection cultivars can be purchased from a garden centre, nursery or garden shop and then planted into a suitable container. You will probably want to purchase your clematis while it is in flower so that the flowering period can be enjoyed immediately. Once flowering ends, clematis from the Boulevard Collection can be pruned down to about 4 in. (10 cm) while the members of the Flora Collection can be pruned to 2.75 in. (7 cm) above soil level. At this point, the support on which the clematis was growing when it was purchased can be removed (and replaced if necessary), after potting on into a larger container.

This hard pruning will encourage the plant to regenerate and it will produce new side stems which will flower again in about six to eight weeks as long as the pruning is carried out between mid spring and midsummer. The new growth will require attention on a regular basis so that it can be trained and tied to the support, with the exception of the Flora Collection clematis which do not require any support.

When growing the clematis indoors I feel that either a terracotta pot or ceramic container would look best, and I suggest growing the clematis on a metal or perhaps bamboo plant support. If you purchase your plant in early spring and prune hard at the end of its flowering period, and it then flowers

Clematis Pistachio 'Evirida' can be grown most successfully in a shady conservatory, planted in the soil or in a large container.

Clematis Cassis 'Evipo020' produces flowers for six to eight weeks as a flowering pot plant in the house.

again after being grown on, the plant should then be left to go into its natural dormancy during the autumn and winter. As mentioned earlier, the plant will need a dormancy period, so remember that it may need a colder environment in which to 'rest' unless the garden room becomes cold during the winter months. It will need a rest period of six to eight weeks before starting into growth again.

In the late winter or spring, whenever the plant is brought back into the indoor environment, the old leaves will need to be removed and the top growth pruned back, as discussed in Chapter 14. The Boulevard and Flora Collection cultivars will need to be pruned down to 6 in. (15 cm) and 3 in. (7.5 cm) respectively. The remaining old stems from the previous season will be the first ones to flower, followed by flowers from the new growth. As new growth commences this should be tied in as it develops. Attention to watering and feeding is most important and a tomato or rose feed can be used.

When these clematis have completed their main crop of flowers, it is possible to prune all stems down to 6 in. (15 cm) above soil level with the Boulevard Collection, and to 3 in. (7.5 cm) for the Flora Collection. If this is done during the period from early summer to midsummer, they will then re-grow and flower again six to eight weeks after being pruned. This second flowering period makes these clematis truly enjoyable for growing indoors; to ensure they flower successfully, they must be kept well watered and fed, to encourage new growth and flower. Once the second flowering crop has finished, allow the plant to go into its natural dormancy period, and give it a cold rest period so that it can again perform well the next season.

At numerous points throughout this book I have explored the possibility of growing other plant material in the container to give added shade to the root system of the clematis. If the area where the clematis is to be grown is hot and sunny, then the same advice stands. However, if the indoor area is shaded it is not necessary and is really a matter of choice. Of course, if there are additional plants in the container which have interesting foliage as well as flower, this is a great advantage during the period after the clematis has finished its first flowering period and has been pruned back.

Assuming that additional plant material is used in the container, it is most important to top-dress the soil in the container at the beginning of each season. Even if other plants are not used, you should remove the top 2–3 in. (5–7.5 cm) of topsoil and replace it with a good-quality potting soil.

From time to time—every two years, ideally—the size of the container in which the clematis is growing should be increased. You could start the first year with a container that is 15 in. (37.5 cm) deep, and the same across, and then every second year increase its size. This is not absolutely essential, but I strongly recommend it; if your clematis is going to flower from very early spring to mid autumn each year, the fresher the soil in the container, and the more space the roots have to develop, the better your plant will perform. When your plant has finally outgrown its container, it can be planted out in the garden.

The Garland Collection cultivars are, I believe, an exceptionally valuable group of clematis. They can perform throughout the season as indoor house-plants and then when they become too old to perform well, they can be planted in the garden (in Zones 6–9). These plants can be obtained from garden centres, nurseries or garden shops, generally in a 6-in. (15-cm) wide pot with the plant's stems trained around a hoop or obelisk. They can be placed in a living room, kitchen, conservatory or garden room in a well-lit position. Your plant will need to be watered as a normal houseplant, not too wet and not too dry, and a houseplant food can be used to keep the plant in a good, healthy condition. The flowering growth of these clematis will be 3–4 ft. (1–1.2 m) and they will continue to grow after the plants have been purchased. As the stems grow, they produce more and more flower buds. Old flowerheads should be removed to encourage more to develop and to open along the stems. As this new growth develops it should be tucked into the hoop or obelisk. Be careful not to break the stems, as it is these growing tips that continue to grow and develop, producing the new flower buds. When the plants finally stop flowering, they can be pruned, re-potted, trained and flowered again, or pruned and planted in the garden.

Let us now assume that you wish to re-flower the plant rather than plant it in the garden. As the last flowers fade away, all of the top growth can be pruned down to within 3 in. (7.5 cm) of the soil level in the pot; prune to just above a leaf-axil bud. Remove all the top growth and the hoop and any dead leaves that are on the remaining stems, and give the plant a good tidy-up. The plant should be removed from its pot and potted into a larger one, which could have a 2.5-in. (5-cm) wider top. Pot into a good quality potting soil and make sure that crocks, stones or pebbles are placed over the drainage holes to assist with good drainage. A larger hoop or other support can be attached to the pot and, as the new growth develops, it must be carefully tied to the hoop or support, or tucked in.

After about eight to ten weeks your clematis should be back in flower. As long as the place where the clematis is growing is light enough (a kitchen windowsill or a sunlit conservatory or garden room would work well), these clematis will continue to flower until Christmas. As the days grow shorter, you will find that the clematis with white or creamy green flowers will take on greener shades. This is normal and is simply due to lower light levels; the clematis flowers will return to their true colours the next season.

Once these clematis have finished flowering, they should be allowed to go into a natural dormancy. Recall that in order for this to happen, they will need to be removed from the indoor location and given a period of six to eight weeks at a colder temperature. (If the temperature were to drop down to 30°F [−1°c or −2°c], this would be ideal.) All of the leaves will die as the plant goes into dormancy, and after the usual six-to-eight-week rest period the plants can be brought back into flower again. At this point you should either re-pot them into a slightly larger pot or at least top-dress the potting soil of the previous season. At this time all top growth will need to be pruned down to within 3 in. (7.5 cm) of soil level. As new growth develops this will then need to be tucked or tied into the support.

The process of re-flowering, re-potting and allowing the plant to have its rest period can continue for several years. When the plant seems to be getting rather tired and does not flower so well anymore, it can then be planted out in a garden location (in Zones 6–9). These clematis are best grown through wall-trained evergreen shrubs or in containers.

Further Options for the Conservatory

The clematis I have mentioned so far in this chapter have been specially bred for their lengthy flowering periods and the great volume of flowers that they produce. As such, they can be very successfully grown in containers or in the soil in a conservatory as described in Chapter 13. But for those who wish to grow clematis other than the Boulevard, Flora or Garland Collection cultivars in the conservatory, there are additional clematis of merit that are worthy of consideration. To explore these further options, I will move chronologically through the flowering seasons, and will assume that most of these clematis will be grown in containers.

Early-Season-Flowering Clematis

The *Clematis cirrhosa* var. *cirrhosa* cultivars look charming growing in containers for three to five years before they become too large and pot-bound. *Clematis cirrhosa* var. *purpurascens* 'Freckles', coming into flower during mid to late autumn, is rather lovely, and its flowers can even last until Christmas. The other cultivars of *C. cirrhosa* flower from midwinter onwards, and give some early season flowers. The Alpina and Macropetala Group clematis, including *C. chiisanensis* 'Lemon Bells', would be delightful if grown in containers and brought into the conservatory or garden room just before flowering. Again, after about three to five years they would need to be replaced and could be planted out into the garden. Clematis belonging to the Montana Group, on the other hand, would become far too vigorous and I do not recommend them for growing in the conservatory.

Midseason-Flowering Clematis

The Regal Evison and Poulsen Collection double large-flowered cultivars would be great fun for growing in a conservatory, where they would provide a good two to three months of flower. *Clematis* Arctic Queen 'Evitwo' (fully double white), *C.* Josephine 'Evijohill' (deep pinkish mauve), *C.* Crystal Fountain 'Evipo038' (blue with whitish petaloid staments) and *C.* Franziska Maria 'Evipo008' (deep blue) would all be attractive and invite lots of interest.

Many of the early large-flowered cultivars would provide a great deal of colour. The best ones for this purpose are *Clematis* Anna Louise 'Evithree', purple with a deeper bar; *C.* 'Doctor Ruppel', deep rose pink with a darker bar; *C.* 'Fujimusume', coloured a delightful blue; *C.* 'H. F. Young', very free-flowering with blue blooms; *C.* 'Niobe', deep red; and *C.* Royal Velvet 'Evifour', deep velvety purple. *Clematis* 'Louise Rowe', a very light blue which displays single, semi-double and double flowers all at the same time, offers good value as does *C.* 'Mrs George Jackman', semi-double white, and *C.* 'Royalty', a very compact semi-double purple.

Clematis cirrhosa 'Ourika Valley' will produce a good crop of flowers when grown in a container in a conservatory or garden room.

Clematis florida var. sieboldiana produces an enormous number of flowers when grown in the sheltered conditions of a conservatory.

Late-Season-Flowering clematis

The late-flowering large-flowered cultivars would be a bit vigorous for our purposes, as would the Viticella Group. However, I recommend trying *Clematis* BONANZA 'Evipo031', a very compact and free-flowering mauve clematis. It is a useful new-wood-flowering cultivar that blooms towards the end of early summer.

Other good late-flowering clematis for adding interest and colour include the scented *Clematis ×aromatica* (purple with a creamy white centre) and *C. flammula* (with almond-scented white flowers), both of which are especially sound choices for growing in a conservatory. *Clematis florida* var. *sieboldiana,* with its passionflower-like flowers coloured white with large purple centres, also consistently docs well in a conservatory or garden room, as would the new florida type, *C.* 'Fond Memories' (pale pinkish white). Finally, the very bright purple-blue *C.* HARLOW CARR 'Evipo004' could be grown well in a container and would reach about 6 ft. (2 m). I am sure that many other clematis could also be grown in containers and then moved into a conservatory or garden room while they are in flower.

Much remains to be learned about the cultivation of clematis indoors; while the ones discussed in this chapter are most certainly worthy of growing as described, breeders have not yet created the ideal 'houseplant' clematis. I hope that breeders will eventually produce evergreen clematis for indoor use—and what a bonus it would be to also have a strong scent to these new clematis! Perhaps in time this will become a reality.

Chapter 9

Clematis for Sun
and Shade

Clematis ROSEMOOR 'Evipo002', a
useful strong-coloured clematis
for a sunny position.

Because gardens around the world vary considerably in their design and in the habitats they create, different types of clematis are required to achieve different objectives from country to country, and from region to region. Some gardeners need clematis for very hot sunny situations while others need clematis that will grow and flower well in fairly heavy shade.

English cottage-style gardens have come very much into fashion in recent times. Perhaps people are trying to create a sense of the past, or evoke a feeling of security, by copying this traditional style, as well as the New England-style gardens from northeastern North America where, very often, soft pastel-coloured flowers are required. Contrastingly, there are more modern minimalist styles where perhaps only strong colours or white flowers may be required. Being very versatile, clematis can fit into a variety of different gardening styles.

In parts of the world where the summers are hot and dry, designers create gardens with ample shade, including shady walkways and shady outdoor living spaces which serve as extensions of the indoor living area. In any garden, the level of sun and shade will vary throughout the day and throughout the year, so the demand is there for clematis that suit all situations.

Before exploring which clematis are best for various aspects, it is important to consider flower colour. When selecting clematis, keep in mind that the darker-coloured flowers—the reds, the purples, the deep blues and the darker-coloured striped flowers—as well as the white clematis, will provide flowers that fade only slightly in direct strong sunshine. Examples include *Clematis* 'Niobe', *C.* ROSEMOOR 'Evipo002' and *C.* 'Gipsy Queen'. The pale-coloured clematis—those with pale pink, mauve, pale blue and the paler-coloured striped flowers, including some of the creamy yellow-flowered clematis—hold their colour better in shady locations and should be grown out of direct strong sunshine. Cultivars such as *C.* 'Silver Moon', *C.* 'Nelly Moser' and *C.* 'Guernsey Cream' fall into this lighter-coloured category.

Another point to consider, however, is that many clematis, especially those that flower very early each season from the previous season's ripened stems, need sufficient sunlight to ripen and create the aged/ripened stems on which those early flowers will be produced. Therefore, while the general rule is that the clematis with deeper-coloured flowers, plus the whites, can be planted in sunny locations while many of the paler ones should be planted in the shade, the exception is that all early-flowering clematis will need some sunlight to ripen the stems in order to produce their early flowers. In the following sections I will give my views on the best clematis for sun and shade, progressing chronologically through the seasons in which they flower.

Early-Season-Flowering Clematis

The evergreen clematis described in this book generally require a sunny location to grow and flower well. These include *Clematis armandii* and the forms of *C. cirrhosa*. The latter go into a summer dormancy in their native habitat in southern Europe, while their stems ripen, re-growing only when the temperature lowers and the rains provide moisture to their root system. They therefore need strong sunlight to ripen their stems and allow them to produce a good crop of flowers. Unfortunately, however, some pale-flowered species and their cultivars do need a sunny position to grow and so the rule of thumb (dark colours for sun and pale colours for shade) does not work every time. *Clematis armandii* has been known to flower in a shady location, but south, east or west would be the best aspects.

It must also be mentioned that the alpina and macropetala types perform well in either sun or shade. Being native to the mountains, they are winter-hardy—but their pale flower colours can cope with the direct sun and do not fade badly, mainly because they flower very early in the season, and therefore can thrive in any location. Although the montana types will perform well in any location, I am sure that a better crop of flowers is produced by plants growing in greater sunlight. If they are growing in trees they will find their way of growing into the sunlight, even if they are planted on the shady side of the tree.

Midseason-Flowering Clematis

The earliest large-flowered single, double and semi-double clematis generally perform well in sun or shade; the deeper the colour of the flowers, the more likely they are to hold their flower colour in a sunny location. If clematis from this group are grown in the shade, they should receive at least three or four hours of good sunlight each day during the growing season.

An important point to remember is that clematis like to grow in a microclimate of other plant material and to have a shady root system—and this is extremely important when clematis are planted in a very hot, sunny location. In a hot location, the plants will need to be watered more frequently, possibly even on a daily basis during the summer months. Of course, this is equally vital when the clematis are being grown in containers, and must not be overlooked.

Keep in mind that as an early large-flowered clematis comes to the end of its first flowering period, the spent flowers should be removed. With a pair of secateurs (hand pruners), cut down to just above the second node. Make sure the plant is kept well watered so that new growth is generated to produce the next crop of flowers. At this time it is important to use a feed at regular intervals—choose a rose or tomato feed, or one specially designed for clematis plants. Again, this is also essential for container-grown clematis.

Most of the semi-double and double midseason-flowering clematis will perform best in a slightly sunny position. They should receive four to five hours of good sunlight per day during the growing season.

All clematis grown in a north-facing location in the northern hemisphere will, of course, flower slightly later than those growing in a sunny location. Due to the lower levels of sunlight, as compared with a sunny position, their early flowers may not display the full depth of colour. Some, such as *Clematis* 'Miss Bateman', will have green stripes down the centre of the sepals. The cream-coloured cultivars, which include *C.* ALABAST 'Poulala' and *C.* 'Guernsey Cream', could all have green flowers early in the season. This is just due to lower light levels and, perhaps, lack of direct sunlight. These unusual green-coloured flowers are of course great fun if you prefer more unusually coloured flowers and enjoy creating flower arrangments with them.

Two very large-flowered cultivars are worthy of mention here, as they perform exceptionally well in North America: *Clematis* 'Blue Ravine' and *C.* 'Ramona'. They seem to enjoy the hot North American sunshine but do not perform so well in Britain—so if your garden is in Britain, be sure to choose a sunny location.

Despite under-performing in British gardens, *Clematis* 'Blue Ravine' often thrives in sunny North American gardens, where it produces immense flowers.

Late-Season-Flowering Clematis

When it comes to the midsummer- and autumn-flowering large-flowered cultivars, the flower colour rule applies. Although some of these clematis may develop powdery mildew if planted in a north-facing location (especially if the air movement is poor), the Viticella Group clematis rarely seem to succumb to mildew in any garden location. As most clematis from the Viticella Group have hot dark colours, they will generally be selected for planting in full sun—they seem especially well suited to being grown in a sunny location, most likely due to the fact that the type species of *Clematis viticella* is native to northern Italy. They are therefore ideal for areas such as southern Europe or California, where they will grow in sun or shade, and perform exceptionally well.

The later-flowering species and their cultivars offer us a good selection of clematis that perform well in sunny locations. Purple *Clematis* ×*aromatica* will do well in a sunlit border, and the scented white *C. flammula* enjoys the sunshine of southern Europe or any mediterranean climate, as does its close relative, the white *C. terniflora* from Japan, and the scented cultivar *C.* ×*triternata* 'Rubromarginata', which has cream-coloured sepals with purple edges.

The Texensis Group cultivars *Clematis texensis* 'Duchess of Albany', *C. texensis* 'Princess Diana' (syn. 'The Princess of Wales'), which is also pink with a vibrant pink bar, and the dusky purple *C. texensis* 'Sir Trevor Lawrence' enjoy the sunshine, as do all of the yellow-flowered tangutica clematis and their yellow relative, *C. tibetana* var. *vernayi* (*L&S 13342*). *Clematis viorna*, whose deep flowers display a range of dull purples and pinks, is very much at home in North America and the warmer, sunny parts of Europe and the British Isles.

In warm areas, such as the European and Californian mediterranean climates, all clematis will flower earlier than they will in cooler climates. Many will flower and then rest during the hottest part of the year, only to come back into flower later in the season as the weather cools down. The practice of growing clematis in hotter climates is still fairly new, so there is much to learn, especially with the new cultivars.

However, one plant that has been proven exceptional for mediterranean climates is the deep-purple-blue-flowered *Clematis* Harlow Carr 'Evipo004'. During trials in California, north of San Francisco, it flowered from mid spring until late autumn, and continued to flower even when temperatures rose above 100°F (38°C). It will even continue to flower as temperatures climb to 110°F (43°C)—an extraordinary plant! At the other extreme, I believe the new Prairie Collection to be extremely winter-hardy, as it consists of cultivars bred from species that are known to withstand temperatures as low as −40°F (−40°C). These also perform well in either sun or shade.

The general rule (darker colours and white for sun, paler for shade) holds good for the late-season-flowering clematis. They should all receive at least three to four hours of good sunlight per day during the growing and flowering season.

In Chapters 10–12 each clematis species and cultivar is fully described, and I advise on the the best location in which to grow them. For quick reference, however, some of the very best choices for sunny and shady locations are listed below.

Early-Season-Flowering Clematis for Sun

C. armandii

C. cirrhosa cultivars

C. alpina cultivars

C. macropetala cultivars

C. montana cultivars

Midseason-Flowering Clematis for Sun— Single Flowers

C. ANNA LOUISE 'Evithree'

C. 'Blue Ravine'

C. BOURBON 'Evipo018'

C. 'Doctor Ruppel'

C. 'Henryi'

C. KINGFISHER 'Evipo037'

C. 'Marie Boisselot'

C. 'Miss Bateman'

C. 'Niobe'

C. PICARDY 'Evipo024'

C. REBECCA 'Evipo016'

C. ROSEMOOR 'Evipo002'

C. ROYAL VELVET 'Evifour'

C. 'Rüütel"

C. 'Warszawska Nike' (syn. 'Warsaw Nike')

Midseason-Flowering Clematis for Sun— Double and Semi-Double Flowers

C. ARCTIC QUEEN 'Evitwo'

C. CRYSTAL FOUNTAIN 'Evipo038'

C. 'Daniel Deronda'

C. FRANZISKA MARIA 'Evipo008'

C. 'Mrs George Jackman'

Late-Season-Flowering Clematis for Sun— Single Flowers

C. 'Barbara Harrington'

C. 'Gipsy Queen'

C. HARLOW CARR 'Evipo004'

C. 'Jackmanii'

C. 'Madame Édouard André'

C. VICTOR HUGO 'Evipo007'

Late-Season-Flowering Clematis for Sun— Viticella Group

C. 'Alba Luxurians'

C. 'Carmencita'

C. CONFETTI 'Evipo036'

C. 'Étoile Violette'

C. GALORE 'Evipo032'

C. 'Madame Julia Correvon'

C. 'Polish Spirit'

C. 'Royal Velours'

C. viticella 'Purpurea Plena Elegans'

Late-Season-Flowering Clematis for Sun— Species and Their Cultivars

C. 'Alionushka'

C. ×aromatica

C. CHINOOK 'Evipoo13'

C. ×durandii

C. 'Eriostemon'

C. flammula

C. GAZELLE 'Evipoo14'

C. ×jouiniana 'Praecox'

C. PETIT FAUCON 'Evisix'

C. recta var. recta

C. terniflora (in the USA)

C. texensis 'Duchess of Albany'

C. texensis 'Sir Trevor Lawrence'

C. tibetana var. vernayi (L&S 13342)

C. ×triternata 'Rubromarginata'

Early-Season-Flowering Clematis for Shade

C. alpina cultivars

C. macropetala cultivars

Midseason-Flowering Clematis for Shade— Single Flowers

C. ALABAST 'Poulala'

C. ANGELIQUE 'Evipoo17'

C. CEZANNE 'Evipoo23'

C. CHANTILLY 'Evipoo21'

C. CLAIR DE LUNE 'Evirin'

C. 'Dawn'

C. 'Fujimusume'

C. 'Guernsey Cream'

C. ICE BLUE 'Evipoo03'

C. 'Nelly Moser'

C. PARISIENNE 'Evipoo19'

C. 'Pink Champagne' (syn 'Kakio')

C. 'Silver Moon'

C. 'Twilight'

Midseason-Flowering Clematis for Shade— Double and Semi-Double Flowers

C. JOSEPHINE 'Evijohill'

C. 'Louise Rowe'

C. 'Proteus'

C. 'Veronica's Choice'

Late-Season-Flowering Clematis for Shade— Single Flowers

C. 'Błękitny Anioł' (syn 'Blue Angel')

C. 'Comtesse de Bouchaud'

C. 'John Huxtable'

C. 'Pink Fantasy'

C. WISLEY 'Evipoo01'

Late-Season-Flowering Clematis for Shade— Viticella Group

C. 'Alba Luxurians'

C. BONANZA 'Evipoo31'

C. PALETTE 'Evipoo34'

C. 'Venosa Violacea'

Late-Season-Flowering Clematis for Shade— Species and Their Cultivars

C. 'Alionushka'

C. GAZELLE 'Evipoo14'

C. MEDLEY 'Evipoo12'

C. SAVANNAH 'Evipoo15'

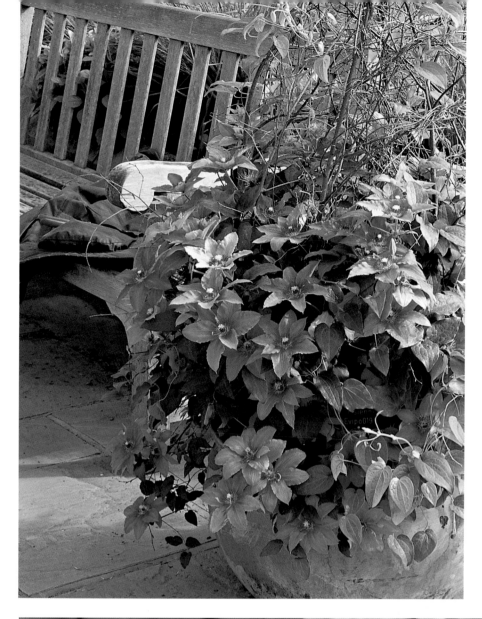

Clematis Parisienne 'Evipo019' is a rewarding midseason-flowering clematis for a shady position in a small garden.

Clematis ×*aromatica* is a charming, scented clematis for a sunny position in the front of a border.

Chapter 10

Early-Season-Flowering Clematis

Clematis alpina
'Frankie'

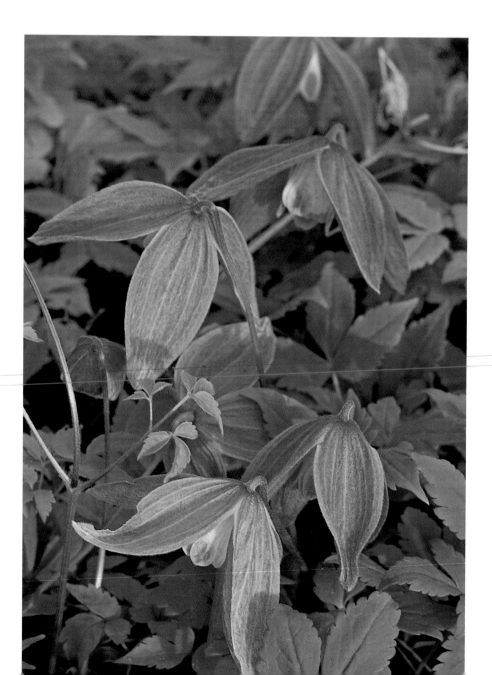

Clematis described in this chapter include the evergreen species and their cultivars; the alpina and macropetala types which belong to the Atragene Group; and the Montana Group. All of these clematis produce their main crop of flowers from the ripened stems of the previous season. They belong to Pruning Group One and require only light pruning after flowering. For full details of pruning please refer to page 237.

Clematis alpina var. alpina

Since its introduction to cultivation in 1792, this deciduous European species has given rise to a wealth of interesting cultivars coloured blue, pink, mauve and white. In most cases, the flowers are nodding and single, with four sepals. However, some are almost fully double, resembling those of the closely related species *C. macropetala* from China. The first flowers are borne in the spring on the ripened stems of the previous season. The alpinas are extremely winter-hardy, withstanding temperatures as low as −31°F (−35°C), and are therefore valuable garden plants for very exposed, windy positions. They can be used to clothe fences at the back of a border, even if north-facing. They also make ideal plants to grow to 4–5 ft. (1.2–1.5 m) over tripods or wooden wigwams in a border. The early spring flowers are followed by highly attractive silky seedheads, and occasional summer and late summer flowers. Height 6.5–10 ft. (2–3 m). Hardy in zones 3–9. ♀

C. alpina 'Constance'

Flowering period mid to late spring. Masses of rich purple-pink semi-double nodding flowers, 2 in. (5 cm) deep with shorter inner sepals (petaloid staminodes) which are cream to purplish pink. Flowers are followed by silky seedheads in summer. The leaves are bi-ternate, with coarse serrated edges. Height to 10 ft. (3 m) on a wall. Zones 3–9. Raised as a seedling from *C. alpina* 'Ruby' by Kathleen Goodman, England, and introduced by the author. ♀

C. alpina 'Cragside'

Flowering period mid to late spring, deep violet 1.75-in. (4.5-cm) bell-shaped flowers with paler margins. Flowers can be double, more like a macropetala than an alpina. Mid-green, toothed leaflets. Height 6.5–8.25 ft. (2–2.5 m). Zones 3–9. Raised by Ed Phillips, Kent, England in 1997.

Clematis alpina
'Pink Flamingo'

C. alpina 'Foxy'

Flowering period mid to late spring. Masses of single, nodding, very pale pink, broad-sepalled flowers, 2 in. (5 cm) deep, each sepal having pointed tips. Sometimes a good second crop of flowers appears later. Light green foliage with serrated edges and delightful seedheads. Height 10 ft. (3 m). Zones 3–9. Raised as a sport from *C. alpina* 'Frankie' by the author. ♔

C. alpina 'Frankie'

One of the most free-flowering alpinas, flowering in mid to late spring but usually with a second crop of flowers later in the season. Mid-blue flowers with broad sepals, 2 in. (5 cm) long, have a very pretty inner skirts. The outer petaloid stamens have pale blue tips. Lots of silky seedheads. Light green bi-ternate leaves, with serrated edges. Looks lovely when mixed with *C. alpina* 'Foxy'. Height 10 ft. (3 m). Zones 3–9. Raised in Lincolnshire, England by Frank Meecham. ♔

C. alpina 'Pink Flamingo'

The longest-flowering alpina, blooming from mid to late spring and again from mid to late summer. The 1.5-in. (4-cm) deep semi-double flowers are pale pink with deep pink veins. Saw-like, serrated leaves. Height 8.25–10 ft. (2.5–3 m). Zones 3–9. Originally a seedling from *C. alpina* raised in Brecon, Wales by Elizabeth Jones. ♔

C. armandii

This very vigorous evergreen Chinese species has become established as a garden plant in the milder parts of the United States and Europe. However, it should not be used to provide an evergreen screen in the garden or the back of a border, due to its naturally untidy habit. Within four to five years of becoming established its lower leaves will die back to a height of 3–5 ft. (1–1.5 m), which looks most unsightly. Its use as a garden plant can be justified if its natural untidiness is remembered, as it makes a marvellous thick screen of foliage for the back of the border growing on a strong solid fence, on support frame or on wires. If you are fortunate enough to have an old non-fruiting apple or pear tree in the border, then *C. armandii*'s elegant evergreen leaves give added interest to the tree during winter, and the white flowers it produces in abundance open before the trees are in full leaf.

Free-flowering from early to mid spring. The clusters of flat, open flowers measuring 1.5–2 in. (4–5 cm) in diameter are creamy white to pure white, with off-white anthers and a hawthorn-like scent. Large, dark green, pointed leaves of leathery texture are bronze-coloured when immature. Young growth is prone to wind damage so needs sheltered, free-draining site. Height 15–20 ft. (4.5–6 m). Zones 6–9.

Clematis
chiisanensis 'Lemon
Bells'

C. chiisanensis 'Lemon Bells'

A very useful garden plant which is long-flowering, but best if the plant can be seen at close quarters as the flowers can become hidden in the foliage. Ideal for a hazel wigwam or metal obelisk at the front of the border.

Flowering period mid to late spring with a few flowers throughout the summer. Pendulous, bell-shaped flowers of four pale yellow, thick, spongy sepals with wine-red bases, 1.5–2 in. (4–5 cm) deep. Wavy-tipped sepals curve outwards from ring of shorter, flattened spoon-shaped (spathulate) staminodes. Attractive, silky green seedheads mature to off-white and become fluffy. Young stems and flower-stalks are dark purple and shiny; bright green, toothed leaves are dull on top and shiny below. Deciduous. Height 6.5–10 ft. (2–3 m). Zones 6–9. Selected at University of British Columbia Botanical Garden in 1992 from South Korean seed sent from Chollipo Arboretum in 1988.

C. cirrhosa var. cirrhosa

In recent years this very variable evergreen European species, which is native to the Mediterranean region of southern Europe and northern Africa, has provided us with some outstanding cultivars. Its flowers are nodding and single, coloured creamy green with brownish red spots or freckles. It must not be thought of as providing an evergreen screen, as in warmer zones it will go into a summer dormancy and shed most of its leaves, as it does in its native location. They re-grow during the late summer or early autumn.

As with *Clematis armandii*, it can be used most successfully at the back of a border, ideally facing south, growing on a wall or solid fence on support wires. Some cultivars such as *C. cirrhosa* var. *purpurascens* 'Freckles' may provide summer flowers in cooler areas and also flower well before the turn of the year, so that it becomes almost an autumn- and spring-flowering plant. If any small trees are grown in the border it can look most attractive flowering before the tree is in full leaf, with long trailing stems dangling from the bare tree branches although, as I have said, a sheltered south-facing site is needed for this to be fully successful. The flowers are followed by large fluffy seedheads which can be fun when used in flower arrangements. It is the fresh new foliage in the autumn that looks best. Generally, cirrhosa cultivars grow to 10–13 ft. (3–4 m) in height, are hardy in Zones 7–9 and need shelter from the wind.

C. cirrhosa 'Ourika Valley'

Slightly scented, unspotted flowers coloured yellow-cream and shaped like nodding bells, 1.5–2 in. (4–5 cm) deep with cream anthers. Rich green leaves. Flowering period late winter to early spring. Height 10–13 ft. (3–4 m). Zones 7–9. Raised by Captain Peter Erskine from seed collected in Ourika Valley, High Atlas Mountains, northern Africa.

C. cirrhosa var. purpurascens 'Freckles'

Produces probably the largest flowers in this group and can be used as a container-grown plant for three to four years before it will become too large. Flowering period autumn to midwinter. Creamy pink flowers 3 in. (7.5 cm), very heavily freckled with red-maroon inside. Larger leaves and longer flower-stalks than species. Height 10–13 ft. (3–4 m). Zones 7–9. Raised by the author from seed collected in the Balearic Islands. ♔

C. cirrhosa var. purpurascens 'Jingle Bells'

Bell-shaped blooms similar to 'Wisley Cream' but far more floriferous. Flowering period mid to late winter. Creamy white nodding flowers, 1.5 in. (4 cm) deep with pale yellow anthers. The foliage is similar to 'Freckles' of which it is a seedling raised by Robin Savill, England. Height 10–13 ft. (3–4 m). Zones 7–9.

C. cirrhosa 'Wisley Cream'

Flowers in mid to late winter with unmarked greenish cream-coloured, 1.5-in. (4-cm) deep bells. Light green, simple leaves. Reported to do well in the northwestern part of the United States. Height 10–13 ft. (3–4 m). Zones 7–9. Raised by Ken Aslet, RHS Garden, Wisley, from seed collected in southern Europe and introduced by the author. ♔

Clematis macropetala var. *macropetala*

C. macropetala var. macropetala

This deciduous climber from northern China and Mongolia has, since its introduction to the British Isles in 1910, given rise to various cultivars in shades of blue, mauve, pink and white. The flowers are mostly nodding and double. It is closely related to the European species *Clematis alpina*, and can therefore be grown and treated as *C. alpina* and its cultivars. This species itself can be very variable but in its better forms it is equally as good as many named cultivars.

As with *Clematis alpina*, the early spring flowers are followed by most attractive silky seedheads which look even more interesting when they are accompanied by the occasional summer flowers that are generally somewhat thinner and smaller in size. The species flowers from mid to late spring with open, pendulous, bell-shaped flowers in blue to violet blue. Numerous staminodes make it appear semi-double. The flowers are 2.5 in. (6 cm) deep. Fluffy seedheads are produced from midsummer to late autumn. Height 6.5 ft. (2 m). Zones 3–9.

C. macropetala 'Markham's Pink'

Clematis macropetala 'Markham's Pink'

A free-flowering plant from mid through to late spring. The deep pink fully double flowers are 2 in. (5 cm) long and the foliage is an attractive pale green. Height 10 ft. (3 m). Zones 3–9. Raised by Ernest Markham, Gravetye Manor, England, and introduced in 1935. ♕

C. macropetala 'Pauline'

Strong-growing, free-flowering cultivar, flowering from mid to late spring. It has extra-large, 2- to 2.5-in. (5- to 6-cm) flowers with mid to dark blue pointed sepals and an attractive, longer, inner skirt of petaloid staminodes. Finely cut, light green leaves. Height 10 ft. (3 m). Zones 3–9. Raised by Washfield Nursery, England in 1966. ♈

C. montana var. montana

A most rampant deciduous species from central and western China, also found in the Himalayas. A highly variable plant in the wild, it was first introduced to the British Isles in 1831. A pink form of the mainly white-flowered species, called *Clematis montana* var. *rubens*, was found by Ernest Wilson in China in the early 1900s. The pink form has given us some outstanding deep pink/mauve cultivars and more recently some semi-double and almost double cultivars have been developed from both white and pink cultivars.

Some cultivars can grow up into trees to about 20–30 ft. (6–9 m), where they look completely natural. However, it makes a most useful plant for covering fences or low walls at the back of a border. Its vigour can be controlled in early summer by hard trimming after flowering, when all new growth should be shortened to 3–4 in. (7.5–10 cm) if possible. If there are any trees or very large obelisks (10–12 ft. [3–3.6 m] high) in the border, this clematis can serve as an attractive focal point in very early summer before most plants in the border are looking their best.

Its flowers are flat and open, somewhat like large stars, and are grouped in pairs or fives, borne directly from the ripened stems from the previous season. The effect of this plant in full flower is quite amazing when, on a mature plant, hundreds of flowers open at the same time. Some cultivars are extremely strongly scented, the evening being the best time to pick up wafts of scent.

These vigorous and rewarding clematis are not suitable for all parts of the United States. Check your area to see if they perform well; some can do well in Zone 6 but need a free-draining soil, whereas most cultivars are suited to Zones 7–9. They flower particularly well in and around the city of Seattle in the USA's Pacific Northwest.

C. montana 'Broughton Star'

Flowering period late spring to early summer. Unusual flowers for a montana: cup-shaped, semi-double to double, 1.5–2.5 in. (4–6 cm) in diameter, coloured deep dusky pink with darker veins. Young foliage bronze, maturing to dark green, deeply serrated. Prefers a sunny position. Good cut flower for small arrangements. Height 13.5–16.5 ft. (4–5 m). Zones 7–9. Raised in 1988 by Vince and Sylvia Denny, Preston, England. Awarded the British Clematis Society Certificate of Merit. ♔

C. montana 'Elizabeth'

Flowering period late spring to early summer. Pale pink, slightly gappy flowers with a satiny sheen, 2.5 in. (6 cm) wide, have a beautiful vanilla scent. Pale yellow stamens of long filaments and spiky anthers. Bronze foliage when young, turns mid-green with maturity. Suitable for sun or partial shade. Height 26.5–33 ft. (8–10 m). Zones 7–9. Raised by Rowland Jackman in 1958. ♔

Clematis montana 'Elizabeth'

Clematis montana
'Freda'

C. montana 'Freda'

Flowering period late spring to early summer. Deep cherry pink, 2.5-in. (6-cm) flowers with dark pink/red margins and contrasting yellow anthers. Compact plant with very deep bronze foliage. A useful montana for smaller gardens. Height 15–20 ft. (4.5–6 m). Zones 7–9. Raised in Suffolk, England and introduced in 1985 by Jim Fisk. ♛

C. montana f. grandiflora

Flowering period late spring to early summer. Pure white 3-in. (7.5-cm) wide flowers, bright yellow anthers. Attractive dark green foliage. Vigorous strong-growing free-flowering clematis ideal for covering large areas. Height 33–36.5 ft. (10–11 m). The hardiest montana known to the author. Zones 6–9. ♛

C. montana 'Jenny'

Synonym: *C. montana* 'Jenny Keay'

Flowering period late spring to early summer. Well-shaped creamy white semi-double 1.5–2.5-in. (4–6-cm) flowers. Develops rich pink highlights when grown in full sun. Very eye-catching. Height 20–26.5 ft. (6–8 m). Zones 7–9.

Clematis montana
var. *rubens*
'Tetrarose'

C. montana 'Mayleen'

Strongly vanilla-scented flowers in late spring to early summer. Rounded flowers coloured satiny pink, 2.5 in. (6 cm) across with contrasting yellow anthers. Attractive bronze foliage. Height 26.5–33 ft. (8–10 m). Zones 7–9. Introduced by Jim Fisk in 1984. ♛

C. montana var. rubens 'Tetrarose'

Flowering period late spring to early summer. Large cup-shaped, deep rosy mauve flowers, 3 in. (7.5 cm) across with thick sepals and a satin sheen as well as a delicate spicy scent. Contrasting cluster of deep yellow stamens. Leaves large and serrated, bronze-green when young, maturing to deep bronze-purple. Height 26.5 ft. (8 m). Zones 7–9. A tetraploid form of *C. montana* var. *rubens* raised at Boskoop Research Station, Holland in 1960. ♛

C. montana 'Warwickshire Rose'

A newish and very useful montana which performs well. Flowering period late spring to early summer. Deep rose-pink flowers, 2–3 in. (5–7.5 cm). Reddish bronze foliage. Height 20–26.5 ft. (6–8 m). Zones 7–9.

Chapter 11 Midseason-Flowering Clematis

Clematis BOURBON 'Evipo018'

The midseason-flowering clematis bloom in late spring and early summer.
I have divided them into four groupings: the single large-flowered cultivars, the
semi-double and double large-flowered cultivars, the Boulevard Collection and
the Flora Collection.

Clematis in this group produce their flowers directly from the previous season's ripened stems. Many produce the occasional summer flowers and a further crop in late summer and early autumn from new stems; these details are
stated in the description of each cultivar. The first crop of flowers is followed
by most attractive spherical seedheads that can be used in summer flower
arrangements, or dried for winter decorations—an additional benefit.

The shapes and sizes of the flowers vary, but these clematis are ideal plants
for growing through wall- or fence-trained evergreen or deciduous shrubs,
other climbers or free-standing small trees or large shrubs. They also make ideal
plants for growing over wigwams, tripods or obelisks in the border, where they
serve as outstanding focal points, giving an added dimension to the border.

These clematis are winter-hardy in Zones 4–9 but in severe winters all
top growth may be killed to ground level. If this occurs, flowering may be
delayed that season by about four weeks as flowers will be produced on the
new stems.

Some of the more compact-growing cultivars can be grown successfully
in containers. These are identified under each cultivar's description. In cold
areas, container-grown clematis will need to be given frost protection by placing them in a shed or garage over winter.

All clematis in this section are deciduous and lose their foliage over winter. All belong to Pruning Group Two and require light pruning at the end
of winter or in early spring, the exceptions being the compact cultivars. For
more details, please refer to page 238.

Single Large-Flowered Cultivars

The single-flowered cultivars are derived from *Clematis patens*, a Chinese
species which has also naturalized in Japan. (Some people believe that the
Japanese forms are native to Japan.) When the species and several Japanese
cultivars of *C. patens* were introduced into Europe in the mid 1800s, it gave

the breeders of that period the chance to create the first new large-flowered cultivars, many of which are still grown in our gardens today.

Clematis ALABAST 'Poulala'

A strong-growing plant with large leaves. Best in a west- or east-facing location as flowers will fade in direct sun (in a south-facing location). Delightful green-cream flowers during late spring in the shade of a north wall. Useful cut flower clematis and a good container plant. Good against a dark background, stunning with purple or blue flowers or foliage.

Flowering period late spring to early summer, and late summer. Round, greenish cream-coloured flowers, 4.75–6 in. (12–15 cm) across, with creamy yellow anthers. Later flowers smaller, measuring 3.5 in. (9 cm). Foliage slightly glaucous. Height 10 ft. (3 m). Zones 4–9. An Evison and Poulsen cultivar, raised in Denmark in the late 1980s. ♔

C. ANNA LOUISE 'Evithree'

Very free-flowering and compact in habit, this plant is ideal for any aspect. An excellent container plant for the patio and small garden, also good as a cut flower. Very useful with a light background and with hosts that have grey- or golden-variegated foliage. Spectacular on a metal obelisk in the middle part of a border.

Long flowering period, from late spring to early autumn. Violet flowers, 6 in. (15 cm) wide with contrasting cerise bar and reddish brown anthers. Height 8.25 ft. (2.5 m). Zones 4–9. An Evison and Poulsen cultivar, introduced by the author in 1993, and named after his second daughter. ♔

C. 'Blue Ravine'

A useful plant for North American gardens where it enjoys the sunshine and can be grown in any aspect. In an English climate it needs a good sunny position to do as well. Very large flowers and large leaves. Best on an obelisk in a border where its stems will ripen well, or up into a small, open tree.

Flowering period early summer to midsummer, and early autumn. Well-formed flowers, 7–8 in. (17.5–20 cm) in diameter, lilac blue suffused with pinkish mauve, anthers red. Later flowers more star-like, with pointed sepals. Large, simple to trifoliate leaves. Height 10 ft. (3 m). Zones 4–9. Raised by Conrad Eriandson in British Columbia, Canada, in about 1978. Parents possibly *C.* 'Nelly Moser' and *C.* 'Ramona'.

C. BOURBON 'Evipo018'

Disinguished by a very dramatically coloured flower. Sadly it does not flower up its stem but will produce a lot of terminal flowers, and it does repeat flower.

Ideal for a sunny border or south-facing fence or wall; marvellous with ceanothus, golden or golden-variegated foliage.

Clematis CLAIR DE LUNE 'Evirin'

Flowering period early summer to midsummer. Vibrant red flowers, 4.75–6 in. (12–15 cm) across, with a strikingly contrasting yellow centre which looks like a spinning wheel. Height 5–6.5 ft. (1.5–2 m). Zones 4–9. Introduced in 2002 by Evison and Poulsen.

C. CLAIR DE LUNE 'Evirin'

A strong-growing plant with pale-coloured flowers that look outstanding in a shady location. Fades rather too much in a south-facing position. Very free-flowering and ideal for a container in shade. Can be grown with grey, golden or purple foliage and any pastel-coloured flowering herbaceous perennials.

Flowering period late spring to early summer and late summer to early autumn. Very pale blue-purple flowers, 5 in. (12.5 cm) across, with paler central bands on sepals and dark anthers. Height 8.25–10 ft. (2.5–3 m). Zones 4–9. An Evison and Poulsen cultivar, introduced in 1997.

C. 'Dawn'

This clematis seems slightly more winter-hardy than most large-flowered cultivars and retains its old stems while other cultivars are killed to the ground. Does equally well in any aspect; ideal for a small garden. Excellent container plant and for the front of a border. The medium-sized flowers do not look out of place trailing at ground level. Ideal with grey or purple foliage and bright blue flowers. Good cut flower and attractive spherical seedheads.

Flowering period late spring to early summer. Pearly white flowers suffused with pink, 4.75 in. (12 cm) across. Deep red anthers. Flowers fade in strong sunlight. Early foliage bronze. Compact and free-flowering. Height 6.5 ft. (2 m). Zones 4–9. Raised by Tage Lundell in Sweden and introduced by the author in 1969.

C. 'Doctor Ruppel'

One of the best 'bicoloured' clematis with striped flowers. Generally holds its colour well but fades slightly in direct sun. Very good on a north-facing aspect. Compact, free-flowering, excellent in containers. Very useful with blue-flowering ceanothus or on purple foliage.

Flowering period late spring to early summer, and late summer to early autumn. Deep rose-pink flowers with darker bar and paler margins, 6 in. (15 cm) wide, light brown anthers. Good cut flower, lovely round seedheads with curly seed tails. Height 8.5–10 ft. (2.5–3 m). Zones 4–9. Argentinian origin, introduced by Jim Fisk in 1975.

C. 'Edith'

Compact habit, suitable for a small garden and an ideal container plant. Flowers very well late spring to early summer, but no repeat flowering. Good with dark background, useful growing on a tripod in the middle of the border. Plant with a deep-coloured annual ipomea. Does well in any aspect.

Flowering period late spring to early summer, and late summer. White flowers with a green bar in late spring, 4.75 in. (12 cm) across (but greenish white flowers on a north-facing aspect). Contrasting dark red anthers, and attractive medium-sized, spherical seedheads. Good cut flower. Height 6.5 ft. (2 m). Zones 4–9. The author's first cultivar, a chance seedling from C. 'Mrs Cholmondeley', introduced in 1974 and named after his mother. ♉

C. 'Fujimusume'

Very free-flowering and of compact habit, superb in containers. Its delightful pale blue flowers mix well with grey foliage and white flowers. Can work well with roses at the base of an archway, ideal for the front or middle of a border on an obelisk at about 4 ft. (1.2 m) and extremely suitable for a small garden.

Flowering period late spring to early summer, and late summer to early autumn. Rounded powder blue flowers with pale yellow anthers, 4–5 in. (10–12.5 cm) across. Height 8.25 ft. (2.5 m). Zones 4–9. Raised by Sejurn Arai of Japan, in 1952. ♉

C. 'Fuyu-no-tabi'

A compact plant which is most suitable for growing in a container or in the middle part of the border on a metal obelisk. Its creamy white flowers need a good strong colour to complement them; reds would be good, picking up the red-coloured anthers of its flowers. Suitable for any aspect, particularly for brightening up a north-facing location or for planting in a white border.

Flowering period late spring to early summer, and again late summer to early autumn. Creamy white full flowers, 6–7 in. (15–17.5 cm), with overlapping sepals and contrasting red anthers. Height 6.5–8.25 ft. (2–2.5 m). Zones 4–9. Raised in Japan by Mrs. Masako Takeuchi in about 1994.

C. 'General Sikorski'

A very free-flowering plant for any aspect. Good on a white-painted obelisk with blue or white flowering hosts, or with golden-foliaged small trees or shrubs. Can be grown with red-flowering roses on an obelisk or on the uprights to an archway or pergola. (If grown in this way it can be treated as a late-season-flowering plant and it will flower a few weeks later on new growth.)

Flowering period midsummer to early autumn. Early flowers 6 in. (15 cm) across, later ones smaller but more profuse. Well-rounded flowers of mauve to deep blue sepals with a hint of pink at the base and yellow anthers. Height 10 ft. (3m). Zones 4–9. A Polish cultivar raised by Wladyslaw Noll, introduced to Britain by Jim Fisk in 1980.

Clematis
'Fujimusume'

C. 'Guernsey Cream'

Extremely free-flowering in late spring, with only a few later flowers. Does very well in the Chicago Botanic Garden, withstanding cold winters and hot summers. Best in east- or west-facing locations, producing almost green flowers in a north-facing position. Useful in the middle of a border for very early colour on an obelisk or against a dark background of purple foliage. Very eye-catching with shrubs that have cream or golden variegated foliage; especially useful for a small garden.

Flowering period late spring to early summer, and late summer. Full, well-formed flowers, 5 in. (12.5 cm) wide, overlapping creamy yellow sepals with primrose bar and yellow anthers. Paler, smaller, 3-in. (7.5-cm) flowers in late summer. Height 8.25 ft. (2.5 m). Zones 4–9. Raised by the author and introduced in 1989.

C. 'Hanaguruma'

A useful, compact, short-growing plant, well suited to container culture. Would need a darkish-coloured under-planting to complement its flower colour, or grey-foliaged summer bedding plants. A Japanese cultivar selected by Goro Josha in 1985. Suitable for any aspect, and useful in windy locations due to its medium-sized flowers.

Flowering period late spring to early summer and possibly again late summer to early autumn. Very rounded flowers which are cerise-pink and have creamy yellow anthers. The medium-sized flowers are only 4–5 in.(10–12.5 cm) wide. Height 4–6.5 ft. (1.2–2 m). Zones 4–9.

C. 'Henryi'

A very popular plant in North America due to its long-flowering, tall-growing habit. Good with variegated ivy (*Hedera* subspecies), on a wall or fence at the back of a border or up into small trees such as magnolias. Suitable for any aspect and a useful cut flower clematis.

Flowering period midsummer to mid autumn. Well-formed white flowers have contrasting chocolate brown anthers and are 6–8 in. (15–20 cm) across. Height 10 ft. (3 m). Zones 4–9. Raised in 1870 by Anderson-Henry of Edinburgh, Scotland. ♛

C. 'H. F. Young'

Very bushy, compact and extremely free-flowering, an outstanding plant for containers. Fades slightly in a south-facing location, otherwise ideal anywhere. Looks good in a border on an obelisk near to deep-blue- or white-flowered herbaceous perennials and with grey foliage. Ideal for the smaller garden.

Flowering period late spring to early summer, and late summer. Pale blue,

5–6-in. (12.5–15-cm) wide, full flowers with pale yellow anthers. Swirls of seed tails on well-formed round seedheads. Height 6.5 ft. (2 m). Zones 4–9. Introduced in 1962, raised by Pennells of Lincoln.

C. Hyde Hall 'Evipo009'

An extremely well-flowered plant in late spring and early summer. Ideal container plant for the patio or small garden. Can be grown in any aspect. Useful in a border growing on a formal-shaped obelisk or with dark colours (purples and blues being ideal), or with white-flowered plants in a white border. It enjoys the sunshine of California where it flowers very well again in late summer.

Flowering period late spring to early summer, and early autumn. Large, creamy white flowers, 5–6 in. (12.5–15 cm) across, sometimes tinged with pink or green. Chocolate-brown anthers. Height 6.5–8.25 ft. (2–2.5 m). Zones 4–9. An Evison and Poulsen cultivar introduced in 2004 and named after the RHS Garden at Hyde Hall.

C. Ice Blue 'Evipo003'

Launched at the 2006 Chelsea Flower Show. An extremely free-flowering plant, it is both very early-flowering and very late-flowering. Best in a north, east- or west-facing location. Produces flowers down its stem. Ideal with purple foliage, on an obelisk in a border, on archways or on a pergola upright. Very useful for brightening up a north-facing position or growing in a

Clematis Ice Blue 'Evipo003'

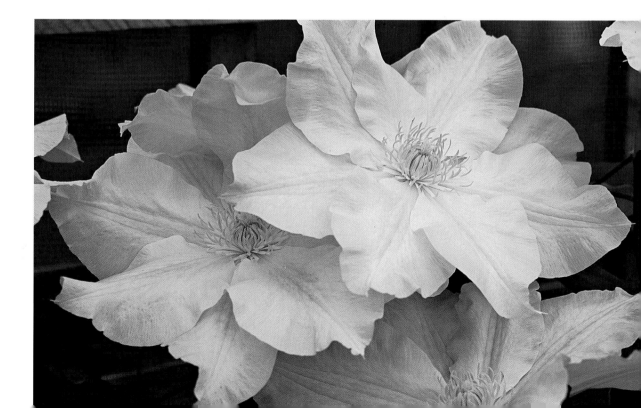

container for a shady location. It will flower at a low height from the previous season's growth and is therefore particularly suited to container culture and for a smaller garden.

Flowering period late spring to early summer, and again in late summer to early autumn. The white early flowers, 6–8 in. (15–20 cm) in diameter, are suffused with pale blue giving it a true 'ice blue' colour. The autumn flowers are smaller in size and sometimes slightly more white. The sepals are offset by creamy white anthers. Height 6.5–8.25 ft. (2–2.5 m). Zones 4–9. An Evison and Poulsen cultivar.

C. 'Julka'

A plant for growing up an obelisk or through grey-foliaged shrubs in the middle part of the border, which is best in partial shade. Raised by Szczepan Marczynski in Poland in the early 1990s, named after his daughter, Julianna, and launched at the Chelsea Flower Show in 2003.

Flowering period early to late summer. The early flowers have bright violet sepals with a red central bar. The later flowers are almost violet-black. Anthers are purplish. The early flowers are 5 in. (12.5 cm) in diameter, while the later ones are much smaller. Height 6.5–8.25 ft. (2–2.5 m). Zones 4–9.

C. 'Kalina'

A free-flowering plant which can be grown in a container or planted to grow up a metal obelisk in the middle part of the border, or perhaps looks better still when grown up into a grey-foliaged host shrub.

Flowering period late spring to early summer, and again in late summer to early autumn. Deep rosy-mauve flowers with pointed sepals, each sepal having a bright rosy-pink central bar which fades towards the tip of the sepal. Flowers, 6–7 in. (15–17.5 cm) in diameter, have a good strong boss of red stamens. Flowers may fade in very sunny position so best on a west or east-facing aspect. Height 6.5–8.25 ft. (2–2.5 m). Zones 4–9. A Brother Stefan Franczak cultivar raised in Poland and introduced about 1989.

C. KINGFISHER 'Evipoo37'

Extremely free-flowering habit, flowering down its stem. Its bright blue colour requires a light background to show off the flowers—grey or golden foliage would be ideal. A useful plant for a formal obelisk in the border, on an archway or at the base of a pergola. Super container plant especially if planted with grey-foliaged herbaceous perennials or white-flowering grey-foliaged annuals. Does not fade in the sun, and is therefore ideal for any location or aspect. A very versatile clematis for the smaller garden.

Flowering period late spring to early summer, and again in late summer to early autumn. Very large spring flowers, 6–7 in. (15–17.5 cm) wide, of intense blue pointed sepals with creamy yellow anthers. Autumn flowers are slightly smaller but produced in abundance. Attractive, spherical seedheads. Height 6.5–8.25 ft. (2–2.5 m). Zones 4–9. An Evison and Poulsen cultivar, launched at th e2007 Chelsea Flower Show.

Clematis KINGFISHER 'Evipo037'

C. 'Lady Northcliffe'

Long- and free-flowering with compact habit. A very good container plant, ideal for the middle part of a border through host plants or grown on a hazel wigwam. Its flowers associate well with pinks and mauves, or pale blues. Blends well with grey or golden foliage hosts. Suitable for any aspect and for the smaller garden.

Flowering period early to late summer, and early autumn. Produces 4.75-in. (12-cm) wide, wedgwood-blue flowers with contrasting greenish yellow

Clematis 'Lady Northcliffe'

anthers which sometimes have black tips. Height 6.5 ft. (2 m). Zones 4–9. Raised by Jackmans of Woking, England, in the early 1900s.

C. 'Marie Boisselot'

A tall-growing plant which flowers over a long period and can continue into late autumn in mild areas. Suitable for any aspect, and ideal for growing into small trees such as magnolias, or on a fence or wall with other plants at the back of the border. Very good cut flower with strong flower stems.

Flowering period early summer to late autumn. Well-rounded pale creamy white flowers with golden yellow anthers, 6 in. (15 cm) across. As flowers mature, colour becomes pure white. Good, strong foliage, remains green well into the autumn. Height 12 ft. (3.5 m). Zones 4–9. Raised in 1885 by Boisselot, France. ♆

C. 'Miss Bateman'

Very compact, this clematis does well in a container, and is also useful as a middle border plant with dark-foliaged hosts. Flowers earlier than most in this section. Suitable in any aspect but the early flowers in a north-facing location will have green central bars to their sepals. Ideal for a smaller garden.

Flowering period late spring to early summer, and late summer to early autumn. Beautiful clear white, fully rounded flowers, 5–6 in. (12.5–15 cm) across, contrasting red anthers. Slightly violet-scented. Height 6.5 ft. (2 m). Zones 4–9. Raised in the 1860s by Charles Noble, England. ♆

C. 'Mrs Cholmondeley'

This very old classic cultivar is sometimes criticized for its rather gappy flowers. However, this criticism can be balanced by the sheer quantity of flowers it produces over a long season. Best on an east-, west- or north-facing location where the flowers fade less. Can be treated as a late-season-flowering clematis and grown up into roses. Flower colour blends perfectly with grey or purple foliage and pale pink flowers. Ideal in a mixed border or on a fence at the back of the border.

Clematis 'Miss Bateman'

Clematis 'Mrs Cholmondeley'

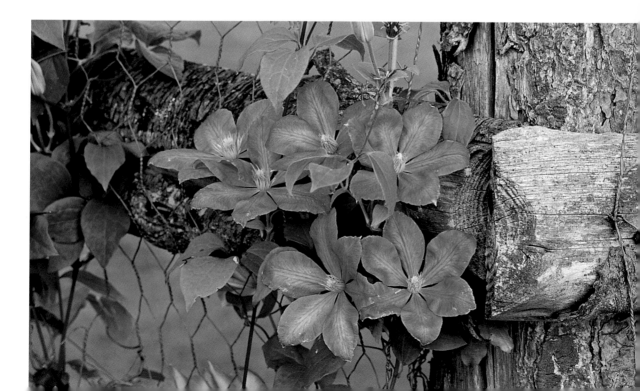

Flowering period late spring to early autumn. Light lavender-blue flowers, 7 in. (17.5 cm) across. Light chocolate-coloured anthers. Medium-sized, spiky seedheads. Zones 4–9. Height 8.25–10 ft. (2.5–3 m). Raised by Charles Noble, England, in 1873. ♔

C. 'Mrs N. Thompson'

A useful middle border plant with good strong-coloured flowers, and a neat habit. Needs a light background for best effect. Ideal for any aspect, works well in small gardens and is good for containers.

Flowering period late spring to early summer, and late summer. Lovely flowers, 5 in. (12.5 cm) wide, bluish purple with purple-cerise bar and red anthers. Height 8.25 ft. (2.5 m). Zones 4–9. Raised by Pennells of Lincoln and introduced in 1961.

C. 'Nelly Moser'

A great favourite around the world due to its dramatic two-tone flowers. The flower colour fades badly in strong sunlight, but it does very well on a north-facing aspect. Contrasts with grey or purple foliage and any pastel-coloured flowers. It is fun with green-white variegated grasses as an under-planting.

Flowering period late spring to early summer, and late summer to early autumn. Pale mauve flowers with deep lilac central bar and dark red anthers measure 6–7 in. (15–17.5 cm) across. Produces large round seedheads. Good

Clematis 'Nelly Moser'

cut flower; suitable for containers and small gardens. Height 8.25–10 ft. (2.5–3 m). Zones 4–9. Raised in 1897 by Moser, France, and now one of the best known clematis. ♛

C. 'Niobe'

This clematis has attained worldwide popularity on account of its deep-coloured flowers and its very free-flowering habit. At home in any aspect—a very good container plant. Looks stunning with yellow or green variegated deciduous or evergreen shrubs, and with a golden-foliaged hop growing on a tall obelisk, or over an archway.

Flowering period late spring to early autumn. Flowers are 6 in. (15 cm) wide, deep wine red with yellow anthers. They can be very dark in hot climates. Long- and free-flowering, it is a good cut flower. Height 8.25–10 ft. (2.5–3 m). Zones 4–9. Raised in Poland by Wladyslaw Noll and introduced by Jim Fisk in 1975. ♛

C. 'Omoshiro'

This plant has a most attractively formed and coloured flower. The white, deep-pink-tinged flowers blend perfectly with pink-, blue- or pinkish white-flowered herbaceous perennials as an under-planting if it is grown up an obelisk. Also marvellous on shrubs with deep purple foliage. The bright-coloured flower are ideal for a shady position.

Flowering period late spring to early summer, and again late summer to early autumn. The 5- to 7-in. (12.5- to 17.5-cm) wide flowers have six to eight sepals, each with a base colour of creamy pink and very deep purple-pink margins with even deeper colour at their tips. Contrasting deep red-purple anthers. Height 6.5–8.25 ft. (2–2.5 m). Zones 4–9. Raised in Japan by Hiroshi Hayakawa around 1988.

C. 'Piilu'

A charming plant with semi-double flowers produced occasionally from the previous season's ripened stems, and single flowers later in the season. A versatile clematis for the small garden, very compact and free-flowering. Ideal for container culture or for growing on an obelisk in the front of a border. Alternatively, it looks lovely when grown through host plants, especially grey- or purple-foliaged ones. Fades in strong sunlight, so is therefore best on a shady north-facing location, or one that faces east or west.

Flowering period late spring to early summer, and again in late summer. Open flowers of six to eight overlapping sepals, 3.5–4.5 in. (9–11 cm) across, pale mauve-pink with deeper pink central bar and cream anthers. Height 4–5 ft. (1.2–1.5 m). Zones 4–9. Raised in Estonia by Uno Kivistik.

C. 'Pink Champagne'

Synonym: *C.* 'Kakio'

A marvellous clematis for growing with blue-flowered ceanothus, either free-standing or against a wall or fence. Flowers fade slightly in full sun but it makes a most attractive plant growing on an obelisk in the border, surrounded by blue or white flowers and grey foliage.

Flowering period late spring to early summer, and late summer to early autumn. Compact yellow anthers and a prominent style contrast with overlapping purplish pink sepals which are darker at the edges, making flowers of 6 in. (15 cm) wide. Attractive medium-sized spherical seedheads. This Japanese cultivar was introduced to Europe in the early 1980s. Height 8.25 ft. (2.5 m). Zones 4–9.

C. 'Ramona'

Best suited to North America, where it enjoys the heat and can be grown in any aspect. In an English climate, plant in a sunny location to get the best results. A useful plant for an obelisk in the border, or on an archway or pergola. Very often seen growing on mail boxes in the United States, where it flowers profusely.

Flowering period early summer to early autumn. Well-formed flowers of pale blue with contrasting dark red anthers, 6–7 in. (15–17.5 cm) wide. Height 10 ft. (3 m). Zones 4–9. Origin uncertain, possibly Holland or the USA. First distributed in 1888 by Jackson and Perkins Co., USA.

Clematis 'Ramona'

C. Rebecca 'Evipoo16'

An outstanding, new, red clematis. Although this plant has a rather large flower it is still very free-flowering as it flowers down its stem. Suitable for any aspect and especially good for a hot sunny location, where its very deep flower colour will become even darker. The striking colour associates extremely well with pale blues, creams and yellows. A good plant for flowering against a golden or variegated golden host shrub at the back of a border. A very colourful plant for container culture but due to its large flower size it is best grown sheltered from strong winds. Plant with creams, pale yellow foliage plants or cream and yellow summer-flowering annuals as an under-planting.

Flowering period late spring to early summer, and late summer to early autumn. Deep velvety red flowers, 6–8 in. (15–20 cm) across, with light chocolate brown stamens. Height 6.5–8.25 ft. (2–2.5 m). Zones 4–9. An Evison and Poulsen cultivar, named after the author's eldest daughter. Launched at the 2008 Chelsea Flower Show.

C. 'Rooran'

This clematis has charming deep pink flowers which look delightful with pale or dark blue-flowering hosts, especially those with grey foliage. For best flower colour, plant in a west- or east-facing aspect.

Flowering period late spring to early summer, and again late summer to early autumn. The deep pink colouring overlays a paler shade of pink, the darker colour being on the margins of the sepals, giving the flower a paler coloured centre which is offset by light brown anthers. A most attractive flower, 5–6 in. (12.5–15 cm) in diameter. Height 6.5–8.25 ft. (2–2.5 m). Zones 4–9. A

Clematis Rebecca 'Evipoo16'

Japanese cultivar raised by Mrs. Masako Takeuchi in about 1995 and named after a city on the Silk Road.

C. ROSEMOOR 'Evipooo2'

This marvellous clematis is destined to become a classic. Very long-flowering with many flowers appearing at the same time. Flowers freely down its stem. Ideal in blue-flowered ceanothus on walls or at the back of a border. Very dramatic on a birch branch obelisk where it could be treated as a late-season-flowering plant, or on a formal metal or wooden obelisk where some of the old stems can be retained. Blends very well with golden-foliaged or yellow-flowered herbaceous perennials. Makes a very full container plant. Great value for money. Holds its colour very well in a very sunny location, south-, east- or west-facing. Named after the RHS Garden Rosemoor, Devon, England.

Flowering period early summer to early autumn. Deep red flowers, 5–6 in. (12.5–15 cm) across, with contrasting yellow anthers. Height 6.5–8.25 ft. (2–2.5 m). Zones 4–9. An Evison and Poulsen cultivar, launched at the 2004 Chelsea Flower Show.

C. ROYAL VELVET 'Evifour'

Clematis ROYAL VELVET 'Evifour'

A fine container plant with compact habit, producing an abundance of flowers in late spring. Best against a light background. Outstanding with grey-foliaged wall-trained shrubs or climbers. Suitable for any aspect, in a border with herbaceous perennials, especially shades of orange. Ideal for a small garden.

Flowering period late spring to early autumn. Flowers are 6 in. (15 cm) across, with rich velvet purple sepals and dark red anthers. Foliage slightly bronze in spring. Height 6.5 ft. (2 m). Zones 4–9. An Evison and Poulsen cultivar, raised by the author and introduced in 1993.

C. 'Rüütel'

A very free-flowering plant which will take a sunny spot; best in a south-, west- or east-facing position. Needs a light background; yellow or golden variegated plant material shows off its dark coloured flowers to best effect. Looks good on an obelisk of birch branches, where it can be treated as a late-season-flowering plant, in the middle part of a border.

Flowering period early to late summer. Flowers are 5–6 in. (12.5–15 cm) wide with six to eight crimson sepals and red-brown anthers. Height 6 ft. (1.8 m). Zones 4–9. Raised by Uno Kivistik, Estonia.

C. 'Signe'

A versatile plant that is suitable for any aspect and associates well with grey, purple or golden foliage. Looks splendid with pink-, purple- or deep-blue–flowering herbaceous perennials when growing up an obelisk.

Flowering period late spring to early summer, and again in early autumn. Six to eight sepals which are a light ice mauve-blue and have pale pink shading. Light brown anthers with a hint of pink. Each flower is 6–8 in. (15–20 cm) in diameter. Height 6.5–8.25 ft. (2–2.5 m). Zones 4–9. Raised in Denmark by A. Antonsen.

C. 'Silver Moon'

Characterized by its unusual flower colour that fades to off-white in strong sunlight. Compact habit, ideal for a container and small gardens. Best in a west- or east-facing aspect and against a dark background. Good with flowers of various pastel colours in a shady border.

Flowering period late spring to early summer, and late summer. Flowers are 6 in. (15 cm) wide, consisting of silvery mauve overlapping sepals with creamy white anthers. Height 6.5 ft. (2 m). Zones 4–9. Raised by Percy Picton and introduced in 1971 by Jim Fisk.

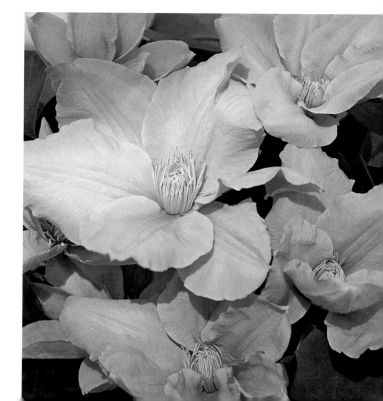

Clematis 'Silver Moon'

C. 'The Bride'

A marvellous clematis for growing in containers or at the base of an archway, or through low-growing shrubs at the front of a border. I believe that this old cultivar should be more widely grown. The rounded white flowers blend with all colours, looking wonderful with pale creams and pinks, or with very dark blues.

Flowering period late spring to early summer, and again in late summer. The 3- to 4-in. (7.5- to 10-cm) wide flowers have white pointed overlapping sepals with pale creamy yellow anthers. Height 6.5–8.25 ft. (2–2.5 m). Zones 4–9. Raised by the famous Jackmans of Woking Nursery before 1924.

C. 'Toki'

A very useful low-flowering plant that Maurice Horn from Joy Creek Nurseries, Portland, Oregon, USA, describes as his best-selling clematis. Ideal for container culture or for planting among low-growing shrubs towards the front of a border. Its white flowers contrast well with any dark-coloured foliage and is, of course, ideal for a white border. Suitable for any aspect.

Flowering period late spring to early summer, and again in late summer. The white-sepalled flowers have soft yellow anthers; the sepals recurve most attractively and are slightly wavy at the margins. Flowers are 4–6 in. (10–15 cm) in diameter. Height 3–6.5 ft. (1–2 m). Zones 4–9. Raised in Japan by Kozo Sugimoto in 1989.

C. 'Twilight'

Clematis 'Twilight'

An extremely good mixed border plant for an obelisk, or for growing with free-standing or wall-trained shrubs. Produces an abundance of medium-sized flowers at one time. Its flowers will blend with most colours and it is suitable for any aspect.

Flowering period late spring to late summer. Open, well-rounded, 5.25- to 6-in. (13- to 15-cm) flowers of deep mauve-pink sepals and yellow anthers. Sepals fade slowly to light mauve-pink. Height 8.25 ft. (2.5 m). Zones 4–9. Raised by Percy Picton in the 1970s.

C. VERSAILLES 'Evipoo25'

An extremely dark-flowered clematis needing a
light background to show off its flowers. Ideal for
a sunny south-facing location, or one facing south-
east or southwest. A handy plant for the middle part
of the border on an obelisk or with grey-foliaged
plants. Good with pink-, cream- or blue-flowered
herbaceous perennials. A good hot colour. Well
suited to the smaller garden.

Flowering period early summer to late autumn.
Elegant maroon red flowers with red anthers fad-
ing to mauve. Flowers 3–4 in. (7.5–10 cm) across.
Height 3–4 ft. (1–1.2 m). Zones 4–9. An Evison and
Poulsen cultivar.

C. VIVIENNE 'Beth Currie'

Very free-flowering and compact. Extremely good
container plant for any aspect, ideal for the smaller garden. Useful front border plant with grey-foliaged hosts, fits well with blue-flowered herbaceous
perennials.

Flowering period late spring to early summer, and late summer to early
autumn. Well-formed flowers, 4–5 in. (10–12.5 cm) across, of overlapping

Clematis VERSAILLES
'Evipoo25'

Clematis Vivienne 'Beth Currie'

plum-purple sepals with crimson central bar and reddish cream anthers. Height 8.25 ft. (2.5 m). Zones 4–9. Raised by Frank Meecham, Lincolnshire, England. Introduced by the author in 1998.

C. 'Warszawska Nike'

Synonym: *C*. 'Warsaw Nike'

An extremely valuable garden plant which is very free-flowering and ideal for any aspect. Needs a light background to show off its dark flowers, marvellous with shades of pink or cream flowering hosts. Very useful mixed border plant on an obelisk to make a colour statement, or on an archway. Looks stunning with cream-coloured roses, where it can be treated as a late-season-flowering plant.

Flowering period early to late summer, and early autumn. Rich velvety red flowers, 6 in. (15 cm) across, with pale yellow anthers. Height 8.25–10 ft. (2.5–3 m). Zones 4–9. Polish cultivar, raised by Brother Stefan Franczak and introduced by Jim Fisk in 1986. ♈

C. 'Warszawska Olga'

A very new cultivar raised by Brother Stefan Franczak in Poland. A useful plant for growing up a formal metal obelisk in the middle part of the border. Blends well with grey or purple foliage, or among other pink-flowered herbaceous perennials. Suitable for any aspect and for container culture.

Flowering period late spring to early summer, and again in late summer to early autumn. Beautiful dusky rose-pink sepals with deeper-coloured margins. Has a large boss of colourful stamens made up of rose-pink filaments topped with golden yellow anthers. The flowers are 5–6 in. (12.5–15 cm) across. Height 6.5–8.25 ft. (2–2.5 m). Zones 4–9.

Double and Semi-Double Large-Flowered Cultivars

The double and semi-double clematis are derived from various double and semi-double forms of *Clematis patens* and its cultivars. All except one of these old double cultivars, *C.* 'John Gould Veitch' introduced in 1862 from Japan, have now been lost to cultivation—and although this is still a lovely and historical cultivar, the double cultivars grown today are vastly superior. Many of the modern-day double cultivars are actually sports from single-flowered cultivars, and perhaps those introduced from Japan years ago were also sports of *C. patens*. It is great fun that some semi-double forms are still to be found growing in the wild in Japan.

Many of the older cultivars which we grow today produce their double flowers only on ripened stems from the previous season, with single flowers being produced on the current season's stems. This is, of course, a great disadvantage for gardeners in cold locations where the top growth of the clematis is killed to ground level each winter and therefore the plants produce only single flowers later in the flowering season. Fortunately, many of the newer double-flowered cultivars do, in fact, produce double flowers on old and current season's stems. This is clearly identified in their descriptions.

Due to the large size of the flowers of some of these cultivars they should be grown only in a sheltered location, away from strong winds. To help protect them further, these large-flowered cultivars should be grown through other wall-trained shrubs or small wall-trained trees. However, all of the double and semi-double clematis selected for this book make exceptional container-grown plants, growing on a 5–6 ft. (1.5–1.8 m) plant support, if sheltered from strong winds. Not all have extremely large flowers, and some can tolerate a certain amount of wind; where this is the case, it is clearly stated in their descriptions.

Clematis ARCTIC QUEEN 'Evitwo'

An exceptional double-flowered cultivar which has an extremely long flowering period. The double and sometimes the later, semi-double flowers are produced on both the old, previous season's ripened stems and on the current growth. This is therefore ideal for cold climates where double flowers will be produced from new growth each year. Suitable for any aspect but when grown on a north-facing location, some early summer flowers may have green outer sepals. Not a very large flower, so can be grown exposed to a certain amount of wind. The creamy white flowers go well with any other colours.

Flowering period early summer to early autumn. All flowers produced are double or semi-double, whether from old or new wood. Flowers 4–7 in. (10–17.5 cm) across, of clear, creamy white sepals and yellow anthers. Attractive seedheads and good foliage. Height 10 ft. (3 m). Zones 4–9. An Evison and Poulsen cultivar, raised by the author and introduced in 1994. ♀

C. 'Beata'

A good plant for a container, with semi-double flowers followed by single flowers. It can be grown in the middle part of a border on a metal obelisk. Best if under-planted with blue- or purple-flowered herbaceous perennials.

Flowering period late spring to early summer, and late summer to early autumn. Semi-double flowers of light mauve-pink sepals with wavy margins in lilac blue, 5–6 in. (12.5–15 cm) in diameter, with yellow anthers. The inner sepals are much shorter. Later flowers are single, with only six sepals. Height 8.25–10 ft. (2.5–3 m). Zones 4–9. Introduced by Brother Stefan Franczak in 1986.

C. CRYSTAL FOUNTAIN 'Evipoo38'

This very unusual clematis is most probably a sport from C. 'H. F. Young'. It occurred in the nursery of Hioshi Hayakawa in Japan and was discovered by the author. An exceptional container plant due to its extremely compact, free-flowering habit. An ideal plant for a small garden, growing through a wall-trained grey- or purple-foliaged shrub. Associates well with white, pink, mauve and dark blue flowers. Always produces the rather exotic double flowers, on both old and current season's stems. Will tolerate a certain amount of wind. Best in a south-, west- or east-facing aspect and most suitable for the smaller garden.

Flowering period late spring to early summer, and late summer to early autumn. Lilac-blue double flowers, 5–6 in. (12.5–15 cm) across, with dramatic fountain-like centre which is paler in colour. The early flowers can be mauve-blue with a green central bar to each sepal. Height 5–6.5 ft. (1.5–2 m). Zones 4–9. Introduced at the Chelsea Flower Show in 2002 by Evison and Poulsen.

C. 'Daniel Deronda'

This strong-growing, very old cultivar has extremely large flowers in early summer. Its rather floppy semi-double and single flowers all appear at the same time in early summer, followed by a good crop of single flowers later in the season. Due to the large size of the early season flowers it is best grown through a wall-trained shrub. The flower colour associates well with plants of most shades, especially yellows, whites and pale blues; some shades of red and orange may clash. The semi-double flowers develop only from the previous season's ripened stems, but it is still worth growing in cold climates despite the risk of having only single flowers. Suitable for any aspect.

Flowering period early summer for semi-doubles and singles, and mid-summer to early autumn for singles. Early flowers 7–8 in. (17.5–20 cm) across, later flowers smaller. Deep purple-blue sepals with plum highlights gradually fade to purple-blue. Creamy yellow anthers. Most unusual and attractive spherical seedheads with a twisted topknot at the apex. Height 8.25 ft. (2.5 m). Zones 4–9. Raised by Charles Noble, England, in 1882. ♈

C. 'Denny's Double'

Early summer flowers of good size. Best grown through a wall-trained shrub at the back of a border or as a container plant. Suitable for any aspect except north. Needs a darker colour to show off its pleasant pale flowers.

Flowering period late spring to early summer, and late summer to early autumn. Pale lavender-blue double flowers from both old and new wood, 5 in. (12.5 cm) across. Flowers fade to light blue. Height 6.5–8.25 ft. (2–2.5 m). Zones 4–9. Raised by Vince Denny, England in 1977, named and introduced in 1993 by John Richards.

C. EMPRESS 'Evipoo11'

An extraordinary-looking clematis, developed as a sport from C. JOSEPHINE 'Evijohill'. An ideal container plant, or for growing through wall-trained shrubs. Makes a good companion clematis to plant in a container with C. CRYSTAL FOUNTAIN 'Evipoo38' due to its similarly shaped spiky flowers. Looks best with grey or purple foliage and its flowers associate well with any other pastel shades. Always produces its double flowers, from both old and new growth. Highly suitable for the smaller garden.

Flowering period late spring to early summer, and early autumn. Pink outer sepals have a darker pink bar; narrow inner sepals give spiky pom-pom effect. Flowers 4.75–6 in. (12–15 cm) across. Height 5–6.5 ft. (1.5–2 m). Zones 4–9. A 2006 Evison and Poulsen introduction.

C. FRANZISKA MARIA 'Evipoo08'

Named after the author's youngest daughter. An extremely free-flowering plant, it flowers again and again from young growth produced behind the terminal flower. It always produces double or semi-double flowers, the fully double flowers being produced from the ripened stems of the previous season. The flower size is not too large and thus can tolerate a certain amount of wind. A very good container plant. Ideal for brightening up grey, golden or variegated foliage; blends well with most other colours and looks good with white. Could be grown successfully on a formal obelisk in a border surrounded by yellow or white herbaceous perennials. Suitable for any aspect.

Flowering period late spring to early summer, and late summer to early autumn. Beautifully shaped, mid-blue-purple flowers with yellow anthers, always double or semi-double, 4–6 in. (10–15 cm) across. Height 6.5–8.25 ft.

Clematis FRANZISKA MARIA 'Evipo008'

(2–2.5 m). Zones 4–9. An Evison and Poulsen cultivar, launched at the 2005 Chelsea Flower Show.

C. JOSEPHINE 'Evijohill'

One of the most exceptional double-flowered clematis, not only because of the number of flowers it produces but also due to its long flowering period and, of course, unusual flower shape which is demonstrably fully double. Outstanding as a container plant or for growing with other wall-trained plants at the back of a border. Long-flowering in very hot regions of North America. Always produces its fully double flowers, from both old and current season's stems, therefore very suitable for colder climates. Can be grown in any location but when grown in a north-facing location its early summer flowers will have a greenish, muddy bronze colouring; then, as the season develops, normal-coloured flowers will be produced. Extremely good value for the small town garden or on the patio in a container.

Flowering period early summer to early autumn, always double. Early flowers are almost bronze, tinged with green and a darker bar. In midsummer the colour becomes lilac with a pink bar. The inner sepals open more slowly giving the flower a layered, pom-pom effect. There are no anthers. Flowers 4–5 in. (10–12.5 cm) across. Height 8.25 ft. (2.5 m). Zones 4–9. Cultivar discovered by Josephine Hill, England, and introduced by Evison and Poulsen in 1998 at the Chelsea Flower Show with an exhibit depicting the château of Napoleon's Josephine. ♚

Clematis JOSEPHINE 'Evijohill'

C. 'Louise Rowe'

A most beautiful clematis, having single, semi-double and fully double flowers, which all open at the same time, in early summer, which is most unusual. The faint pale blue colour fades in strong sunlight, and therefore is best on a west- or east-facing location, growing through other wall-trained shrubs. As with so many clematis, it looks outstanding with grey foliage, and dramatic with purple foliage; dark blue or white flowers and perhaps orange-coloured herbaceous perennials are useful associated colours. A special plant for container culture in a prominent place on the patio, especially if under-planted with grey foliage and white or very dark blue lobelia during the summer months.

Flowering period early summer (single, semi-double and double), and mid to late summer (single). Flowers 5–6 in. (12.5–15 cm) across; colour varies from pale mauve to nearly white depending on light levels. Anthers are cream-coloured. Height 6.5–8.25 ft. (2–2.5 m). Zones 4–9. Introduced by Jim Fisk in 1984.

C. 'Mrs George Jackman'

One of my great favourite clematis, it was raised in 1877 but would meet most of the criteria we look for in today's value-for-money clematis. Unfortunately though, its semi-double flowers are produced only on the previous season's ripened stems. Makes a very good container plant, and can be grown on a formal obelisk in the border or through wall-trained plants at the back of the border. Suitable for any location; ideal for brightening up north-facing

Clematis 'Mrs George Jackman'

locations. A very useful cut flower clematis. Due to its medium-sized flowers it can tolerate a certain amount of wind and is ideal for the smaller garden.

Flowering period early summer (semi-double), and mid to late summer (single). Almost perfect flower shape, fully rounded, 6 in. (15 cm) in diameter, overlapping creamy white sepals taper to pointed tips. Light brown anthers. Height 8.25 ft. (2.5 m). Zones 4–9. Introduced by George Jackman and Son, 1875. ♈

C. 'Proteus'

Clematis 'Proteus'

Another very old cultivar (from 1876), which can produce fully double, semi-double or single flowers in early summer, and a good crop of single flowers later in the season. It was not in my original list for this book but the plant growing in Charis Ward's garden at Abbey Dore proved exceptional in 2006. She grows it almost at ground level on a chain that is hung between two archways at the edge of a patio/eating area—so, after seeing it flowering for at least three months, and looking so magnificent, I had to include it! Best in a sunny location so its old stems get well ripened to produce the double flowers. Unfortunately, in cold climates it will produce only single flowers, unless it is grown in a container and taken inside each winter.

Clematis 'Royalty'   Flowering period early summer (double and semi-double), and mid to late summer (single). Double flowers may have a mixture of green or purple-pink outer sepals and soft pinkish purple inner sepals. Semi-doubles lack green outer sepals and singles are a soft mauve-pink with pale yellow anthers. Early flowers 6–8 in. (15–20 cm) across, later flowers 4–6 in. (10–15 cm). Height 10 ft. (3 m). Zones 4–9. Raised by Charles Noble, England.

C. 'Royalty'

A marvellous plant for a container, raised by John Treasure at Burford House Gardens, England. Compact with lots of semi-double flowers in early summer followed by a good crop of single flowers later in the season. Can be grown on an obelisk in the front of a border, or over grey foliage shrubs. Looks good with herbaceous perennials that have white, cream, blue, bright yellow or orange flowers. Ideal for the small town garden or on a patio. Suitable for all aspects except north-facing. Unfortunately the semi-double flowers are produced only from the previous season's ripened stems.

Flowering period early summer (semi-double), and mid to late summer (single). Rich purple-mauve double flowers with purple-blue inner sepals are
Clematis 'Veronica's   4–5 in. (10–12.5 cm) across, while later single flowers are 3 in. (7.5 cm) across.
Choice'   All have a central boss of yellow anthers on attractive purple filaments. Not suitable for north-facing aspect. Height 6.5 ft. (2 m). Zones 4–9. Introduced in 1985. ♛

C. 'Veronica's Choice'

Raised by Walter Pennell in Lincoln, England. A beautiful frilly flower which has double and semi-double flowers in early summer from the previous season's ripened stems, followed by single flowers later in the season on the current season's stems. The medium-sized flowers tolerate wind and it is best planted in a west- or east-facing location. The flower colour blends with all pastel shades and with dark blues, but it needs a dark background to show off the pale flowers.

Flowering period early summer (double), and mid to late summer (single). Primrose-scented flowers are pale mauve-lavender with a hint of pink. Doubles are 6–7 in. (15–17.5 cm) across and singles 4–5 in. (10–12.5 cm) across. Overlapping sepals have very wavy edges, giving flowers a frilly appearance. Height 8.25 ft. (2.5 m). Zones 4–9. Raised by Pennells of Lincoln and named in 1973.

The Boulevard Collection

One group of new compact free-flowering clematis, forming the Boulevard Evison and Poulsen Collection, have been developed from the old early large-flowered cultivars for the purpose of growing in containers and in the smaller garden generally. They are able to flower very freely both from the ripened stems of the previous season and from the current season's growth; moreover, as well as producing many flowering stems, there are from five to seven (and sometimes more) flowers per stem, flowering from the terminal flower first.

These clematis, therefore, are ideal for growing in colder climates, because even if their prior season's ripened stems have been killed to ground level, they will re-grow in early spring and produce flowers on new growth within eight weeks—a great advantage over the older cultivars for such climates.

Their many possible uses make them very garden-worthy and exceptionally valuable when space is at a premium. They can be grown in containers as described in Chapter 5, and work very well in small spaces where they can be planted in the soil to grow through other wall-trained shrubs or in a border on birch tree branch obelisks. They may also be grown on shrubs in the central to front part of a border, making them quite versatile plants.

Clematis ANGELIQUE 'Evipo017'

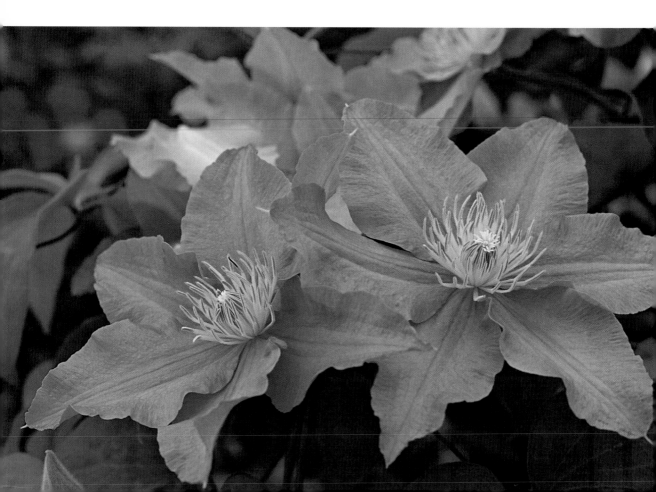

With regard to the annual pruning of the Boulevard Collection clematis: while they naturally belong to the midseason-flowering category, I have found that they perform better when they are treated as being late-season-flowering. To prune them, simply carry out what Suzie McCoy, who gardens in Pennsylvania, has delightfully referred to as a "pony tail cut": in one hand, gather up all the top growth just 12 in. (30 cm) above ground or soil level, and then cut off all stems above this point using a pair of hand pruners or garden secateurs. Some early flowers will be produced from the older stems and these are followed by new growth which will help provide the next, continuous crop. If treated in this way, these clematis will be restricted to within 3–4 ft. (1–1.2 m) of growth each year and will remain very bushy and compact. They can be treated in the same way whether they are container-grown or planted out in the garden. Regarding timing, remember that "when the crocuses bloom, it's time to prune"—another gem from Suzie McCoy.

Clematis ANGELIQUE 'Evipo017'

Prodduces good fresh green foliage and is very free-flowering. Suitable for any aspect. Best against a dark background but almost equally good with paler-coloured hosts, if that is the planting scheme. If grown in a container, looks lovely with a dark blue, white, red or orange under-planting.

Flowering period early to midsummer, and late summer to early autumn. Pale lilac-blue flowers, 4.75–5.5 in. (12–14 cm), with light brown anthers. Height 3–4 ft. (1–1.2 m). Zones 4–9.

C. CEZANNE 'Evipo023'

Suitable for any aspect, it fades less when placed out of full sun, and is very useful for a north-facing position to brighten up a darker area. Its pale colour allows it to be planted with any host plant, or with any herbaceous perennials.

Flowering period early to midsummer, and late summer to early autumn. Very free-flowering. Attractive sky blue single flowers measure 5.5–7 in. (14–17.5 cm) across, with overlapping sepals and yellow anthers. Height 3–4 ft. (1–1.2 m). Zones 4–9.

C. CHANTILLY 'Evipo021'

Its rather pale colour with hints of pink fade in strong sunlight, but it is superb for a north-facing location and works well on an east- or west-facing position. Beautifully rounded flowers and always a great favourite of visitors to the Chelsea Flower Show. Looks wonderful with creamy pink flowers in the border on an obelisk or through pale-blue-flowered shrubs or purple-foliaged hosts.

Flowering period early to midsummer. Very free-flowering. Delightful,

Clematis CHANTILLY
'Evipoo21'

single and occasionally semi-double, very delicate, pale pink flowers, 4–6 in. (10–15 cm) across, with more pronounced deeper pink central bar as the sepals fade in colour to white. Creamy brown anthers. Height 3–4 ft. (1–1.2 m). Zones 4–9.

C. FLEURI 'Evipoo42'

A strong-coloured plant that performs extremely well. It is very uniform in its habit, flowering down its stems. As its colour is similar to that of *C.* PICARDY 'Evipoo24', any aspect except north would be suitable. Best against a light background and ideal for small gardens and containers.

Flowering period early to midsummer. Velvety flowers are a deep purple-red with a red central bar, 5–6 in. (12.5–15 cm) across; very free-flowering. It has a large boss of creamy white anthers on red filaments. Height 3–4 ft. (1–1.2 m). Zones 4–9.

C. OOH LA LA 'Evipoo41'

A useful addition to the range, pink-striped with attractive light green foliage. The medium-sized flowers have six to eight sepals, which have a darker central band, and contrasting dark red anthers. A very free-flowering plant which is uniform in habit. If you choose to plant several clematis together in a large container, this cultivar looks extremely good with *C.* PARISIENNE 'Evipoo19' and *C.* ANGELIQUE 'Evipoo17'.

Flowering period early to midsummer. Delicate, dusky pink flowers, 4–5 in. (10–12.5 cm) across, made up of pointed, frilly-edged sepals. Height 3–4 ft. (1–1.2 m). Zones 4–9.

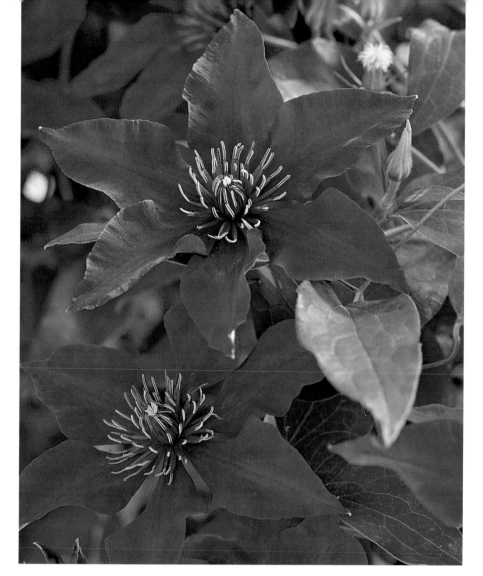

Clematis FLEURI
'Evipo042'

Clematis OOH LA LA
'Evipo041'

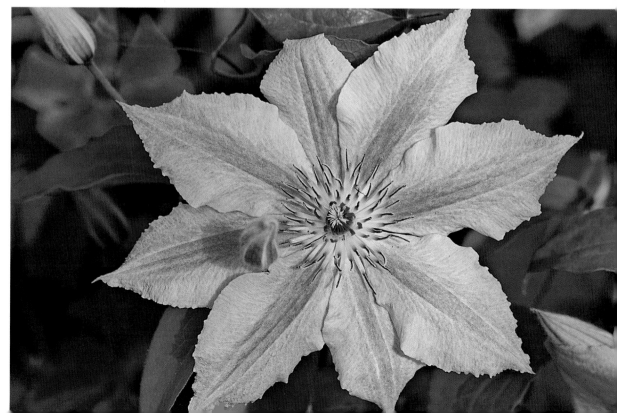

C. Parisienne 'Evipoo19'

Perhaps a rather typical blue clematis with a red centre, but the sheer volume of flowers it produces makes it a very valuable garden plant. Suitable for any location, it works well in a border with yellows, oranges or purples, and with grey foliage and white flowers. Alternatively, grow it in a container and use such colours as an under-planting.

Clematis Picardy 'Evipoo24'

Flowering period early to midsummer, and late summer to early autumn. Very free-flowering. Pale, violet-blue flowers, 4.75–5.5 in. (12–14 cm) across, with overlapping wavy-edged sepals and attractive red anthers. Height 3–4 ft. (1–1.2 m). Zones 4–9.

C. Picardy 'Evipoo24'

A truly outstanding plant, extremely well-flowered. Suitable for south-, west- or east-facing locations; its flower colour makes it perhaps too dark for a north-facing location. Probably best against a light background but would also look at home in a purple border and contrasts very well with yellows. Superb in a container or in a border, and exceptionally good for a very small garden where there is space for only one or two clematis.

Flowering period early to midsummer, and late summer to early autumn. Very free-flowering. Unusual dusky red flowers with a brighter red bar on the sepals and reddish brown anthers, 5–6 in. (12.5–15 cm) across. Height 3–4 ft. (1–1.2 m). Zones 4–9.

The Flora Collection

Two new compact plants—*Clematis* Bijou 'Evipoo30' and *C.* Filigree 'Evipoo29'—are currently the only members of the Flora Collection, and are very low-growing, 'dwarf' clematis. However, many more Flora Collection cultivars will become available in the next few years.

These clematis are brilliant plants for the small garden, as they are well suited for container culture and for growing in the front of the border through

Clematis Bijou 'Evipoo30'

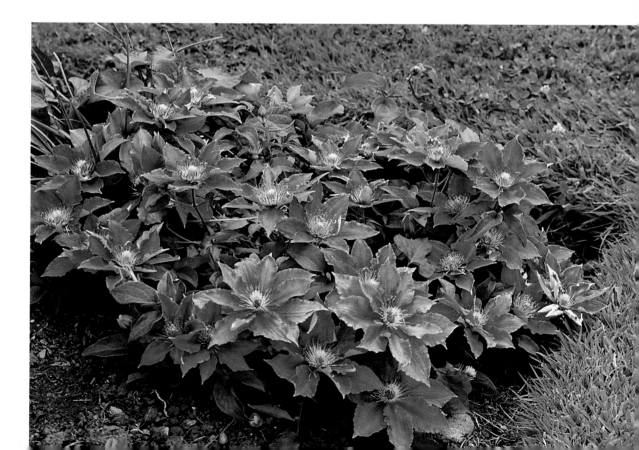

other plants or by themselves. Alternatively, they are superb for growing in small containers for the balcony, and in hanging or wall baskets. They grow to less than 12 in. (30 cm) high and are basically mound-forming, so leave them unsupported or use some short pea-sticks to lift them off the soil, if you wish. In the late summer they sometimes put on a few extension growths. These stems should be removed unless the plants are growing in hanging or wall baskets, when it is rather charming to have some trailing stems. Otherwise, trim back all stems in late winter or early spring to about 9–12 in. (22.5–30 cm).

C. BIJOU 'Evipoo30'

Suitable for any aspect except a very shady north-facing location. Its pale colour blends perfectly with all other colours. When grown in a container, it needs one with only a 12 in. (30 cm) diameter and the same depth. Alternatively, grow it with other very low-growing herbaceous perennials or low-growing summer-flowering bedding plants.

Flowering period early to midsummer. Very free-flowering. Classic open flowers, 3–4.75 in. (7.5–12 cm) across, keep shape well. Small, pointed, ruffled sepals in pale violet/mauve with slight pinkish bar. Pink-tipped anthers in flowers that open to a lovely rosette shape. Height 12–15 in. (30–37.5 cm). Zones 4–9.

C. FILIGREE 'Evipoo29'

Its habit is extremely similar to that of C. BIJOU 'Evipoo30', and it can be grown in a similar way. Both make exceptional plants growing naturally at the front of a border or even in a very narrow border where they can, in fact, give shade to the root systems of the normal tall-growing clematis.

Flowering period early to midsummer. Exceptionally free-flowering. Single and semi-double flowers, 4–5.5 in. (10–14 cm) across. Silvery blue sepals with ruffled edges. Red/brown anthers. Height 12–15 in. (30–37.5 cm). Zones 4–9.

Clematis FILIGREE
'Evip0029'

Chapter 12

Late-Season-Flowering Clematis

Clematis 'Błękitny Anioł'

The late-season-flowering clematis are an extremely valuable group of garden plants, varying widely from the large-flowered cultivars to the very free-flowering Viticella Group to the short-growing herbaceous types. All produce their flowers on the current season's stems from midsummer onward to mid autumn, and belong to Pruning Group Three which require hard pruning (see page 240). I have sub-divided them into three groups, based on their cultivation and their uses as garden plants: the late large-flowered cultivars, the Viticella Group and the late-flowering species and their cultivars.

Late Large-Flowered Cultivars

These most useful, very free-flowering cultivars can be grown at the back of a border through wall-trained trees and shrubs to great effect. Due to their bright colours, they are extremely effective when used as focal plants, making a colourful statement on birch tree branches in the form of a 5- to 6-ft. (1.5- to 1.8-m) obelisk in a border. They associate marvellously with roses, either free-standing or climbers and ramblers on poles, archways, arbours and pergolas, or on more formal obelisks in the border. Plants of this subgroup lend themselves to being grown with free-standing shrubs in a border, but are not ideal for container culture due to their taller growing habit.

They all belong to Pruning Group Three and so require hard pruning during late winter or early spring. Most are hardy in Zones 3–9.

C. 'Barbara Harrington'

Very free-flowering over a long period; ideal for archways with cream-coloured roses. Good at the back of the border with golden or golden-variegated foliage shrubs, up into small trees or on an obelisk either by itself or with other climbers such as *Dicentra scandens*. Suitable for any aspect.

Flowering period midsummer to early autumn. Cerise-coloured flowers, 4 in. (10 cm) across, have pointed sepals with a dark border, and contrasting yellow anthers. Height 10 ft. (3 m). Zones 3–9. Raised as a sport from *C.* 'Comtesse de Bouchaud' by Dominic Harrington in Wisbech, England, and very similar in habit to its parent. ♀

Clematis 'Comtesse de Bouchaud'

Clematis 'Błękitny Anioł'

Synonym: *C.* 'Blue Angel'

An exceptional, free-flowering clematis that is one of the best for growing on archways. Its rather pale colour tends to fade in bright sunshine but it produces so many flowers that this can go almost unnoticed. Very good on obelisks and through dark-coloured roses, on purple foliage shrubs or up into small trees in a border. Suitable for any aspect.

Flowering period mid to late summer. Pale lavender blue flowers, 4–4.75 in. (10–12 cm) across, with crimped margins and greenish yellow anthers. Height 13 ft. (4 m). Zones 3–9. Polish origin, bred by Brother Stefan Franczak. ♀

C. 'Comtesse de Bouchaud'

This classic French cultivar produces a wealth of flowers and looks good in any location. Useful on north-facing walls with other shrubs or climbers, on archways and on obelisks. Its colour blends well with grey- or purple-foliaged plants and it is perfect with pale blue, pink or pale mauve flowers.

Flowering period midsummer to early autumn. Rounded flowers, 5 in. (12.5 cm) across, bright mauve-pink with cream anthers. Sepals are deeply textured with a satin sheen, blunt tips and crimpled edges. Height 10 ft. (3 m). Zones 4–9. Raised by Morel in France in around 1900. ♀

C. 'Ernest Markham'

This clematis has a very dramatic magenta colouring and is best suited to a south-, southeast- or west-facing position. It does not flower in a north-facing aspect. However, in a sunny border it is dramatic when flowering on an obelisk or at the back of the border. Best with creams or yellows, or against purple foliage.

Flowering period midsummer to mid autumn. Roundish magenta flowers, 4–5 in. (10–12.5 cm) wide, of six to eight broad, overlapping sepals, with light brown anthers. Height 10–13 ft. (3–4 m). Zones 3–9. Raised by Ernest Markham but flowered after his death and named by Rowland Jackman in 1937. ♀

Clematis 'John Huxtable'

C. 'Gipsy Queen'

An extremely old cultivar that still holds great garden value. Suitable for any aspect but is ideal in a bright sunny spot where it retains its deep colour. Best against a light background where its colour is shown to best effect, golden or golden/silver variegated foliage being superb. Useful border plant on an obelisk, especially with pale pink colours; great with roses.

Flowering period early summer to early autumn. Flowers on old and new wood. Deep velvety violet flowers with dark red anthers. Early flowers are 6 in. (15 cm), later ones 4–5 in. (10–12.5 cm) in diameter. Height 10 ft. (3 m). Zones 3–9. Raised in England by Cripps and Son in 1877. ♛

C. 'Jackmanii'

One of the oldest cultivars still grown. Produces a marvellous quantity of flowers. Performs very well in the colder parts of northern Europe and North America. Sometimes gets mildew in sheltered positions; best in south-, west- or east-facing locations. A natural companion for any type of rose, especially with pink, cream, yellow or deep red cultivars. Useful in a blue/purple border, on an obelisk surrounded by yellow- or pink-flowered herbaceous perennials, or at the back of a border on golden foliage.

Flowering period midsummer to early autumn. Semi-nodding, dark, velvety, deep purple flowers, 4 in. (10 cm) across, fade with age to a good bluish purple. Creamy green anthers. Height 10 ft. (3 m). Zones 3–9. ♛

C. 'John Huxtable'

An exceptional late-flowering white clematis, raised from *C.* 'Comtesse de Bouchaud', which can be used in the garden in the same ways. Suitable for any aspect. Great in a white border on an obelisk or up into a small tree. Looks special with white climbing roses and deep reds. Useful at the back of a border to draw the eye towards it, especially against purple foliage.

Flowering period mid to late summer. Creamy white flowers, 4 in. (10 cm) across, offset by yellow-white anthers. Height 8.25–10 ft. (2.5–3 m). Zones

3–9. Raised by John Huxtable, Devon, England, and given to the author by Rowland Jackman to introduce in 1967. ♀

C. 'Madame Édouard André'

Due to its compact habit, it is excellent to grow in a container, providing colour on the patio, particularly with suitable under-planting of cream foliage or flowers. An ideal plant for enhancing a small garden late in the season. A good mid-border plant on an obelisk or on a golden foliage shrub. Suitable for all locations except north.

Flowering period mid to late summer. Slightly cup-shaped flowers, 4 in. (10 cm) across, of pointed red sepals, which fade to mauve-red, and contrasting creamy yellow anthers. Height 8.25 ft. (2.5 m). Zones 3–9. Raised in 1892 by Baron Veillard, France.

C. 'Perle d'Azur'

This plant is a great favourite because of its rather special flower colour. Somewhat gangly in its habit; good at the back of a border against a dark background. Perfect for roses of all colours and forms. Outstanding on grey-foliaged buddlejas and good on an obelisk at the back of a border. It is badly susceptible to mildew in some seasons, so protect against this. Best not to use on a north wall because of this threat.

Flowering period early summer to early autumn. Mid to light blue, semi-nodding flowers with a hint of pink at the base; sepals almost translucent. Pale yellow anthers. Height 12 ft. (3.6 m). Zones 3–9. Raised in 1885 by Morel, France.

C. 'Pink Fantasy'

A compact plant that can be grown in a container for the patio to give much-needed late flowers, but needs a good cream colour (or perhaps grey) as an under-planting. Ideal for a smaller garden. Best out of full sun due to premature fading. Perfect for a north-facing location. A good mixed border plant in a shady position on an obelisk or with blue flowers or purple foliage.

Flowering period midsummer to early autumn. Flowers of pink sepals with peachy pink highlights and dusky red anthers are 4 in. (10 cm) wide. Height 6.5–8.25 ft. (2–2.5 m). Zones 3–9. Introduced to Europe from Canada in 1975 by Jim Fisk.

C. 'Rhapsody'

A good bright colour, but flowers and foliage can look a little floppy. Super with roses, especially cream, yellows or pale pinks. Suitable for any aspect and for growing with golden or silver variegated shrubs at the back of a border. Blends with grey foliage and looks special in a blue border.

Flowering period early summer to early autumn. Displays 4- to 5-in. (10- to 12.5-cm) wide flowers of sapphire blue (colour deepens with age) and splayed open creamy yellow anthers. Height 8.25 ft. (2.5 m). Zones 3–9.

Clematis 'Rhapsody'

C. WISLEY 'EVIPO 001'

Introduced as part of the RHS Bicentenary Plant Collection. An exceptional plant for growing with deep pink or red roses, on archways or pergolas. Contrasts well with cream or yellow foliage and looks dramatic with purple-foliaged shrubs or small purple-foliaged trees. Produces a great abundance of flowers over a long period.

Flowering period midsummer to early autumn, very free-flowering. Semi-nodding, violet-blue, 3.5- to 4 in. (9- to 10 cm) flowers with yellow anthers. Height 8.25–10 ft. (2.5–3 m). Zones 4–9. An Evison and Poulsen cultivar, launched at the 2004 Chelsea Flower Show.

The Viticella Group

Probably one of the most versatile groups of clematis for garden use around the world, the viticellas are valued for their winter-hardiness, their ability to do well in hot, sunny climates, their wide use in the garden and the great volume of flowers they produce over a long period of time.

Clematis in this group are hardy in Zones 3–9 and are extremely useful in very cold areas in North America and northern Europe. They also do well in mediterranean climates, as found in southern Italy and California. For the most part (with very few exceptions) they are not suitable for long-term container culture, but are marvellous for growing with all types of roses and through a great variety of shrubs and climbing plants. Clematis from this group are very effective with certain trees as hosts, but are equally suitable at ground level through low-growing or ground cover plants such as heathers or flat spreading junipers.

Clematis 'Alba Luxurians'

Though its green-tipped sepals are disliked by some, I feel that they are an interesting feature. Can be grown in all positions mentioned above in the introduction to this section. Suitable for all locations, and looks appealing in *Sorbus* (mountain ash), especially those with grey-foliage. Useful for brightening up a north-facing wall and on open fences, but most spectacular as a focal plant growing on a birch branch obelisk in a border when on its own. It looks charming when grown with dark red roses on an archway or pergola.

Flowering period midsummer to early autumn. Nodding, open flowers, 3 in. (7.5 cm) in diameter, of white sepals with green tips early in the season, and purple-black contrasting anthers. Height 10 ft. (3 m). Zones 3–9. Raised around 1900 by Veitch and Sons, England. ♚

C. Avant-Garde 'Evipo033'

An exciting plant with a flower that appears double due to its petaloid stamens. Probably best grown into a small tree or shrub where the flower can be looked up into rather than being grown at ground level. It does equally well on an archway or pergola for the same reason. Needs a light-coloured background to show off its flowers. Suitable for any location. Arose in a Dutch nursery as a sport from *C.* 'Kermesina'; discovered by the author.

Flowering period midsummer to early autumn. Deep red flowers, 2 in. (5 cm) across with central pom-pom of pink petaloid stamens. Height 10 ft. (3 m). Zones 4–9. Introduced by Evison and Poulsen in 2006.

C. 'Betty Corning'

A charming plant discovered by Betty Corning in the USA in 1932 and most likely to be a cross between *C. crispa* and *C. viticella*. Its nodding flowers are freely produced. It is best placed on an obelisk or allowed to grow up into a small tree in a border, but close enough at hand to be able to see the flowers nearby and to enjoy their slight scent. Makes a full plant despite growing to only about 6.5 ft. (2 m). Not suitable for growing at ground level as the beauty of the flowers cannot be fully enjoyed.

Flowering period midsummer to mid autumn. Bell-shaped flowers, 2 in. (5 cm) in length. Inside the flower is a light pinkish mauve while the outside is a pale pinkish blue. Anthers are pale yellow. Height 6.5 ft. (2 m). Zones 3–9. ♉

C. 'Black Prince'

Its very dark colour requires a light background to give contrast to its flowers. Looks good with golden-foliaged heathers or clambering through potentillas at low level, blending with yellow or white flowers. Is seen at its best with grey-foliaged plants near the front of a border or on an obelisk surrounded by yellow or cream flowers. Suitable for all locations except a shady north wall where it would not show up well.

Flowering period mid to late summer. Semi-nodding, deep claret reddish purple flowers, 2–3.5 in. (5–9 cm) across, with maroon stamens. Outer surface of sepals silvery and hairy, stems covered with white hairs. Height 8.25–10 ft. (2.5–3 m). Zones 3–9. Raised in Christchurch, New Zealand by Alister Keay.

C. BONANZA 'Evipo031'

Quite a large-flowered viticella type, more resembling a large-flowered cultivar. A very free-flowering plant which, due to its compact habit, can be grown in a container to give later colour on the patio. The plant is also of great value growing towards the front part of a border on a 5-ft. (1.5-m) high birch branch obelisk where it would flower for several months, making a colourful statement. It could also be used to give added colour to a grey- or purple-foliaged host, especially if they had associated plants with cream or pink flowers. Highly suitable for any aspect this clematis has a great long-term future and is superb for the smaller garden.

Flowering period midsummer to early autumn. 3-in. (7.5-cm) wide blue-purple flowers with pale yellow anthers. Height 5–6.5 ft. (1.5–2 m). Zones 4–9. An Evison and Poulsen cultivar, introduced at the 2006 Chelsea Flower Show.

C. 'Carmencita'

A viticella of stunning colour and very suitable for any aspect. Looks marvellous on fences at the back of a border with light-coloured hosts, especially golden or silver variegated shrubs. Good with cream or yellow roses on an archway, pergola or by itself on a birch branch obelisk in a border. A very useful plant for growing with ground cover plants, especially golden-foliaged heathers.

Flowering period midsummer to early autumn. Semi-nodding, satin-textured carmine flowers, 2 in. (5 cm) across, with black anthers. Height 12 ft. (3.6 m). Zones 3–9.

C. Confetti 'Evipo036'

This clematis features a charming nodding flower, produced in great numbers. Suitable for any aspect. Best grown up an archway or pergola, or into small trees in the border. If possible, plant it so that the full beauty of its flowers can be enjoyed from below. Looks good on an obelisk by itself and under-planted with light-coloured foliage or flowers, pale cream shades being ideal.

Flowering period midsummer to early autumn. Nodding, deep pink flowers, 1.5 in. (4 cm) across. Height 10 ft. (3 m). Zones 4–9. An Evison and Poulsen cultivar, introduced at the 2006 Chelsea Flower Show.

C. 'Étoile Violette'

Raised in France by Morel in 1885 but still one of the most free-flowering clematis available. When fully established, it is almost too dense in habit to grow over heather, such is its profusion of foliage and flowers. Looks stunning growing up into a variegated holly or on a fence or wall at the back of a border. Ideal for growing up into an old apple or pear tree where its stems covered with flowers can come tumbling down from the tree. Its flowers hold their colour well in full sun so it is suitable for any aspect.

Flowering period midsummer to early autumn. Semi-nodding, violet-purple flowers with contrasting yellow anthers are 3 in. (7.5 cm) wide and have a reddish tint when young. Height 10–13 ft. (3–4 m). Zones 3–9. ♀

C. Galore 'Evipo032'

Flowers are large and somewhat gappy, but produced in great profusion. It is suitable for any aspect except north-facing, due to its rather dark-coloured flowers. A light background is therefore needed; it looks very pleasant with pale creams or pale pinks. Makes a large block of colour growing on a large obelisk in a border, especially with light-coloured foliage or flowers planted at its base. It is great fun when allowed to trail over grey foliage, such as flat-spreading junipers.

Flowering period midsummer to early autumn. Deep purple flowers, 3 in. (7.5 cm) across, with contrasting yellow anthers. Height 10 ft. (3 m). Zones 4–9. An Evison and Poulsen cultivar, introduced at the 2006 Chelsea Flower Show.

Clematis GALORE 'Evipo032'

C. 'Kermesina'

A free-flowering plant, suitable for any aspect. Its colour shows best against a light background and it can be grown through medium-sized trees or large shrubs, or as a focal point on an obelisk.

Flowering period midsummer to early autumn. Semi-nodding, rich, deep red flowers, 2.5 in. (6 cm) across. The four blunt sepals, which can have green tips early in the season, recurve at the edges and have a white blotch at the base. The anthers are almost black. Height 10 ft. (3 m). Zones 3–9. Raised by Victor Lemoine, Nancy, France, in 1883. ♥

C. 'Madame Julia Correvon'

A stunning plant on an obelisk in a border where its dramatically coloured flowers make a very loud statement. Looks outstanding in a red border either trailing through other plants or growing vertically. Suitable for any aspect. Holds its colour extremely well in direct sun. It can be grown with purple-foliaged hosts or left to sprawl around at ground level through golden-foliaged heather or yellow potentillas.

Flowering period midsummer to early autumn. Semi-nodding rich red 3-in. (7.5-cm) wide flowers have pale pink reverse with a white central bar. Pale yellow stamens. Height 10 ft. (3 m). Zones 3–9. Raised in 1900 by Morel, France. Lost to cultivation until found again by the late Christopher Lloyd, OBE, VMH, plantsman and author, in the garden at Hidcote Manor in Gloucestershire. ♛

C. 'M. Koster'

Sometimes this clematis is criticized for its rather gappy flowers. However, it has a charming pale pink colouring and looks splendid on a tall obelisk when grown in a wide mixed perennial border. It is also very dramatic when grown on a pillar, archway or pergola with cream-coloured roses, especially when they are both flowering at the same time.

Flowering period midsummer to early autumn. Semi-nodding, deep mauve-pink flowers, 4 in. (10 cm) across. As the four to six sepals mature, the margins roll back on themselves and the tips recurve so the sepals look thinner and the flower gappy. Height 12 ft. (3.6 m). Zones 3–9. Selected and introduced by Koster in about 1895.

C. PALETTE 'Evipo034'

Its delicate veined flowers can blend with grey or purple at the back of the border, growing up into an open-framed old apple tree or a white-fruiting mountain ash or growing down at ground level over white or pink summer-flowering heathers. Suitable for any aspect. Good for brightening up a north-facing wall, through a silver variegated host. Ideal for a small garden to give late summer flower.

Flowering period midsummer to early autumn. Striking 2-in. (5-cm) flowers of blue-edged sepals fading to white with blue veins on the inner parts, and black anthers. Height 10 ft. (3 m). Zones 3–9. An Evison and Poulsen cultivar, introduced in 2006 at the Chelsea Flower Show.

C. 'Polish Spirit'

A most rewarding clematis with good foliage, even at lower levels. Suitable for any aspect with good vigour, but too rampant to be grown over other

ground cover plants. Must have a light background to show off its many flowers. Looks good with orange-fruiting *Sorbus* species or up into cherry trees in the border, giving them added interest long after their flowers have gone. One of the most foolproof clematis which is really guaranteed to grow and flower well for everyone.

Flowering period midsummer to early autumn. Semi-nodding, rich purple-blue 3-in. (7.5-cm) wide flowers have a satin sheen when young. Blackish red anthers. Height 10–13 ft. (3–4 m). Zones 3–9. Raised by Brother Stefan Franczak in Poland and introduced by the author in 1989. ♔

Clematis PALETTE 'Evipo034'

Clematis 'Polish Spirit'

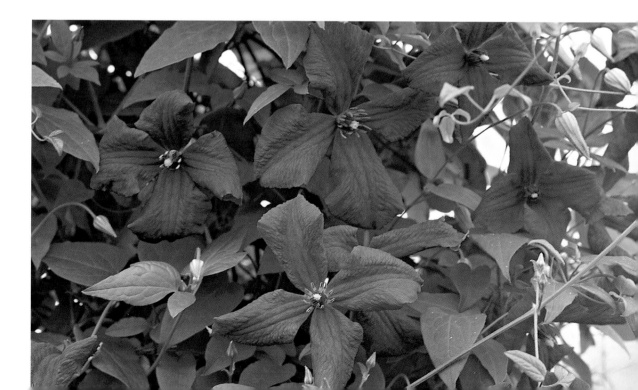

C. 'Royal Velours'

A most stunning deep-coloured flower that must have a lighter background for best effect. Looks very dramatic in a red border on an obelisk or clambering through other hosts. It also contrasts well with creams or yellows and light-blue-flowered host plants, or does well as a plant growing over light-coloured heathers, or grey- or golden-foliaged junipers. A very special plant needing a special place in the garden. It is always admired for its regal colour. Suitable for all locations except north-facing walls, where its colour is too dark.

Flowering period midsummer to early autumn. Semi-nodding, deep velvety purple flowers with a satin sheen and greenish red anthers, 2–2.5 in. (5–6 cm) across. Height 10 ft. (3 m). Zones 3–9. Raised in 1914 by Morel, France, and introduced by William Robinson and Ernest Markham at Gravetye Manor. ♛

C. 'Venosa Violacea'

A clematis raised before 1884 which has extra-special veined flowers. In very hot climates the veins merge to produce an almost purple flower, but it is still very much worth growing. Suitable for all aspects but best in good light conditions which are not too shady. Ideal with a grey background, cream or yellow variegated foliage. Looks very pleasant with pale blue or cream flowers. Associates charmingly with pale pink climbing roses or growing at ground level on grey-foliaged junipers.

Flowering period midsummer to mid autumn. Semi-nodding, 4-in. (10-cm), white flowers with purple veins which become more intense towards the edges of the sepals. Black anthers. Height 10 ft. (3 m). Zones 3–9. Raised by Lemoine, France. ♛

C. viticella 'Hågelby White'

A useful white-flowered viticella, ideal for the white border to give summer colour. Can be grown through dark-foliaged host plants or up a birch branch obelisk.

Flowering period early to late summer. Dainty, nodding, white flowers, 2 in. (5 cm) across, are not prone to green tips like C. 'Alba Luxurians'. Height 8.25–10 ft. (2.5–3 m). Zones 3–9. Found in Hågelby Park, Stockholm, Sweden, and introduced in 1998 to mark the tenth anniversary of the Swedish Clematis Society.

C. viticella 'Purpurea Plena Elegans'

This charming clematis, believed to have been grown in the sixteenth century in European gardens, should be grown more widely. It is very free-flowering, and looks good with pale green or golden foliage. Best grown up into small trees or through large shrubs where its delightful, fully double flowers can be fully enjoyed. It produces long trailing stems that make ideal trails for arranging in pedestal flower arrangements. Suitable for almost any aspect but not in dark, shady, north-facing locations.

Flowering period midsummer to early autumn. Nodding, dusky violet-purple flowers, 2.5 in. (6 cm) across. Occasionally has green outer sepals or sepal tips. Height 12 ft. (3.6 m). Zones 3–9. ♛

Clematis viticella 'Purpurea Plena Elegans'

Clematis 'Arabella'

Late-Flowering Species and Their Cultivars

This last group of clematis ranges from the short-growing herbaceous perennial clematis to the extremely vigorous members of the Tangutica Group which can reach up to 20 ft. (6 m) or more into trees. They all flower on the current season's stems from midsummer onwards and belong to Pruning Group Three. When a tangutica is growing 20 ft. (6 m) or so into a tree then it need not be pruned down to ground level each spring—that is generally left to Mother Nature! However, if it is possible to reduce its vast top growth, this should be done, perhaps every other year. As the following clematis are so varied and their garden uses likewise are varied, my recommendations for their use in the garden are detailed with their descriptions. All of these clematis are deciduous and the majority, but not all, are hardy in Zones 4–9.

Clematis 'Alionushka'

A valuable mixed border plant which is almost a herbaceous perennial and can be treated as such. Prune back to almost soil level in late winter or early spring. Suitable for any aspect. A good middle border plant that looks well on a birch branch obelisk, or towards the front of the border where it should be allowed to find its own way around among other plants just above ground level. It has a non-clinging habit. Blends well with other pinks or mauves, and with whites or deep purple-blues. Can be grown with *C.* Petit Faucon 'Evisix' on an obelisk. Looks stunning when grown on grey- or purple-foliaged hosts but is too dense in habit for growing on winter- or summer-flowering heathers. Suitable for the smaller garden.

Flowering period midsummer to early autumn. Delightful nodding 2.5- to 3-in. (6- to 7.5-cm) long flowers of rich, satiny pink with a deeper pink central bar. The four wavy-edged sepals are deeply grooved and have recurved tips which twist attractively as they age. Height 3–5 ft. (1–1.5 m). Zones 4–9. Raised in the Ukraine in 1963. Awarded the British Clematis Society Certificate of Merit. ♛

C. 'Arabella'

An extremely long-flowering herbaceous perennial that can flop around on host plants but is best if grown on a low birch branch obelisk, pea-sticks or herbaceous plant supports. Can get mildew in very sheltered locations, therefore best growing in a south-, east- or west-facing aspect. A very good plant for the middle to front of a mixed border. Can be grown at the base of climbing roses; its flowers associate well with any other pastel colours, and it looks good as an under-planting with red or pink roses. Suitable for the smaller garden.

Flowering period early summer to early autumn. Semi-nodding, round flowers, 3–3.5 in. (7.5–9 cm) wide, deep mauve-blue fading to light blue. Yellow anthers. Height 5–6.5 ft. (1.5–2 m). Zones 4–9. Raised in England by Barry Fretwell, introduced in 1990. ♛

C. ×*aromatica*

An extremely old cultivar from the mid 1800s but still a rather pretty and useful garden plant. It should be treated as a herbaceous perennial. Suitable for any aspect except north-facing. A very good front-of-border plant for growing on a birch branch obelisk, or for scrambling over plants with grey or light-coloured foliage. Looks well with cream or yellow herbaceous perennials or with an under-planting of yellow-foliaged summer bedding plants. Pretty as a cut flower in a vase of mixed flowers. Suitable for the smaller garden.

Flowering period early summer to early autumn. Very dark green leaves and dark violet-purple flowers, 1.5–2 in. (4–5 cm) wide, with yellow anthers. The four narrow sepals make a gappy, star-like flower, strongly vanilla-scented. Height 5–6.5 ft. (1.5–2 m). Zones 4–9.

C. 'Buckland Beauty'

A fun herbaceous plant belonging to the Viorna Group. It needs to clamber up into light-coloured plant material or, even better, it can be grown on a birch branch obelisk in the middle part of the border, close enough that the nodding urn-shaped flowers can be admired at or below eye level. Best in a sunny location such as a south-, west- or east-facing aspect. Prone to some mildew in shady locations. Requires hard pruning in late winter or early spring.

Flowering period early to late summer. The small, nodding, 1-in. (2.5-cm) wide flowers are a very deep mauve-pink, almost red. The four thick, fleshy sepals are creamy pink at their edges. They recurve to expose the pale yellow inside. Young leaves are light green but they darken with age. Height 5–10 ft. (1.5–3 m). Zones 4–9. Raised by Everett Leeds in Buckland, Surrey, England in 1997.

C. CHINOOK 'Evipo 013'

A most free-flowering plant from the Prairie Evison and Poulsen Collection, suitable for the middle part of a border. Its bell-shaped flowers are perhaps best displayed if the plant is grown up into a birch branch obelisk, where it will flower for several months, making a useful colour statement. Ideally, it should be planted in association with white- or cream-flowered grey-foliaged herbaceous perennials, or perhaps ones with pale pink or light blue flowers. David Jewell at the RHS Garden, Wisley, found another way of growing this cultivar, not in the border but in a 2-ft. (60-cm) wide container. During the hot summer of 2006 this plant continued to flower for at least six weeks. A very useful addition to the range of clematis that can be grown on the patio. Suitable for any aspect and the smaller garden.

Flowers and habit resemble those of the Integrifolia Group clematis. Mid-purple-blue, nodding flowers, 1.5 in. (4 cm) wide, have sepals that twist as they open out, revealing a boss of yellow stamens. Flowering period midsummer to early autumn. Height 3–4 ft. (1–1.2 m). Zones 4–9.

C. ×durandii

A very old cultivar from 1874. Herbaceous in habit, it should be pruned to ground level each year. Suitable for any aspect. Needs support of a host plant or an obelisk. The flowers are very large for such a plant but have a very strong colour which looks marvellous with creams or yellows and contrasts well with grey or golden foliage. Try it also with deep purple foliage for a great effect. Can be used as a cut flower and lasts well. Has a non-clinging habit. Suitable for the smaller garden.

Flowering period early summer to early autumn. Flowers are semi-nodding, flat, open, indigo-blue and 3–4 in. (7.5–10 cm) across with a striking boss of white filaments, blue at the base, topped by cream anthers. Height 3–6.5 ft. (1–2 m). Zones 5–9. ♥

C. 'Edward Prichard'

An interesting herbaceous perennial raised in Australia as a result of crossing *C. tubulosa* var. *davidiana* and *C. recta* var. *recta*. Hard prune in early winter or late winter/early spring. A useful front-of-border plant, best grown up into pea-sticks or a short birch branch obelisk or through herbaceous perennial plant supports. It has largish pinnate leaves each with five leaflets and the small individual flowers are borne in clusters. It can be under-planted with darker, contrasting flowers or foliage, or planted against a purple or red background. Suitable for the smaller garden.

Flowering period late summer to mid autumn. Pale mauve, scented flowers, 1–1.5 in. (2.5–4 cm) across. Height just over 3 ft. (1 m). Zones 5–9.

C. 'Eriostemon'

A marvellous mixed border plant of non-clinging habit. Probably the first hybrid clematis ever raised, the result of crossing *C. integrifolia* var. *integrifolia* with *C. viticella* in about 1830. Ideal for the back to middle section of the border. Needs to be grown on a stout support due to its vigour. Suitable for any aspect except a dark north-facing location. Its deep colour needs a light colour to show it off to greatest effect; creams, whites and pale pinks are best. Prune to ground level each year.

Flowering period midsummer to early autumn. Semi-nodding, semi-open deep purple-blue flowers, 2–3 in. (5–7.5 cm) across, with greenish cream-coloured anthers. Height 6.5 ft. (2 m). Zones 3–9.

*Clematis
'Eriostemon'*

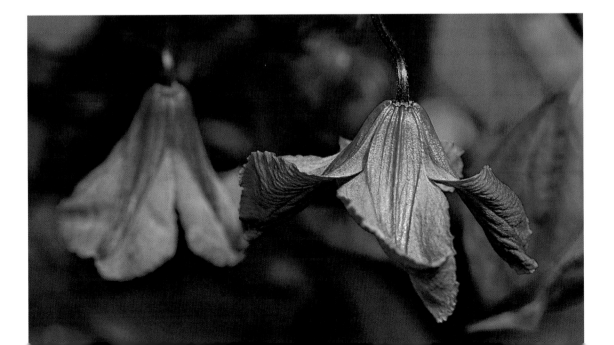

C. flammula

A variable species, sometimes almost evergreen in habit, producing tiny, almond-scented flowers which look outstanding against a dark green background such as the Common English holly (*Ilex aquifolium*). It can be grown up into a dark-foliaged evergreen or planted so that it grows up an obelisk with a dark background to it. Under-plant with pale or dark blue herbaceous perennials or plant in a white border. Needs a well-drained soil to do well; does not like cold, wet soils during winter. A plant worth growing for its scent alone.

Flowering period midsummer to mid autumn. White, star-like flowers, 1 in. (2.5 cm) across, of four narrow, blunt sepals and creamy white anthers. Height 15 ft. (4.5 m). Zones 6–9.

C. florida cultivars (The Florida Group)

The Chinese species *Clematis florida* has given rise to some highly useful cultivars. Its immediate cultivars or botanical variants are prone to sporting in gardens—which is not a disadvantage but quite charming, especially once they have established and their flowers all bloom together. As garden plants they are hardy in Zones 6–9 and are best grown through wall-trained evergreen shrubs on a west- or south-facing aspect. They also make dramatic container plants for the patio, conservatory or garden room. Some, when grown in small pots, make outstanding indoor flowering pot plants. (For more information, see Chapter 8.) All plants belonging to the Florida Group require hard pruning in late winter or very early spring.

C. CASSIS 'Evipoo2o' A stunning new, fully double cultivar which is generally grown as a flowering houseplant in the first instance and then planted out in the garden or in a container for the patio, conservatory or garden room (see page 115). For maximum effect, when grown outside, plant it to grow through a golden- or silver-variegated evergreen wall-trained shrub for maximum effect on a west- or south-facing wall or fence.

Flowering period early summer to early autumn outside, and until late autumn or early winter under glass. Flowers are 4 in. (10 cm) in diameter with six outer sepals and a very full centre. Each sepal is veined with purple mauve throughout on a creamy base. In hot weather and bright sunlight the colour and veining is much more distinct, creating an exciting flower. The flowers are borne along the stem and as the stem develops so do more flower buds and flowers. Can grow up to 10 ft. (3 m). Zones 6–9.

C. florida var. *sieboldiana* This has probably one of the most dramatic flowers of all clematis, due to the deep purple colour of its petal-like staminodes that fill the central part of the flower. Best grown as described above, which is rather frustrating; if only it were a stronger-growing and more hardy garden plant, more people could enjoy its unusual flower colouring. I've grown it in a delightful combination with pale-blue-flowered ceanothus on a west-facing wall but it has never had the vigour that I would have liked. I suggest growing it in a container with a good under-planting of white or purple to bring out its colours. In cold climates, the container should be protected indoors over winter. However, as a conservatory plant it is very successful.

Flowering period early summer to early autumn outside, until late autumn under glass. 4-in. (10-cm) wide flowers of six sepals, creamy white in summer and creamy green in autumn, with a dramatic central boss of purple, petaloid stamens, 2–2.5 in. (5–6 cm) across, which remain for a week or so after the outer sepals have dropped away. Height 6.5–8.25 ft. (2–2.5 m). Zones 6–9.

C. 'Fond Memories' A large-flowered plant with a *C. florida* habit that has perhaps limited use in the garden except in mild areas when grown through evergreen wall-trained shrubs on a south- or west-facing location. However, as a container-grown plant for the patio, conservatory or garden room, it makes a very desirable plant when in full flower. An under-planting with grey, purple or pink would complement its rather delicate colouring.

Satiny, pale pinkish white flowers with rosy lavender margins and deep rosy mauve reverse, 5–7 in. (12.5–17.5 cm) wide. Flowering period early to late summer. Height 6.5–8.25 ft. (20–2.5 m). Zones 6–9. Introduced by Thorncroft Clematis Nursery in 2004.

C. Peppermint 'Evipo005' A fully double cultivar which is generally grown as *C.* Cassis 'Evipo020', in the first instance as a flowering houseplant. In the garden it looks most attractive when grown through evergreen, grey- or purple-foliaged wall-trained shrubs on a south- or west-facing location. Looks very good at the back of a white border.

Flowering period from early summer to early autumn outside and until late autumn or early winter under glass. The flowers are 3–4 in. (7.5–10 cm) in diameter, fully double and creamy white. During early summer and early autumn the flower colour is more greenish cream but as daylight and light intensity increase, it becomes whiter. Continues to flower along its stem as more growth is produced. Can grow to 6.5–10 ft. (2–3 m). Zones 6–9.

C. Pistachio 'Evirida' This plant was raised as a sport from the author's form of *C. florida* and has been introduced as a houseplant by the Evison and Poulsen clematis development programme. After its use as a houseplant is over, it can be planted outside to be grown through an evergreen wall-trained shrub on a west- or south-facing wall or fence. Alternatively it can be grown in a container for the patio, conservatory or garden room. Very free-flowering, it continues to flower along its stems as new growth is produced. Since its introduction in 1999 it has become very widely grown as a flowering houseplant.

Flowering period early summer to mid autumn outside, and late spring to late autumn or early winter under glass. One of the most free-flowering members of the Garland Collection of indoor clematis. The rounded 3.5-in. (9-cm) wide flowers have six overlapping sepals which are creamy white in summer and creamy green in spring and autumn. The central part of the flower is made up of pinkish grey anthers and a tuft of aborted stigmas replaces the styles, which are absent. Can grow up to 10 ft. (3 m). Zones 6–9.

Clematis Viennetta 'Evipo006'

C. Viennetta 'Evipo006' The most popular Evison and Poulsen indoor-flowering clematis to date. Its flower form and colour resembles the ever-popular *C. florida* var. *sieboldiana* but its central tuft of petal-like staminodes is larger and more full, somewhat dome-shaped. After its use as a houseplant has ended, it can be re-grown in a large container for use in the conservatory or garden room, or planted into a larger container for the patio or deck garden. Alternatively it can be grown through an evergreen wall-trained shrub on a west- or south-facing location. It looks most pleasing with purple-, blue-, mauve- or pink-flowering hosts, especially those with grey foliage.

Flowering from early summer until mid to late autumn outside and from late spring to early winter under glass. The flowers are 4 in. (10 cm) across; the outer six sepals are creamy white in summer and creamy green in spring and autumn or early winter. The large, domed central boss of purple petal-like staminodes gives the flower its dramatic appearance. It has a long flowering period; new buds and flowers are continually produced along its flowering stem, as long as the daylight lasts long enough and light levels are good, sometimes lasting outside into late autumn. Can grow up to 10 ft. (3 m). Zones 6–9.

C. fusca var. fusca

A fun plant to have as a border plant due to its downy-covered, nodding, bell-shaped flowers. Not the most dramatic of flowers, but unusual and best placed at the front of the border. Some forms are short-growing, below 3 ft. (1 m), while others need the support of some pea-sticks or a herbaceous plant support. Its habit is non-clinging and it looks rather pleasant with an under-planting of cream-coloured flowers. Suitable for any aspect and for the smaller garden. Hard pruning required.

Flowering period midsummer to early autumn. Small flowers, 0.75–1.25 in. (2–3 cm) deep, made up of four thick, brown sepals. The inside, seen only when the sepal tips recurve, is cream or occasionally light blue. Height 3–6.5 ft. (1–2 m). Hardy in Zones 5–9.

C. fusca var. violacea

A variant of the species, coming from northern China and Korea. Somewhat taller in habit, growing to 6.5 ft. (2 m), and more of a climbing plant than the species. Again, an interesting plant which is not going to create a lot of colour in a border, but will be valued by serious plantsmen. Best grown on a wigwam frame or on a birch branch obelisk in the middle part of the border. The flowers are followed by the most delightful, large, spiky seedheads which start green and turn to orange before they ripen fully. Suitable for any aspect. Hard pruning required.

Flowering period midsummer to mid autumn. Larger flowers than the species, 1.25–2 in. (3–5 cm) long, and not so hairy. Sepals are purple-brown outside and purple-blue inside, with creamy green anthers. Height 6.5–10 ft. (2–3 m). Hardy in Zones 5–9.

Clematis GAZELLE 'Evipo014'

C. GAZELLE 'Evipo014'

A Prairie Collection cultivar with fresh green foliage, this clematis will grow up to almost 6.5 ft. (2 m). Non-clinging habit but produces its flowers on extremely strong stems. It looks marvellous on a birch branch obelisk in a white border, or it can be grown at the base of an archway in association with other annual or perennial climbers. Its creamy white colour associates well with all colours. It can be grown at the base of red- or purple-flowered viti-cella clematis, where its differently shaped flowers give added charm. Suit-able for any aspect, it is a good choice for the smaller garden.

Flowering period midsummer to early autumn. Resembles *C. integrifolia* var. *integrifolia* in flowers and habit. Nodding white flowers, 2.5 in. (6 cm) across, with a boss of yellow stamens. Slightly scented and sepals twist as they open out. Height 6.5 ft. (2 m). Zones 4–9.

C. HARLOW CARR 'Evipo004'

A clematis introduced as part of the RHS Bicentenary Plant Collection. It is of non-clinging habit but clambers up through its host or support. It produces an extraordinary number of flowers over a very long period; in California, for instance, it flowers from early spring until mid to late autumn. It enjoys tem-peratures as high as 100°F (38°C) and continues to flower in these conditions. A most useful plant for growing up into roses, especially pinks, creams and reds. Marvellous with grey or golden foliage and brilliant for giving interest and colour to grey-, green- or golden- foliaged conifers towards the front of the border. Suitable for any aspect and for the smaller garden.

Flowering period early to late summer. Semi-nodding, dark violet, open flowers, 3 in. (7.5 cm) across, of four narrow, twisted sepals. Stamens have dark brown anthers and white filaments. Height 6.5 ft. (2 m). Zones 4–9.

C. heracleifolia 'Roundway Blue Bird'

A selection from *C. heracleifolia* made by John Phillips of Roundway, Devizes, Wiltshire, England. It has a very dark blue flower, is a sub-shrub and a very useful mixed border plant, growing only to about 3 ft. (1 m) in height. It can be left unstaked; a plant for the front of the border. Ideal when mixed with creams, whites or grey foliage.

Flowering period midsummer to mid autumn. Strongly scented, tubular, flowers, 0.75–1 in. (2–2.5 cm) long. Sepals recurve with age to reveal paler blue inside and yellow anthers on white filaments. Height 3 ft. (1 m). Zones 5–9.

C. integrifolia var. integrifolia

A very useful herbaceous perennial which is non-clinging as it has simple elliptical leaves which do not have petioles. The bell-like flowers help to bring added interest to the front of a mixed or herbaceous border. It is best supported with pea-sticks or a herbaceous plant support. Some forms or cultivars are short-growing and can be allowed to flop around at ground level; it really depends on the border, whether it is formal or informal. This species and its cultivars are suitable for any aspect. Their various flower colours are all pastel shades and therefore blend perfectly with most colours. They are effective when grown underneath roses in a rose border, where their flowers will add interest and charm. The species and cultivars should be pruned as any other herbaceous perennial, therefore if the border is tidied up in the autumn and other, nearby plants are pruned back to ground level, these clematis can be treated similarly. They are all suitable for the smaller garden.

Flowering period midsummer to early autumn. Nodding, bell-shaped flowers, 1.5in. (4 cm) deep, are borne on long flower-stalks. The four sepals vary from mauve blue to deep blue and have very pointed tips which recurve outwards. Height 2–3 ft. (60 cm–1 m). Zones 4–9.

C. integrifolia 'Alba'

A form of the species with pure white, scented flowers, 1.5 in. (4 cm) deep. Often grown from seed and so can be variable and revert to the blue form of the species. Flowering period midsummer to early autumn. Height 2 ft. (60 cm). Zones 4–9.

C. integrifolia 'Hakuree'

A long-flowering white integrifolia, raised by Mr. Hiroshi Hayakawa in about 1992. An outstanding plant for a white border and for growing towards the front of the border supported by pea-sticks or herbaceous plant supports.

Flowering period early summer to autumn. The four white sepals are often bluish white at the beginning of the flowering season, but during the heat of the summer they become white. The flowers are strongly scented—of gardenias, according to Maurice Horn. Height 2–2.5 ft. (60–80 cm). Zones 4–9.

C. integrifolia 'Hanajima'

A very useful front-of-border, short-growing pink cultivar. It blends well with other pink, white or blue-flowered herbaceous perennials. It can be supported by pea-sticks or left to flop around.

Flowering period early summer to early autumn. The rosy pink flowers, 1.5 in. (4 cm) deep, have creamy yellow anthers and sepals that twist at their tips giving it a distinct charm. Height about 2 ft. (60 cm). Zones 4–9. Raised by Mr. Kazushije Ozawa in Japan about 1986.

C. integrifolia 'Pangbourne Pink'

*Clematis
integrifolia
'Pangbourne Pink'*

A larger-flowered selection of *C. integrifolia* 'Rosea', flowering from midsummer to early autumn. Deep pink-mauve, open bell-shaped flowers, 2–2.5 in. (5–6 cm) across. Height 2 ft. (60 cm). Zones 4–9. ♀

C. integrifolia 'Rosea'

A pale pink or mauve pink selection with 1.5-in. (4-cm) deep flowers. Height 2 ft. (60 cm). Zones 4–9. ♛

C. 'Jan Fopma'

Named after a famous Dutch nurseryman, this is an interesting plant for the front of the border. It needs to be grown over a low birch branch obelisk or through low-growing shrubs with grey- or light-coloured-foliage. It will not create a vast display of colour but is a clematis that is just that little bit different, and worthy of a place among other unusual plants. Suitable for the smaller garden; best in a sunny location.

Flowering period midsummer to early autumn. Small, nodding, bell-shaped flowers which are a deep glossy purple-red and have deep dusky pink margins. The 2-in. (5-cm) wide flowers are borne in clusters. Height 4–5 ft. (1.2–1.5 m). Zones 4–9.

C. ×jouiniana 'Praecox'

An extremely good plant for smothering the ground—truly a ground cover clematis. It is the result of crossing *C. tubulosa* and *C. vitalba*. It is non-clinging and can be grown either at ground level as a ground cover plant, or upright against a wall or fence, where it will require some tying-in to wires or other supports. It therefore can be grown at the back of a border where it makes a fairly dense screen and will look most effective. It can also be grown up a 6.5-ft. (2-m) high birch branch obelisk to give height and interest in the middle part of a border. It has a woody base, some of which can be retained each spring at the time of pruning when all the previous season's stems are removed to almost ground level.

When grown at ground level it is quite vigorous and can swamp its neighbours, therefore you must allow it an area about 8.25 ft. × 6.5 ft. (2.5 × 2 m) in which to spread. This vigour can be used to great advantage for covering unsightly objects at ground level such as old tree stumps. It is extremely useful for clambering down sloping banks and covering them with foliage and flower.

Flowering period midsummer to mid autumn. Bluish white flowers, 1.5 in. (4 cm) across, with deep mauve towards the tips of the narrow sepals, and creamy white anthers. Large trifoliate, dark green leaves with serrated margins. Height 10 ft. (3 m) on a wall, 20 in. (50 cm) grown at ground level. Zones 3–9. ♛

C. MEDLEY 'Evipo012'

A Prairie Collection cultivar, suitable for any aspect and a great choice for smaller gardens. Its pink bell-shaped flowers look rather fine when grown against a purple background, possibly with an under-planting of deep blue-flowering herbaceous perennials mixed with grey foliage.

Flowering period midsummer to early autumn. Resembles *C. integrifolia* var. *integrifolia* in flower and habit. Slightly scented, light pink, nodding flowers, 1.5 in. (4 cm) wide, with yellow stamens. Sepals twist as they open out. Height 3–4 ft. (1–1.2 m). Zones 4–9.

C. Petit Faucon 'Evisix'

A different and good-value mixed border clematis. It has a non-clinging habit, growing to only about 3 ft. (1 m). Its deep purple, nodding flowers need a light-coloured background to show them off. Best grown on a birch branch obelisk or on a wigwam support in the middle to front of a border, where it will flower for at least three months. The flowers are followed by attractive silky seedheads, extending the period when it is contributing greatly to the garden. Best in a south-, west- or east-facing position.

Flowering period midsummer to mid autumn. Stunning, nodding, blue-purple flowers, 3–3.5 in. (7.5–9 cm) across, with slightly twisted sepals maturing to deep blue. Golden-yellow anthers mature to creamy white. Height 3 ft. (1 m). Zones 4–9. An Evison and Poulsen cultivar, raised in 1989. Awarded the British Clematis Society Certificate of Merit. ♛

Clematis Petit
Faucon 'Evisix'

C. 'Pink Ice'

An extremely colourful plant that can be grown at the forward part of a border on a birch branch obelisk. It contrasts brilliantly with grey-foliaged herbaceous perennials and ground cover plants, especially those with white flowers.

Flowering period midsummer to mid autumn. An integrifolia-type, non-clinging plant with open, semi-nodding, vibrant pink flowers of four well-separated, slightly twisted sepals and creamy yellow stamens, 2.5–3 in. (6–7.5 cm) across. Suitable for any aspect. Height 3–6 ft. (1–1.8 m). Zones 4–9. Raised by Malcolm Oviatt-Ham, UK, in 1995. Awarded the British Clematis Society Certificate of Merit. ♔

C. recta var. purpurea

A good selection of this purple-foliaged form of *C. recta* var. *recta* is an extremely valuable mixed border plant, and can be grown as recommended for the species (see below). It is best to acquire a plant that has been grown from a root division of a proven form, or select a good-coloured form in a garden outlet. Seedlings grown from a good form will be variable, but you can be lucky! The plant is prized for its young purple foliage; it looks its best before the flowers are produced by which time the foliage has turned greenish purple. Once the plant has flowered, cut it back hard to ground level in summer to obtain a further flush of attractive young foliage. A good form can also be raised by sowing seeds of the species. About ten per cent of these seedlings will have purple foliage, and it is then a matter of selection. Suitable for the smaller garden.

Flowering period early to late summer. Scented, white flowers as in the species. Height 3 ft. (1 m). Zones 3–9.

C. recta var. recta

A herbaceous perennial clematis that adds greatly to a mixed border. Can be allowed to scramble around at ground level but I believe that it looks best growing up through a plant support such as a hazel or willow wigwam, or just use pea-sticks to keep it off the ground. The plants offered in plant outlets are generally grown from seed, which means that they can be variable. If possible, find a friendly gardener who has a good flowering form and ask if you can have a root division from his or her plant. The better clones are very free-flowering, producing masses of tiny star-shaped white flowers in terminal panicles (flowerheads). It can be positioned in a border to grow with dark-coloured neighbours. Plant it towards the front of the border so that you can enjoy what is quite a strong hawthorn scent. Suitable for any aspect and for the smaller garden.

Flowering period early to late summer. White, star-like flowers, 1.25 in.

(3 cm) across, of four narrow sepals and creamy white anthers. Height 3–6.5 ft. (1–2 m). Hardy in Zones 3–9.

C. SAVANNAH 'Evipo015'

An outstanding amount of flower is produced by this Prairie Collection cultivar. It is darker in colour than C. MEDLEY 'Evipo012' and most useful for providing a big splash of colour on a birch branch obelisk in the central part of a border, over a long period. Suitable for any aspect and for the smaller garden.

Flowering period midsummer to early autumn. Resembles C. *integrifolia* in flower and habit. Deep pink, nodding flowers with twisted sepals, 2.5 in. (6 cm) across, and yellow stamens. Height 3–4 ft. (1–1.2 m). Zones 4–9.

Clematis SAVANNAH 'Evipo015'

C. *tangutica* 'Bill MacKenzie'

An excellent plant for covering large areas on a wall or fence at the back of the border. Probably best grown on its own or up into a tree. Its yellow flowers followed by large silky seedheads bring colour and interest well into the autumn months. Ideal for a yellow border or for giving contrast to red, purple or dark blue herbaceous perennials, which can be grown in front of it. Suitable for any aspect.

Flowering period midsummer to late autumn. Open, bell-shaped, 2.5- to 3-in. (6- to 7.5-cm) flowers of four broad, yellow sepals with pointed tips and brown anthers on reddish filaments. Attractive, silky seedheads. Height 16.5–20 ft. (5–6 m). Zones 4–9. ♔

C. tangutica 'Helios'

A very useful tangutica cultivar for the smaller garden. It grows to only about 5 ft. (1.5 m) and, with an interesting flower shape (as the flowers mature they become flat with recurving tips), it can be used as a plant at the front of a border, growing up into a willow or hazel wigwam. Looks good with dark or pale blue herbaceous perennials and dark orange colours. Suitable for any position.

Flowering period midsummer to mid autumn. Lantern-like yellow flowers, 1.5–2.5 in. (4–6 cm) across, with creamy yellow anthers on dark purple-brown filaments. Large silky seedheads. Height 5 ft. (1.5 m). Zones 4–9.

C. tangutica 'Lambton Park'

A good large-flowered cultivar which can be grown on a strong plant support in the middle section of the border. It looks charming when grown on a large dome-shaped 6.5-ft. (2-m) high birch branch obelisk, particularly if its neighbours are herbaceous perennials with pale blue, dark blue or orange flowers. Its seedheads are very useful for summer flower arrangements or for drying for winter decorations. Suitable for any aspect.

Flowering period early summer to mid autumn. Coconut-scented, bright buttercup-yellow, cowbell-shaped flowers, 2 in. (5 cm) wide, with yellow-green anthers. Large silky seedheads. Height 10–13 ft. (3–4 m). Zones 4–9. ♔

C. terniflora

An extremely vigorous species which is native to parts of China, Korea and Japan. In many parts of the United States and Canada it is considered an invasive weed. However, in the British Isles it is less vigorous and will flower well only after hot summers. In the USA and Canada it is known as the 'sweet autumn clematis' due to its rather strong and pleasant scent. It was previously known, incorrectly, as *C. paniculata* or *C. maximowicziana*. In the British Isles it needs to be grown in a good sunny location where it can grow up into a tree or possibly cover an arbour, archway or pergola alongside or at the back of a border. In North America it can be grown in any location where it will develop and flower very well. In central Europe it is best planted in a good sunny location, and it will thrive in southern Europe as does the closely related species *C. flammula*.

Flowering period late summer to mid autumn. Small, star-like, white flowers, 1 in. (3 cm) wide, hawthorn-scented with four narrow sepals and white anthers. Flowers borne in panicles. Silky seedheads. Height 20 ft. (6 m). Zones 5–9.

C. texensis cultivars (The Texensis Group)

Some of the following cultivars were raised originally in the late 1800s by crossing the species *C. texensis* with late large-flowered cultivars such as *C.* 'Star of India'. They are marvellous garden plants and have various uses in the garden. Some have miniature tulip-like flowers, while others have nodding bell-shaped flowers. Their uses in the garden are detailed with their individual descriptions.

C. texensis 'Duchess of Albany' A strong-growing plant with a delightful miniature tulip-shaped, satiny pink flower. I believe that it is best grown at ground level at the front of the border where you can look into its charming flowers. Ideal for growing over low-growing ground cover shrubs, or flat-spreading junipers. Looks stunning with grey foliage and pale blue flowers. Once established, it can be quite vigorous and so needs a large border where it can develop; alternatively, you can plant it at the back of a border growing up a fence or on a wall where its flowers can still be admired. Suitable for any position.

Clematis texensis 'Duchess of Albany'

Flowering period midsummer to mid autumn. Upright miniature tulip-like flowers, 2- to 2.5-in. (5- to 6-cm) deep, with pink anthers. The four satiny sepals are deep candy pink on the inside with a deeper pink bar, and paler pink on the outside. Lasts well as a cut flower due to its thick flower-stalk (pedicel). Height 10 ft. (3 m). Zones 3–9.

C. texensis 'Étoile Rose' A clematis that was nearly left out of my selection because it can be seriously affected by powdery mildew. However, it thrived in the hot English summer of 2006, with no trace of mildew. Its charming bell-shaped, nodding flowers persuaded me, I am afraid, that it should be included! However, you should remember that there is a good chance it will be subject to mildew in some years. If you use a fungicide to control mildew on roses then treat this clematis at the same time from the beginning of the growing season. It needs the support of a fence, or a host plant which has an open framework. It looks really marvellous with grey foliage, pale blue or pale pink flowers. Suitable for any aspect except a shady position or a north-facing location.

Flowering period midsummer to early autumn. Stunning flowers, 2.5 in. (6 cm) across, are of deep satiny pink on the outside and vibrant, pale scarlet pink on the inside, while the anthers are pale yellow. Height 10 ft. (3 m). Zones 4–9.

C. texensis 'Pagoda' A very fine plant once established. It has masses of flowers during the summer months and certainly enjoyed the hot summer of 2006 in England. Because of its nodding flowers this plant needs to be grown up into a small tree at the back of the border, or through a purple-foliaged host shrub, where its delightful flowers can be admired. It also looks especially fine on a fence or up the base of an archway, arbour or pergola, when one can view the flowers from close quarters. Looks good with cream and mauve-pink flowers, and associates well with climbing roses on a pole or up a formal obelisk in the border, where it will create great interest. Best in a south-, west- or east-facing position.

Flowering period early to late summer. Pagoda-shaped, nodding flowers of creamy pink-mauve with a deeper mauve-purple band tapering to the tip, with creamy pink inside and darker veins throughout. Creamy green anthers in 2.5- to 3-in. (6- to 7.5-cm) wide flowers. Height 10 ft. (3 m). Zones 4–9. Raised by John Treasure at Burford House Gardens, Shropshire, England, by crossing *C. texensis* 'Étoile Rose' and *C. viticella*. ♛

C. texensis 'Princess Diana' (Synonym: *C. texensis* 'The Princess of Wales'.) A beautiful cultivar, raised by Barry Fretwell, England, in 1984, from crossing *C. texensis* with *C.* 'Bees Jubilee'. It can be grown in a similar way to *C. texensis*

Clematis texensis
'Princess Diana'

'Duchess of Albany', but is less vigorous and perhaps better for the slightly smaller garden. Its darker-coloured flowers require a light background for contrast, looking good with grey-foliaged heathers or low-growing herbaceous perennials at the front of a border. Suitable for any position except north-facing.

Flowering period early to late summer. Miniature tulip-shaped flowers, 2.5 in. (6 cm) long, of four luminous pink sepals with a deep vibrant pink central bar. The outside of the sepals are a pale whitish pink, again with a deep pink central bar. The maroon anthers are on cream filaments. Height 8.25 ft. (2.5 m). Zones 4–9. ♀

C. texensis 'Sir Trevor Lawrence.' Raised in 1890 at the same time as *C. texensis* 'Duchess of Albany' by Jackmans of Woking, England, when they crossed *C.* 'Star of India' with *C. texensis*. It resembles *C. texensis* 'Duchess of Albany' in habit, and can be grown in a similar way. Its darker-coloured flowers benefit from a light background that provides contrast; grey is the obvious choice, but it also looks delightful when grown with golden, golden or silver variegated foliage or golden flat spreading junipers.

Flowering period midsummer to early autumn. Miniature tulip-like flowers, 2–2.5 in. (5–6 cm) long, dusky purple-red inside with a scarlet central bar, and whitish pink (in shade) to reddish pink (in sun) outside, with reddish pink veins running the length of the sepals. Yellow anthers. Height 10 ft. (3 m). Zones 4–9.

C. tibetana var. vernayi (L&S 13342)

A really delightful form of the species collected by Frank Ludlow and George Sherriff in Lhasa, Tibet in 1947; it is sometimes referred to as the 'orange peel clematis' due to its thick sepals. (Very often, seedling clematis from *C. tangutica* or *C. orientalis* are labelled incorrectly as the 'orange peel clematis' but these seedlings are not the true 'orange peel clematis'. The true 'orange peel clematis' is quite distinct due to its finely cut, very glaucous foliage.) *Clematis tibetana* var. *vernayi* (*L&S 13342*) is a plant that is not over-vigorous for this group of yellow-flowered clematis and is very useful for the smaller garden. It can be grown on a birch branch obelisk in the middle section of the border, or through large-leaved rhododendrons, or up into purple-foliaged small trees, where its yellow flowers give a marvellous contrast.

Flowering period midsummer to mid autumn. Nodding, globular, four-sepalled, golden-yellow flowers, 1.5 in. (4 cm) across. The thick sepals have been compared to lemon rind. Height 10 ft. (3 m). Zones 4–9.

C. ×triternata 'Rubromarginata'

A very old, small-flowered cultivar, raised in 1862 by Cripps and Son in England, by crossing *C. flammula* and *C. viticella*. An outstanding, vigorous plant

Clematis tibetana var. vernayi (L&S 13342)

for growing by itself in a sunny position at the back of a border on a fence or wall. Alternatively, it looks delightful growing up into a small, purple-foliaged tree or into an old apple or pear tree in the border. Perhaps, if the prime reason for growing it is its strong hawthorn scent, then it can be grown on a strong archway, arbour or pergola, where it can be enjoyed at close quarters.

Flowering period midsummer to early autumn. Star-like white flowers, 1–1.5 in. (3–4 cm) across, with wine-red margins and creamy red anthers. Height 10–13 ft. (3–4 m). Zones 5–9. ♔

C. tubulosa var. davidiana

Formerly *C. heracleifolia* var. *davidiana*. A herbaceous clematis which is well suited for growing at the front of the border where it forms a large clump after several years. It is generally self-supporting. The hyacinth-like flowers are very pleasantly scented and the large leaves also become fragrant as they dry and die away in the autumn. The large leaves are a feature in their own right and the blue flowers look good with cream or white flowers, either as a permanent planting or with summer-flowering annuals. Hard pruning required.

Flowering period late summer to mid autumn. Pale powdery blue, tubular flowers, 0.75 in. (2 cm) long and 1.5 in. (4 cm) wide, that open out towards the tip. Pale yellow anthers on white filaments. Height 3 ft. (1 m). Zones 5–9. A clone of the species, collected near Beijing in 1863 by Père David, a French missionary.

C. tubulosa var. davidiana 'Wyevale'

Formerly *C. heracleifolia*. var. *davidiana* 'Wyevale'. A very good selection of the species that can be used in a similar way. Its larger flowerheads are a great attraction to butterflies during the summer months. Both forms may be propagated by digging up the rhizomes that form underground as the plant spreads and becomes a larger clump.

Flowering period midsummer to mid autumn. Tubular mid-mauve-blue flowers, 1.25 in. (3 cm) long with recurving frilly tips. Yellow stamens. Height 3–4 ft. (1–1.2 m). Zones 5–9. Raised by Wyevale Nurseries, Hereford, England, in the 1950s. ♔

C. viorna

A species from eastern North America that is very variable and is also known as the 'vase vine' or 'leather flower'. Its pitcher-shaped flowers need to be viewed at close quarters to be fully appreciated. These charming flowers look good when growing on a birch branch obelisk, or a hazel or willow wigwam at the front of a border. A good deep-coloured form looks great with creams or light orange-coloured herbaceous perennials as an under-planting. Best in a sunny location; can get powdery mildew on a shady north-facing position. Very attractive, large, spiky seedheads during the late summer or early autumn.

Flowering period midsummer to early autumn. Pendulous, pitcher-shaped, 1.25- to 1.5-in. (3- to 4-cm) deep flowers vary in colour from violet, through dull purple to pink. The four thick sepals recurve to reveal creamy yellow margins and yellow anthers. Height 6.5 ft. (2 m). Zones 4–9.

C. VICTOR HUGO 'Evipo007'

This tall-growing, non-clinging, deep-purple-flowered clematis is ideal when grown against a light-coloured background, as otherwise its flowers get lost due to their very deep colour. Best if grown in a sunny location up an obelisk, either formal or informal, with a pale cream, pale pink or pale blue background of herbaceous perennials, or with pale-coloured summer-flowering climbing annuals to provide contrast. It will make a very bold statement on a vertical support in the middle part of a border. Very long-flowering.

Clematis VICTOR HUGO 'Evipo007'

Flowering period early summer to early autumn. Deep purple flowers of four to six sepals, 2.5–3.5 in. (6–9 cm) wide, with dark violet-tipped stamens. Height 6.5–10 ft. (2–3 m). Zones 4–9. Introduced by Evison and Poulsen during 2002, the bicentenary of Victor Hugo's birth.

Chapter 13   # Cultivation

Clematis flammula, a species
from southern Europe, is best
suited to a free-draining soil.

I strongly believe that when cultivating our gardens we should look to plants in their natural habitats for guidance and inspiration. When a clematis is planted out in the garden with its root system growing 'naturally' in the soil, for instance, we should remember that clematis in the wild grow most successfully when their root system is shaded by some other plants (or even by a large pile of stones or a boulder).

When we grow clematis in containers on a balcony, on a terrace or on a deck area, we cannot refer back to equivalent situations in the wild, as one would be hard-pressed to find balconies or deck gardens in the wilds of China or Japan. But we can still remember the basic points about shading the root system of clematis even if they are growing in a more contrived way in pots or containers, by adding additional plant material to grow in the container with them to provide that much needed shade to the root system, creating a microclimate for the clematis to enjoy.

As I have mentioned earlier, very often when I have been looking for clematis in the wild, I have seen seedlings that have established themselves in crevices or cracks in walls or rocky outcrops. Somehow their roots have found moisture, and not only do the plants survive, but they grow extremely well. I have seen *Clematis tangutica* in Western Sichuan, China, growing out of scree on a rocky landslide, with its root system buried by 2–3 ft. (60–90 cm) of stone. This is what one might describe as giving the plant a shady root system!

Clematis tangutica in the wild in China.

Clematis are scramblers. They are happy growing over a host plant, at low or higher levels. If no support is available then they will make a mound of stems, growing on themselves. Therefore all except the non-clinging types which are herbaceous perennials in their habit, such as *Clematis integrifolia* var. *integrifolia*, will benefit from some type of support whether it is man-made or another plant, tree or shrub.

Deep, well-drained soil is best. Clematis like plenty of water but certainly do not relish soggy, wet root systems. Some like very well-drained soils; for instance, *Clematis flammula* enjoys the free-draining limestone-type soils of southern France.

Shade at the root systems is, as everyone should now know, absolutely vital—this we see in their natural habitat. Therefore, additional shade needs to be given to the plant's root system after planting. Clematis love a micro-climate with other plant material at their base, which provides shade and moisture. You should not attempt to plant a clematis against a south-facing wall or fence at the back of a border where no shade can be given to the root system. We know from our production of clematis in Guernsey and from our customers around the world that if soil temperatures reach 80°F (27°C) then the clematis plant's root system stops growing. We also know that native clematis species which grow in mediterranean climates, as found in some parts of Europe and California, go into a summer dormancy and re-grow only when the temperatures cool and the rains come. Do not subject your large-flowered clematis cultivars to such conditions!

Considering the conditions that clematis naturally prefer, you might wonder why and how can clematis grow well in containers in hot climates. The answer is that with the correct choice of container and with the use of other shallow-rooted plant material, it is possible. Later in this chapter this will be described in detail.

Once a clematis' roots are planted in the shade, the top will find its way naturally into the light and sunshine. If clematis are planted in a shady position they require only about three to four hours of good sunlight per day to grow successfully. Therefore, north-facing walls in the northern hemisphere can provide a good site for growing clematis (in association with other plants, of course).

A point to remember is that only the white, deep blue, deep purple and red large-flowered clematis should be planted to flower in full sun. These will keep their colour well. However, the pale blues, pale mauves and pinks and some of the paler striped clematis, such as *Clematis* 'Nelly Moser', can be utilized to brighten up a shady wall or fence at the back of a border where the sun will not prematurely bleach out the flowers.

Buying Your Clematis

Gardeners nowadays are able to purchase the clematis of their choice through mail order, internet sales, eBay, special newspaper offers and so forth, without actually seeing the plant beforehand. These can work well if you know the company, but do be selective. Sometimes, a very low-priced plant may take a long time to become established and strong enough to plant out into the garden.

It is usually best to select the plants yourself by going to the garden centre or plant nursery. Contrary to popular belief, it is not vital that the plant be large and tall; rather, the most important criterion is that it should be strong at its base. Also, ask yourself whether it is bushy or very thin; the thin plants have probably not been pruned as young nursery plants, and these are the ones to avoid. When you buy a large plant in a two- or three-gallon pot in North America or a two- or three-litre pot size plant in Europe, you are hopefully buying time—a more mature plant. If you buy strong healthy plants in a quart (10.5-cm) pot you will need to grow these plants on, possibly for one year, before you can safely plant them out in the garden. On the other hand, if you intend to grow the plant in a container for the terrace or patio garden, then a smaller plant will work. It will grow perfectly well as long as the plant is pruned hard as a young plant, so that it produces multiple stems and is well furnished at its base.

The most important parts of your clematis are its root system, which needs to be well established in the container, and the bottom 12 in. (30 cm) of the plant's growth, which must be strong with basal stems.

Planting Out Your New Clematis

If you live in a mild climate and autumn planting is possible, this is the ideal time to plant and it saves on watering the following spring. Nowadays, however, the best selection of clematis are offered in garden centres in the spring months.

Before purchasing your new clematis you will have selected the planting site or container and decided which type or colour will best suit the location where the plant will grow. Recommendations on the most suitable clematis for individual sites can be found in Chapters 6–9. Likewise, my recommendations for the most successful clematis for containers, hanging baskets, planters and the like, are found in Chapters 5 and 7.

When planting the clematis in the garden, it is important to choose the most appropriate site. Once your host plant or planting combination has been decided, or if you are to clothe a fence or wall at the back of your perennial or shrub border, you will know roughly where you want to plant your clematis. The optimum position to plant your clematis is in a spot where its root system will be in the most shade at midday. Plant behind the host plant or support, if possible, where the root system will receive the most natural shade. If the soil where you intend to plant has not been dug or had additional fertilizer mixed with it recently, then some preparation work will need to be done before planting.

Before you start to prepare the planting site, take the clematis you have purchased and are about to plant and place it in a bucket of water so that the

Clematis JOSEPHINE
'Evijohill' at the
back of a narrow
border where its
root system is very
well shaded by
Astrantia.

root ball is completely submerged for at least twenty minutes, but not longer than thirty minutes. In this way the root ball will be able to take up water, which will help considerably after planting and give your clematis a good start in its new home. If you do not do this, the root ball may be very dry and then, after planting, it is almost impossible to wet thoroughly, making your plant much less likely to establish well.

Having selected the ideal planting site you then need to dig a hole, measuring at least 18 in. (45 cm) deep by 18 in. (45 cm) in diameter if possible. If you are planting between the roots of an old apple tree (for instance), you should prepare a hole as large as you are able. If you have decided to plant underneath a laburnum, or perhaps a hawthorn or lilac tree, then these small trees do have very fibrous root systems and you may need to remove some of these tree roots. This will not harm the tree, but will give the clematis a chance to establish in its newly prepared site.

If your planting site has a very heavy clay soil, you will need to break up the sides and the base of the hole with a garden fork. If this is not done, then your clematis will be growing in what is effectively a clay pot rather than the open ground.

If you have some well-rotted garden compost, place this in the bottom of the hole to a depth of about 5–6 in. (13–15 cm) and also fork it well into the base of the hole. This will give the clematis roots moisture, fibre and food when they reach it. The rest of the hole can be back-filled with old potting soil from the previous season's annuals, or you can use new potting soil. Alternatively, you can make your own mix of one part peat or peat substitute, one part coarse sand and one part good loam or topsoil from your garden; also use a general fertilizer or, if your prefer, an organic fertilizer such as fish meal, blood and bone. Firm the refilled hole with your feet (the heel is best), or your fists. A hole large enough to take the clematis' root ball can then be dug out.

When I plant new clematis I like to plant the clematis in its new position slightly deeper than the soil level in the container. An extra depth of 2–2.5 in. (5–6 cm) is sufficient. This will keep the basal buds of the plant moist. The buried stems will also produce extra roots, making the plant stronger. If the plant should succumb to clematis wilt—and this affects only some of the large-flowered cultivars (more information about this later in this chapter)—then your clematis will re-grow. Likewise, if the top growth should become damaged or totally broken off at soil level during cultivation of the surrounding area, then your plant will have the chance to re-grow from the dormant buds which will have developed below soil level. I very often advise friends who are planting a clematis that they should think of it as a climbing perennial plant which needs to develop a root crown below ground level. Having planted the clematis those extra few inches/centimetres deeper and firmed the soil around its root system with your hands, you must consider the top growth and attaching it to its host or support.

Clematis will be sold in plant and garden centres growing on a range of different plant supports, varying from a single bamboo cane, to two or three canes, to those on a trellis or even a cedar stake power-stapled to the side of the flowerpot. If you have purchased your clematis when it is in full leaf, and possibly flowering, you may prefer to just plant the clematis and then deal with the task of disentangling it from its nursery support the following spring when you need to prune the plant. However, if you are purchasing your plant while it is dormant during the late winter or spring or perhaps the late autumn, you may wish to deal with the problem at the time of planting. If the clematis is sold growing on a single cane, then it is perhaps best to remove it from its support immediately after planting by just untying it from the support. Please be careful not to kink or damage the stems while you are doing this.

Whenever you decide to move the plant from its nursery plant support and attach it to its new support or host plant, it is important to ensure that the stem or stems are firmly secured and not allowed to just blow around in the breeze. I prefer to remove the plant from the support and then place a single strong stick, stake or bamboo cane in front of the stems, so that the support can protect the stems which would be between the support and the host plant or host support. Just lean the support stick or cane towards something to which it can be tied. During cultivation of the soil, by forking or hoeing, the fragile stems will then be somewhat protected from accidental damage.

If you decide at the time of planting to leave the nursery support in place, then just lean this against the host tree, shrub or host support. It really depends on your taste and type of gardening as to whether you wish to remove the nursery support or not. Importantly, do tie the nursery support to something so that the clematis stems are not left to blow in the wind, and certainly make sure the clematis stems are secured to something that is not going to move around in the breeze. At this point, any damaged stems on the clematis should be removed down to a strong pair of leaf-axil buds.

Clematis 'Étoile Violette' is well secured at its base as it clambers up into a golden variegated holly.

All of this does sound a great deal of work but it is important that, if you are planting your clematis to grow up into a large shrub or small tree, the clematis stems should have the correct support to which they can attach themselves. If you intend to attach the clematis to a low branch of a tree, then do be sure to place a strong stake in the soil near the root ball and tie the stake to a low branch, so the clematis is not uprooted by the first strong wind after planting.

You will not have forgotten all of the previous comments about your clematis requiring a shady root system. If you are planting in a border which is, or will be, full of herbaceous perennial plants then I am sure there will be plenty of shallow-rooted plants to give your clematis that added shade to its root system. If not, then plant a group of plants about 12 in. (30 cm) from the root crown of the clematis.

For best results, choose plants that will provide shade and add interest by virtue of their foliage, form or flowers, or even their seedheads. Examples include *Artemisia arborescens* 'Powis Castle' and other grey-foliaged shallow-rooted plants as well as *Alchemilla mollis*, with its mounds of rounded leaves and feathery sprays of flowers. Genera with potential clematis companions include *Erica* (heather), *Calluna* (ling) and *Daboecia* (Irish heath), which are summer- or winter-flowering; *Ajuga* (with attractive flowers and foliage); *Bergenia* (with large evergreen leaves that turn colour during winter and have early spring or summer flowers); *Heuchera* (with many different foliage colours); and *Lamium* (with silver and greenish grey foliage). These are just a few from which to make your selection and are covered in more detail in the chapters dealing with combining clematis and other plants (Chapters 4, 6, 7 and 9).

Once all the planting has been carried out and the clematis is tied securely to its host, the last job is to water everything in well. For a planting site that includes the clematis and shade plants you will need to use 2 gallons (7.5 litres) of clear water, preferably using a watering can or hose pipe with a fine rose, thus avoiding puddling the soil too much.

Replanting Established Clematis

It is quite easy to dig up and replant an established large-flowered clematis or an herbaceous clematis such as *Clematis integrifolia* var. *integrifolia* or *C. tubulosa*. However, it is not really recommended that you dig up and replant an established species or small-flowered cultivar if it has a fibrous root system. If such a plant is only one to two years old then, with care, this might be possible. The fibrous-rooted types include *C. armandii*, *C. cirrhosa* var. *cirrhosa* and other evergreen types, the alpina and macropetala types, the montanas and late-flowering types such as *C. tangutica*. However, the viticella types which have a root system similar to the large-flowered cultivars can be moved successfully.

The best time to do this is during the late winter or very early spring, after the worst frosts have gone and before bud break. First remove the top growth down to 24 in. (60 cm) and tie the remaining stems securely to a strong bamboo cane or stake. Place the stake near to the root crown to a depth of at least 6 in. (15 cm) but avoid damaging the root crown of the clematis.

The root ball will be at least 18 in. (45 cm) wide by about the same depth. With

Clematis ANNA LOUISE 'Evithree'. An established large-flowered cultivar such as this clematis can be transplanted in the very early spring if required.

a spade, dig carefully and deeply around the root crown, about 9 in. (23 cm) from it. Get the spade underneath the roots if possible. With help, lift out the root ball with as much soil as possible onto a sack or plastic sheet and transport it to the new planting site. If the soil conditions are dry, then water the clematis well two days before you attempt to transplant it.

The preparations for the new planting site should be the same as those carried out before planting a new clematis, except that much less additional potting soil will be required. Again, plant an extra 2.5 in. (5 cm) deep. Make sure the clematis stems are secured, water in well and surround with some additional plants to give shade to the root system.

Moving an established clematis may cause the plant to take time to re-establish, so be patient. Plenty of water will be required in the coming spring and during the following summer if the weather is hot and there is very little rain. Additional feeding will also help with the re-establishment. Use a general purpose fertilizer to your preference, but not one high in nitrogen; a well-balanced feed is best. You can also use a rose or tomato feed as these work well and are easily obtainable in garden centres.

Planting in a Container

Today, many people have limited open garden space, or have less time to spend on the cultivation of their gardens and prefer to grow plants in containers. Some people living in towns and cities—even those in small apartments—wish to grow plants for their enjoyment and to extend their indoor living space by developing an outside area on a patio, where they can have lunches, create a barbecue area and spend some enjoyable time among plants.

The best clematis for growing in containers to give the desired effect are the early large-flowered cultivars and those very recently developed by Evison and Poulsen, and these have been detailed in Chapter 5 in which I give detailed advice on selecting the best clematis plants for containers. In this section, I will focus on selecting the best container.

It is important to select a container with a thick wall, to give the plant's root system protection and coolness from the summer sun, and to provide insulation and added protection during the winter months if the container is to be left outside. Therefore, the use of plastic pots is not acceptable, but there is available today a great wealth of other types of container from which to select. These include frost-hardy terracotta pots, prefabricated stone containers, wooden half barrels, ceramic pots and more. It is most important that the container should have very good drainage holes. Some beautifully coloured ceramic containers have no drainage holes at all. These are not acceptable; the roots of the clematis would soon succumb to root rot problems and die.

The minimum container size should be 18 in. (45 cm) square, the larger the better. The 18-in. (45-cm) wide container would need to have one large drainage hole 2 in. (5 cm) in diameter, or three smaller ones of 1-in. (2.5-cm) diameter.

In areas with high levels of rainfall it would also be advisable to place two household bricks under the container, thus lifting it off the floor surface and giving the best drainage advantage, as well as extra air movement around the container itself. When preparing the container, stones or broken clay flowerpot pieces should be placed over the drainage hole or holes, to stop the compost from clogging them up, though this is also sometimes caused by earthworms. Some type of coarse material, such as peat fibres or well-rotted garden compost, can be placed over the stones. The container can then be filled to within 2 in. (5 cm) of its rim with a good grade potting soil. A fibrous one is best so that there is good aeration, which your clematis' root system will enjoy. Firm the compost by using your fists.

As with the preparation for planting in the soil, during all of this work you should soak the root ball of your clematis by placing it in a bucket of water for twenty minutes. Once the container is ready for planting and the root ball soaked, the clematis can be planted. Again, plant the clematis that extra 2–2.5 in. (5–6 cm) deep, thus burying the lower stems. If you wish, the lower leaves can be removed.

To give more shade to the root system of the clematis and add interest to the container, plant other shallow-rooted low-growing shrubs or perennials around the edges of the container. Those plants recommended in Chapter 4 for giving shade to a garden clematis can be used. Alternatively, I have found the use of summer bedding plants interesting, because a different coloured planting scheme can be used each year. Grey-foliaged and pastel-coloured flowering plants all blend perfectly with most clematis flower colours. In the autumn, if you are able to keep your clematis container out all winter, you can remove the summer annuals, top-dress the container with fresh potting soil to a depth of 2–3 in. (5–7.5 cm), and then replant with winter-flowering pansies, wallflowers or polyanthus, adding some spring-flowering bulbs such as daffodils or tulips. All of the best clematis for growing in containers are deciduous, so giving that extra colour and interest during the winter months, while the clematis is dormant, brightens up that part of the garden, patio or terrace area.

In cold areas of northern Europe or North America, clematis grown in containers will need winter protection to avoid frost damage. This is dealt with in Chapter 5. Also included there is advice on the selection of supports for growing clematis in containers and the selection of host plants for larger containers.

Watering

Watering your newly planted clematis is a 'must', and even more important when growing plants in containers. In a garden situation it is always best to plant in the late summer or autumn if you live in a mild climate, as this really saves considerably on the watering required the following spring. However, in areas in northern Europe or North America where the winters are very cold then this is not possible.

As new growth appears on your newly planted clematis in early spring, be sure to check to see if the garden soil is moist enough. If not, then be sure to water the clematis and additional plants to help them establish well before the heat of the late spring and summer sun.

For plants newly planted in a container, this attention to watering will be needed again from early spring to help them establish. Watering should be checked each day—watering in the morning is always best, and the container will need a good soaking. An 18-in. (45-cm) diameter container will need at least 1 gallon (3.75 litres) of water every other day unless there has been plenty of rain.

Established plants in the garden will also need additional watering in dry, rainless weather during the spring and summer months to keep them in healthy condition, providing them with enough moisture so that they can continue to grow, especially after their first crop of flowers have died away. This will give them added vigour to put on new growth for the second crop of flowers and is essential for established plants growing in containers.

Feeding

Clematis require good nutrient levels if they are to perform correctly and provide additional growth for further crops of flowers or the continuation of flowering. A general-purpose fertilizer is best; I prefer organic ones, such as blood, fish and bone. Do not use a high-nitrogen feed, as this only encourages lots of growth and not flowers. Instead, you can simply use a rose or tomato feed at the rate advised on the packaging. If well-rotted farmyard manure or well-rotted garden compost is available, then these make ideal mulch feeds for plants growing in the garden if applied in the late winter or very early spring. This can be placed around the clematis to a diameter of 2 ft. (60 cm), but do avoid placing the mulch near to the stem of the clematis as this could cause the rotting of the stem. If used to a depth of 2–3 in. (5–7.5 cm) then this too will act as shade to the root system as well as a mulch.

The best time to apply other feeds or fertilizers is from very late winter to early spring as the weather becomes warmer and new growth commences on your clematis. I have found that it is best to stop feeding clematis just before they come into flower, as feeding during the flowering period only encourages the flowers to go over (die away) more quickly and shortens the flowering period. However, with the newly introduced clematis cultivars which have a very long or almost continuous flowering period, the reduction of feeding during flowering is not ideal as this does not replenish depleted food levels in the soil. Therefore I believe that it is very important to give a good feed prior to flowering in late winter/early spring and then to reduce the feed

Clematis JOSEPHINE 'Evijohill', growing on a fence at the back of a narrow border. Additional feeding after the first flowers fade ensures extra, later flowers.

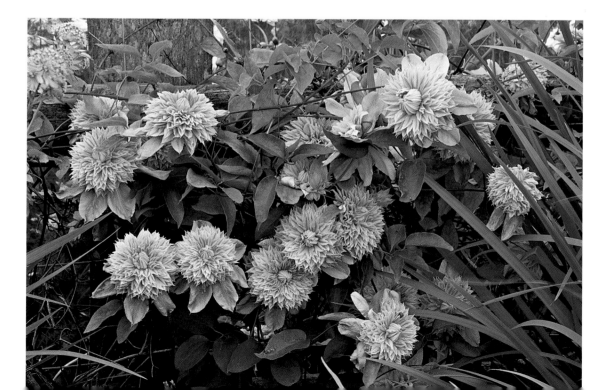

levels, but not to stop feeding. This encourages extra growth and flower later in the season.

It is, however, important to stop feeding by late summer so that the clematis are allowed to go into their natural dormancy and allow the top growth to ripen fully, especially with the early-flowering species and early large-flowered cultivars. Watering can also be reduced by mid autumn unless the garden soil conditions are very dry. However, the watering of plants in containers will need to continue until sufficient winter rains provide the correct moisture levels for the soil.

Training

It is most important that your clematis be correctly trained in early spring as new growth commences. Your clematis can grow up to 1 in. (3 cm) per day in ideal growing conditions, so attention to detail is important at this stage. Because of the speed of new growth and its very brittle nature, winds can easily damage new growth; the stems can simply snap off, which is most perplexing and frustrating. Spending a few moments every two or three days can avoid such damage: as new growth appears, just tie this into the host support or host plant. Try to spread the new stems out to evenly cover the required area. If clematis are being grown over low-growing plants then it is also important to secure their stems. This applies to plants scrambling about through other herbaceous perennial plants, especially if the clematis are actually non-clinging types such as *Clematis* Harlow Carr 'Evipo004'.

Where clematis are growing up old apple or pear trees in a border (these generally should be the hard pruning types, from the late-season-flowering group) then it is important that their vigorous new stems should be trained safely onto the lower branches of the trees. Strong green string firmly anchored to the ground and onto the lower branches is all that is required so that the stems can be attached. The string can be renewed annually or, if you prefer, a column of chicken wire can be placed around the tree trunk, but be careful that the tree trunk does not grow into the chicken wire.

The training of clematis growing on supports or on host plants when they are in containers is of course vital. You must pay close attention to detail at this time of rapid spring growth. The aim is not to get the growth to the top of the support as fast as possible, but rather to evenly clothe the lower parts of the support so that the flowers and subsequent growth are spaced attractively around it.

Winter Protection

If you are the type of gardener that craves a challenge, then you may wish to grow a certain clematis that is on the borderline of hardiness in your climate or Zone. If that is the case you may wish to grow one of the evergreen types to add interest in your garden in springtime. Should you rise to this challenge then it is best to grow such a plant in a dry, well-drained soil where the conditions will help to ripen the stems and 'dry out' the root system a little before winter. If such a plant is growing in soil conditions that are damp and feed levels are high, then your clematis will continue to grow well into the autumn period and then will be more likely to succumb to frost damage. It may also help to get your plant through the winter undamaged if you take steps to protect the foliage from frost or from cold winds during the worst months of the winter.

If we continue to look chronologically at the flowering seasons of the different groups of clematis, we move from the evergreens to the very winter-hardy alpina and macropetala types which will stand temperatures as low as $-31°$F $(-35°$C$)$. These will come through most winters. Again, the drier the plant and the more ripened its stems, the more hardy the plant will be.

The montanas come next—and you can either grow these well or not at all, so check to see if they grow in your neighbourhood. *Clematis montana* f. *grandiflora* seems the most hardy that I have grown, at $-4°$F $(-20°$C$)$, but in that instance its root system was in a dry area underneath a raised deck.

Clematis montana f. grandiflora, capable of surviving low temperature if its root system is in a dry area.

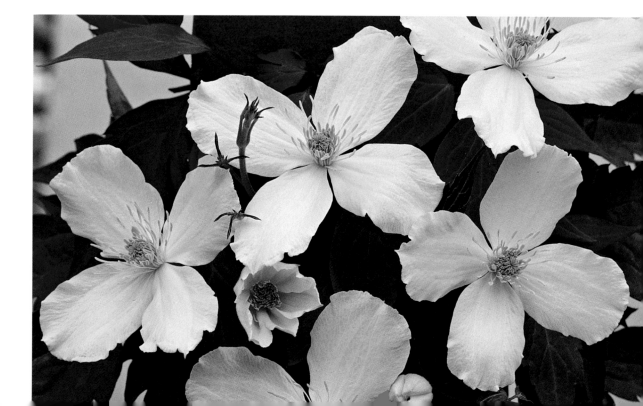

The early large-flowered cultivars growing in a garden location will come through most winters in the British Isles without winter damage, but this is not the case in some parts of the northern United States and Canada, or in northern Europe. Here, during a normal cold winter, their top growth will be killed to ground or snow level. If this happens, the flowering period will be delayed by about six weeks and the flowers produced will be smaller than if they were coming directly from the previous season's ripened stems. The semi-double or double-flowered ones may produce only single flowers as most of the older double-flowered cultivars produce their double flowers only from the ripened stems from the previous season. Therefore, if you are growing these in a borderline Zone area, the use of a horticultural fleece (or something similar) will offer protection to the old stems, helping to prevent desiccation by wind.

As an alternative method of protection, I know of people who actually lower the old stems down to ground level and cover them with straw or branches from evergreen trees to give that added protection, unless snow cover is guaranteed. Unfortunately, stems could be damaged during this process unless it is carried out very carefully.

If you are growing clematis in containers in cold areas, then you could sink the container into the garden soil over winter and cover the top growth with fleece. This can only help a little, so it is really best to move the container into a garden building which has frost protection, or into an outhouse or garage in very cold areas.

After the first frost of the winter it makes sense to move the container indoors and keep the soil moist but not wet. If any summer flowering annuals have been planted in the container with your clematis these should be removed at this time. Keep the soil moist through the winter, not wet, but do not allow it to dry out completely. This will keep the clematis in a dormant state and protect both the root system and top growth. The container can then be moved out to its summer location when the worst of the winter's frosts have passed. You should then make sure that the soil is very well watered, top-dress the container with new potting soil to a depth of 2–3 in. (5–7.5 cm), prune the clematis and tie in old stems.

The late-flowering species and the late large-flowered cultivars are perhaps among the most winter-hardy types. The exceptions are the Florida Group clematis which will certainly need winter protection when grown in containers (and when used as garden plants in cold areas). I always prefer to grow this group of clematis through wall-trained evergreen trees or shrubs, as this gives them additional winter protection.

Do not leave the protective horticultural fleece on your plants too long. If you do, this will encourage soft early growth which will then be damaged by

Clematis 'Madame Julia Correvon', a particularly winter-hardy type for colder gardens, flowering on a fence at the back of a border.

late frosts or cold winds. It is always best to remove it as the leaf-axil buds start to become active and swell. Then, the annual pruning can take place.

Concerning the watering of container-grown clematis at the end of winter or in very early spring, I believe it is important that any watering is carried out early in the day, allowing the container to 'drain off' before nightfall. This gives the root system of the clematis the chance to go into the evening and night with warmer, drier roots.

Gardeners in many cold areas also like to mulch the root systems of their plants to give them added winter protection. If you prefer to use a wood chip mulch or other mulching material then do so, but do give the immediate area around the root crown some space so that air is able to pass around the basal stems. Otherwise, the basal stems could rot over winter. Determining when to carry out this work is simple: when the leaves turn brown, it is time to mulch.

Combatting Clematis Wilt and Mildew

Fortunately, clematis do not succumb to many diseases. However, many gardeners associate clematis with one infamous affliction: clematis wilt. While this problem can be most frustrating to anyone cultivating clematis, it is only the large-flowered cultivars that are affected. None of the clematis species or small-flowered cultivars are vulnerable to clematis wilt.

The cause of clematis wilt is a fungus known as *Phoma clematidina*. Generally it affects only young clematis plants, unless a garden area is badly infected (in which case older plants can be seriously damaged). The fungus is usually soil-borne and it appears to affect the clematis at or near soil level. It most probably enters the clematis plant through a crack in a stem or through previous damage or weakness, or has been splashed onto the stems by watering or heavy rain. In basic terms the fungus starts to break down the cell structure, stopping the sap from reaching the area above the infection. This causes the clematis plant or individual stem to collapse.

Clematis wilt normally attacks plants in early summer to midsummer when they are growing quickly in periods of high humidity. The wilt takes hold very suddenly—literally overnight. A stem or the whole plant can be affected; the foliage and stems just collapse, affecting the tip growth and young leaves first, and then the affected plant turns black very quickly.

I have met several gardeners who thought their plant was suffering from clematis wilt—but when I asked them whether it had collapsed from the top or if the leaves were drying off from the base of the plant, I was told that the leaves were going yellow and dying from the base of the plant upwards. This is not clematis wilt, but just that the plant is suffering from lack of moisture and needs a drink of water!

If your plant has suffered from clematis wilt, then immediately remove all affected stems and every leaf, and burn them. Once you have removed all dead stems and leaves, it is then a good idea to drench the soil area to a diameter of 24 in. (60 cm) around the root system with a copper-based fungicide. This should help to destroy any remaining fungal spores. (Use as directed on the fungicide packaging.) Continue to drench the same area at monthly intervals and this should help prevent future problems.

If the root ball has been planted that extra 2.5 in. (6 cm) deeper, then a root crown will have been built up below soil level and new stems should grow from basal buds or buds well below soil level. When new growth appears, allow it to develop to two or three nodes, 9–12 in. (23–30 cm) tall, and then the tip growth should be removed. This 'soft' pinch will encourage side-shoots to be developed, building up the stem structure of the plant. As the plant starts its recovery, treat it as a newly planted clematis with regard to feeding, watering and pruning.

If you have experienced clematis wilt in parts of your garden in previous years, then it is best to take precautions against future attacks. As new growth appears in springtime, drench the foliage on the lower parts of each clematis plant, up to say 24 in. (60 cm) high, together with the surrounding soil area to a 24 in. (60 cm) diameter, with a copper-based fungicide at monthly intervals. This should help prevent further damage and spread of fungal spores.

If a plant fails completely from clematis wilt, it should be removed and burned. The soil should be dug up and replaced before attempting to replant with another clematis; then, carry out the preparations described in the Planting Out Your New Clematis section earlier in this chapter. Before refilling with fresh soil, the hole made by removing the old soil and clematis root ball, and the surrounding soil area, should be drenched with a copper-based fungicide. Certainly after replanting, a further drench over the lower foliage and soil area with the copper-based fungicide would be a useful precaution, offering added protection to your newly planted clematis. Do remember that if you wish to grow clematis that are more resistant to wilt, choose a viticella type such as *Clematis* 'Polish Spirit'. Should you become extremely frustrated with clematis wilt problems, bear in mind that some of the more modern large-flowered cultivars such as *C.* PICARDY 'Evipo024' and *C.* ANGELIQUE 'Evipo017' can be grown very successfully in containers.

Mildew can also be extremely frustrating, and in some years it can be much more prevalent than in others. Powdery mildew generally affects only some of the late-flowering cultivars such as *Clematis* 'Jackmanii', *C.* 'Perle d'Azur' and *C.* 'Ville de Lyon', but it can also be very troublesome on some cultivars from the Texensis Group such as *C. texensis* 'Étoile Rose' and *C. texensis* 'Pagoda'.

Once mildew is present then there is very little that can be done to cure the problem. Therefore, preventative measures should be used. If you have experienced mildew on your clematis previously, take preventative action early in the season to avoid the problem. A selection of control measures is usually available in garden centre shops; you can choose any that are recommended for use on roses, and use in accordance with the instructions on the container.

Mildew can plague *Clematis* 'Perle d'Azur' (left) and *Clematis texensis* 'Étoile Rose' (right).

Pest Control

Naturally, clematis are vulnerable to the same spectrum of pests that affect other garden plants. Bear in mind that the pest control methods described below can be applied to other plants as well as clematis.

Insects, Mites and Molluscs

In greenhouses, conservatories and garden rooms, the following pests may cause problems: aphids, white fly and red spider mite. All of these can be controlled through the use of natural predators or with chemicals; your local independent garden centre or nursery staff will be able to advise you on what is most effective in your area.

Aphids are generally most troublesome in late spring or early summer as they develop quickly on soft new tip growth. They leave distorted leaves and stems behind, which is unsightly. Therefore, they should be controlled at an early stage.

White fly can be a great nuisance if it is allowed to spread; it leaves nasty black marks and deposits on foliage, which spoils the look of the plant. Luckily, white fly is easy to control with natural predators.

Red spider mite normally affects plants when soil conditions are very dry and they are having a good breeding season. Again, a severe attack and infestation can look unpleasant. This can be identified by the leaves becoming somewhat blotchy and paler in colour on the surface, and by a large build-up of pinkish red mite covering the underside of the leaves. This will cause distorted foliage and flowers, and must be controlled at an early stage.

Quite frequently I am told about clematis plants with holes in their leaves and flowers. Usually it is impossible to identify the culprit, but I suspect that earwigs are very often responsible. Earwigs are night prowlers, hiding during the daytime in cracks and crevices in brickwork or old timber frames near to the plants. Therefore, if you are growing clematis through a host plant on an old building wall at the back of a border, you must be prepared for possible damage from earwigs.

To control earwigs, there are various chemical sprays on the market—but I prefer not to use them. Unless there is a massive infestation, I find that an alternative, old-fashioned method favoured by many older gardeners works well: if a small pot (4 in. [8 cm] in diameter) is stuffed with moss and upturned on a stick close to the plant, the earwigs will hide in the moss during the daytime. Then it is simply a matter of shaking them out of their hiding place onto the floor and treading on them—perhaps not a control method for everyone!

When it comes to slugs and snails (both of which are molluscs), some gardens are worse affected than others. The ideal conditions for spring damage are in damp gardens where there is plenty of shade, especially after a mild winter. I suppose that for those pests which have waited around most of the winter for a feast of nice juicy green clematis stems, it is like us waiting for the first crop of asparagus in the spring! They graze the soft new growth, especially the low, fat leaf-axil buds, removing them completely. There are many old remedies, such as placing a shallow container of beer near to the plants, or placing abrasive material around the plants. I have also recently been told that using copper filings or copper wire, which slugs and snails apparently dislike, helps to keep them away from those succulent stems.

Clematis montana 'Mayleen', whose flower buds can be damaged by small birds in search of insects.

Animal Pests

Mice seem to be attracted to clematis stems during the winter or early spring, when pieces of stem are removed at ground level and either left on the ground or used for nesting material. Very often there is no evidence of damage until the clematis fails to come into growth in the spring; then, when the top growth is checked it is discovered that a length of stem has been removed, leaving it without any connection to the plant's root system. If the clematis has been planted those extra few inches deep at the time of planting, then it will almost certainly grow again from below soil level.

If mice are around in large numbers, clematis growing in association with low-growing or ground cover plants can be the worst affected. If good hunter cats are around the garden, this is most helpful; otherwise, mousetraps placed in pipes can be effective. Another cure I have used is to place a clay drainpipe on its end and let the clematis grow up through the pipe. Once the stems become thicker and more woody they are less attractive to mice, and then the drainpipe can be broken and removed. When growing clematis in association with winter-flowering heathers in south Shropshire, England, I remember that we once ended up with some exceedingly bushy, well-furnished viticellas which grew and flowered very well due to 'mouse pruning'—but that is an unusual outcome!

Small birds can cause great damage to some of the early-flowering clematis such as members of the Montana Group. It appears that the birds enjoy the fat leaf-axil buds as they search for small insects. In doing so, a whole crop of flowers can be destroyed as each bud is totally damaged. Very little can be done to avoid this relatively uncommon problem.

If rabbits are able to get into your garden, they can cause similar damage to that wreaked by mice and they continue to cause damage to young clematis growth until there is plenty of other vegetation for them to eat. Upturned land drains can be employed, but a more pleasing idea is to use a collar of chicken wire to a diameter of 9 in. (23 cm) or so and to a height of 24 in. (60 cm). Place this over the top of the root crown of the clematis, allowing the clematis to grow up through the collar. This becomes almost unnoticeable as it becomes weathered in a garden setting and it can be left in place.

Deer, I am told, enjoy eating clematis (as they enjoy eating so many other plants). However, I have no personal experience with prevention of damage by deer and I suggest that you gather local knowledge of how best to avoid or limit the problem.

During the summer of 2006, I noticed a new problem with my *Clematis viticella* at home in Guernsey. Our Maran hens (a French breed that lays beautiful dark brown eggs) decimated the lower part of this clematis up to a height of 3 ft. (90 cm), but it was only the flower buds and the flowers themselves that the hens obviously enjoyed. While the climbing rose through which the clematis grew, as well as the clematis foliage, were left alone, every flower and flower bud of the clematis was eaten; they jumped up to the flowers, pecked them off and ate them. This problem was, I think, rather uncommon—but it amused us, and proved we have some fit hens!

Although these various prescriptions for dealing with pests and diseases may seem rather extensive, the problems are not great in themselves. As long as you are aware of what may occur when you grow clematis, you can be prepared to deal with them before a small inconvenience becomes a major problem.

Chapter 14 # Pruning

Clematis alpina 'Foxy',
a member of Pruning
Group One.

The pruning requirements of clematis cause more concern and worry than any other aspect of their care, sometimes baffling experienced clematis growers as well as beginners. Admittedly, due to the variation between different groups and types of clematis, there is no single easy-to-follow rule for the annual pruning of all clematis. Luckily, however, pruning clematis need not be altogether confusing.

The First Spring After Planting

All clematis, whichever group they belong to, need a severe haircut at the start of their first full season. This simply involves removing all top growth down to 12 in. (30 cm) above soil level. It will encourage good basal growth and help to develop a plant with a good bushy base. If this is not done, then the result will be a plant with just one—or, at best, two—stems growing straight up to 6 ft. (2 m) and a 'bird's nest' effect above; after three to four years there will be no fresh growth on these stems and the plant will look unsightly.

However, if you happen to have purchased a very large plant which was well furnished with basal stems and growing in a two- or five-gallon pot, then the hard pruning will not need to be that drastic. In the first spring after planting, top growth can be left to a height of 24 in. (60 cm) on such a plant. Late-summer-flowering plants would be the exception, and these would need to be pruned down to about 12 in. (30 cm) of soil level each spring, including the first.

From the second spring after planting onwards, you should carry out one of the following three annual pruning regimes, according to your clematis' flowering season. Following these guidelines will help your clematis to produce as many flowers as possible.

Pruning Group One
(Early-Season-Flowering: winter to late spring)

The Pruning Group One clematis produce their flowers on short flower stems, either singly or in clusters directly from the previous season's ripened stems. These are the evergreen types such as *Clematis armandii*, the alpina and *macropetala* types including *C. alpina* 'Foxy', and the Montana Group, one of which is *C. montana* 'Freda'.

Naturally, no pruning should be done until these clematis have completed their flowering, as this can damage the flowering stems. The annual pruning, then, should be undertaken very soon after flowering, when any dead or damaged stems can be removed. Within about one month after the last flowers have fallen, these clematis will start to put on new, vigorous growth. If the plants are under five years old from planting, then this new growth will be most welcome as you will be aiming to clothe an area of wall or fence, or to get the plant up into a tree. On the other hand, if your clematis is well established and has achieved its height requirements you may well be aiming to keep the plant within its allotted space, in which case this new growth can be reduced during the midsummer months.

However, it is important that some of this new growth (ideally about 6 in. [15 cm]) should be left on each stem, as upon ripening it will provide the flowering stems the following spring. Since these new stems need to be ripened by the end of the summer, the reduction of new growth must not be carried out later than midsummer. Of course, if you have a *Clematis montana* or any of the other spring-flowering clematis established and growing well up into a tree, then just leave Mother Nature to take care of your plant. It is not necessary to climb up into the tree to prune the clematis!

To sum up Pruning Group One: tidy up these clematis after flowering, or just leave them unpruned.

Pruning Group Two
(Midseason-Flowering: late spring to early summer)

The second Pruning Group consists of the earliest large-flowered single, semi-double and double-flowered clematis which are midseason-flowering. (Although the new Boulevard Evison and Poulsen Collection clematis are midseason-flowering, they should be pruned differently; for more details please see page 171). Like the early-season-flowering clematis, this group produce their main crop of flowers from stems ripened the previous season. However, they may also produce from 6 in. (15 cm) to 24 in. (60 cm) of new growth before their flowers open, depending on the cultivar. Mostly their flowers are terminal—that is, they have one flower per stem.

The pruning of this group should be carried out at the end of winter or very early in spring, before new growth begins. Clematis belonging to this group basically need a good tidy-up. All dead and weak stems should be removed down to just above a strong pair of leaf-axil buds.

When you approach a clematis from this group at the end of winter, you are confronted with a tangled mass of old, dead-looking stems and perhaps a few old brown leaves. It is something of a puzzle as to where and how to prune such a plant. Usually I cut away the upper tangled mass of stems that have flopped back over themselves so that I can see what really needs to be done. I then look at what is left and cut away all the dead stems which have no fresh green leaf-axil buds visible. Any thin stems should also be removed at this point. On each remaining stem I then cut back to the strongest pair of leaf-axil buds; these buds will produce the first flowers within two to three months. To encourage fresh growth to be produced from the base of the plant, I always prune two or three stems down to 12–24 in. (30–60 cm) each year. These are usually the thinner weaker stems rather than those that will bear the most flowers. All dead leaves should be removed at this point and all stems tied to their host or support, so that when new growth commences it has a firm base and is not damaged by strong winds.

In areas where the winter is severe, this work should only be done if all top growth is not killed by hard frosts. If you are gardening in such climates, it is best to wait until you can see if any stems have survived. If no green leaf-axil buds are visible then it is a simple matter of cutting away all the previous season's top growth down to ground level. New growth will then be produced as spring develops and it will all need to be tied into its host or support.

In short: at the end of winter/early spring, care for your Pruning Group Two clematis by cutting back the dead and weak stems down to a strong pair of leaf-axil buds.

Clematis 'Proteus', gracing a chain, belongs to Pruning Group Two.

Clematis 'M. Koster', flowering on an obelisk alongside *Philadelphus,* is part of Pruning Group Three.

Pruning Group Three
(Late-Season-Flowering: midsummer to autumn)

All of the Pruning Group Three clematis produce their flowers almost entirely from the current season's stems—so they need all the previous season's stems to be removed before the plant starts into new growth each year.

Very simply, these clematis need to be pruned down to just above the base of the previous season's stems at the end of winter or very early spring before the new growth begins. This should be about 12 in. (30 cm) above ground level.

As new growth commences, the stems should be tied into their host or support. If a large plant of, for example, *Clematis terniflora* were to grow 20 ft. (6 m) or more into a large old apple tree, for instance, then it could be left unpruned; however, in time this would become a great tangled mass. Conversely, some of the herbaceous clematis such as *C. integrifolia* var. *integrifolia* or *C.* Chinook 'Evipo013' should be pruned down to ground level as one would prune any other type of herbaceous perennial plant.

Clematis 'Royal Velours', *C.* 'Madame Julia Correvon' and *C.* 'Venosa Violacea', flowering on heathers, belong to Pruning Group Three but when grown in this way should be trimmed back before winter so their host can be enjoyed.

Where some such clematis are used in a border among other herbaceous or low-growing evergreen shrubs, it would be best to trim these back before the onset of winter so that the border or evergreen shrub is left looking tidy during the winter months. Likewise, if a Viticella Group clematis is growing up into an old apple or pear tree, most of its top growth can be removed pre-winter so that the tree looks uncluttered during the winter months. The final pruning can then take place at the end of winter or in very early spring. The same type of pruning is needed when Viticella Group clematis are grown in association with winter- or summer-flowering heathers.

Caring for Pruning Group Three, then, is straightforward: remove all the previous season's stems to just above ground level at the end of winter or very early spring, just before new growth commences. (Try not to do this too late, but beware of pruning too early as new growth may commence in mild weather only to be damaged by late frosts.)

It helps to keep in mind that the pruning requirements are based on a simple fact—that is, the earlier a clematis flowers, the closer the flowers are produced to the previous season's stems. Therefore, the earlier in the season the clematis species or cultivar flowers, the less pruning is required.

Chapter 15   # Propagation

Clematis HYDE HALL 'Evipo009' can be
propagated by inter-nodal cuttings
in very early summer.

Clematis can be reproduced from seed, by division, by layering, through the use of inter-nodal cuttings or by grafting. Grafting is carried out very infrequently in commercial production these days. It is generally used only to reproduce an old cultivar which, perhaps, is difficult to strike from cuttings or for which layering is extremely difficult; this might be due to the age of the clematis plant and the woody nature of its stems. Therefore, I will concentrate on methods of reproduction by seed, division, layering and from cuttings.

In several of the following sections, reference is made to the use of flowerpots and other containers, and in all such cases having good drainage is imperative. The container needs to have adequate drainage holes and you should place small stones, broken crocks, sharp grit or pea gravel over these holes to ensure that they do not get blocked.

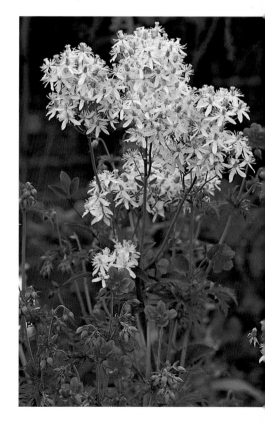

Clematis recta var. *recta*, seen here with double blue geraniums, is easily reproduced from seed.

Seed

Clematis species can be reproduced from seed quite easily, but there will be some variation in the seedlings. For instance, *Clematis recta* is very variable in the wild and its seedlings are also variable (in fact, about ten per cent of its seedlings have purple foliage). Some variants make extremely attractive plants for the border. As a consequence, when I have the chance to grow clematis species from seed, I always prefer to flower out all seedlings and choose the best plant, which I then propagate from cuttings so that I can reproduce the selected clone.

The small- and large-flowered cultivars, being hybrids, do not come true to type from seed; they are always variable. For example, it is quite common to take seed from a large-flowered blue clematis and get a pink or perhaps white-flowered seedling. Many clematis introduced by nurserymen and clematis breeders in the last one hundred and fifty years have been produced from open-pollinated flowers (termed 'chance seedlings'). Therefore these cultivars can be reproduced true to type only from plants grown from layers or cuttings, or by division in the case of herbaceous types.

I should also point out that some species cross-pollinate very easily with some other species, and to be sure your species seedlings are true to type they need to be grown at some distance from one another. The species which cross-pollinate very easily are the evergreen New Zealand types and the American pitcher-shaped species such as *Clematis crispa* and *C. pitcherii*. I have also found interesting interspecies hybrids in the wild in China where, for instance, *C. tubulosa* and *C. brevicaudata* have produced a fine plant similar to *C.* ×*jouiniana* 'Praecox'. Therefore, beware: clematis species grown closely together in a garden location may produce offspring that are not true to type, but the exciting possibility is that the seedlings may produce some fascinating results.

Clematis ×*jouiniana* 'Praecox' flowering with a low-growing pink geranium. This cultivar can be reproduced by cross-pollinating two species clematis.

I prefer to collect the clematis seed as soon as it becomes ripe on the plant. It should still be fresh and must not be over-ripe. If this happens the seed may go into a lengthy dormancy, causing a long delay in germination. Therefore, you should collect the seed before the seed tails become too fluffy and the seed dark brown. Some people choose to place seed into a cold store before sowing. If possible, I try to avoid this due to the risk of putting the seed into that unwanted dormancy. However, it is important to time the seed sowing carefully so that the seedlings do not germinate just before the onset of winter. If this happens and the seedlings do not have the chance to become an integrated plant—working correctly from roots through to leaves—then the seedlings may just 'damp off', suffering from botrytis. It should be noted, though, that seeds collected from the evergreen types, *Clematis alpina*, *C. macropetala* or *C. montana,* can be sown as soon as they are ripe. They should then germinate and become established well before the winter.

Most of our seed sowing in the nursery in Guernsey is done in December or early January, so it is harvested in late September or October and then held in a household refrigerator. However, seed collected in the late summer or early autumn can be sown straightaway as it will not germinate until the spring months. Our delay in sowing is due mainly to workload factors in the autumn.

The length of time seeds take to germinate varies greatly. The seeds that germinate the most rapidly are those of species belonging to the subsection Meclatis: *Clematis tangutica*, *C. tibetana* and others. They will germinate within two weeks of sowing. The large-flowered cultivars (when grown to produce new cultivars) may take over twelve months to germinate. Some species, such as *C. campaniflora,* will perhaps produce a few seedlings quite quickly, but then the main germination could take a further year—so be patient.

Two other tips: firstly, if you wish to grow some of the later flowering species from seed, such as *Clematis flammula* or *C. terniflora*, you may have to help with the ripening of the seed due to their late-flowering habit. In early autumn you may need to detach a length of stem from the plant so that the seed can be ripened in a warm, sunny spot. Cut a stem about 24 in. (60 cm) long, remove the leaves and then hang the stem downwards from its base, with good light and ventilation (for example, in an old greenhouse). The seed should ripen after a few weeks.

Clematis var. *alpina* in seed.

Secondly: you should watch carefully any seed you wish to harvest, ensuring that the seed does not get blown away by strong winds. (This can happen—I know from experience!) To avoid such a problem, place a muslin bag or fine net bag over the seedhead to keep it intact.

When you feel that the time is right, harvest the seed. This is done by simply detaching the seed in a handful from the old flower-stalk (pedicel). The seed should break away easily and then each seed should be cleaned by removing the fluffy seed tail. You may need a pair of sharp scissors to do this, but do take care not to damage the seed.

Depending on the quantity of seed to be sown, this can be done in a flowerpot or seed tray with good drainage holes covered with small stones or sharp grit. Fill the container to within 1 in. (2.5 cm) of its rim with good quality seed compost. Firm with your hands, level off and firm again with a flat board or, if you are using a flowerpot, use the base of a smaller pot to obtain a level surface. Water the seed compost and allow it to drain off before sowing. Place the seed evenly over the soil but do not be tempted to sow too thickly as this may cause a problem with the seedlings being too overcrowded before they are pricked off. Cover the seeds with a thin layer (0.25 in. [0.6 cm]) of finely sieved compost and water them in with a watering can fitted with a fine rose.

If you have plenty of space where you intend to germinate the seed and have extra time when you are sowing, then the seed can be sown one per Jiffy 7 pot or similar. These small peat pots, which measure 1.5 in. deep by 1 in. across (4 × 2.5 cm), are ideal for sowing clematis seed and they help tremendously at the time of potting on, saving a great deal of time later since pricking out is not necessary. The whole pot can just be planted into the growing-on pot and losses are consequently greatly reduced.

Whether you use a seed tray, flowerpot or the small peat-type pots in which to germinate your seeds, you will need to place then in an area where they can stay for perhaps six or twelve months. A heated greenhouse or outside coldframe can be used (a greenhouse will obviously help with faster germination). However, one important point to remember is that mice adore clematis seed, so the seed containers do need to be protected from them. The old-fashioned method of placing a piece of clear glass over the flowerpot or tray helps in this respect, as well as keeping the seed compost warmer. If you do this, place a sheet of newspaper or brown paper on top of the glass. Where peat pots are used, these need to be stood in a large box where a sheet of glass can be placed over them. The seeds will need to be checked on a regular basis to see if they need water (do not let them dry out) and, of course, they also need to be checked for germination.

The next job is to prick out or pot on the seedlings—a highly satisfying task. Again, the timing of this is important; it should not be done just before winter. Clematis, as young plants, do not need to be over-potted and should be potted in time for the seedlings to be well established before winter. If you have sown the seed individually in the little peat pots then potting them on into a 3-in. (7-cm) pot is a simple job. Use a potting-on compost that is of good quality and has good aeration, again making sure that the pot has good drainage holes. If the seedlings have germinated in a flowerpot or seed tray, they are ready to be potted-on as soon as they have produced two or three pairs of properly formed leaves. They should be handled with care—use thumb and finger to transplant them by handling just the leaf. Be careful not to touch the stems as these, like the stems of tomato plants, are very fragile and easily bruised. Use a dibber or small stick to lift the seedlings from the seed tray or pot and use it again to replant them. While you are doing this, take care not to disturb the soil surface totally as there may still be seed at the point of germination which may be destroyed if you are too clumsy. Leave the seed pots and trays for a few extra months as further seeds may germinate.

Water in the transplanted seedlings and, if the day is hot and sunny, shade them from direct sunlight. Until the seedlings have re-rooted themselves they all need shade (up to sixty per cent) and regular watering, but do not over-water them as this may cause them to 'damp off' and die.

Once the seedlings have re-established themselves and started to grow away, it is important that they be 'stopped'—once they have reached about 4 in. (10 cm), pinch out the growing tip. This will help the plant to become more bushy at its base, as more stems will develop from the leaf-axil buds. As new growth develops, tie this into an 18-in. (45-cm) split cane, pinching out the plant again at about 6 in. (15 cm) so that it develops a good bushy framework of stems.

When the roots fill the small pot it can be potted on into a larger pot, again using a good quality potting compost. The plant should then grow on in this pot and can be planted out the following spring. If the seedling is from a clematis species that may produce a variation among its seedlings, you may wish to flower the plant before planting it out into the garden. Your new plant can be planted in the garden as described in Chapter 13.

Division

Generally reproduction by division is used only with herbaceous-type clematis that are more difficult to propagate by cuttings. Some clematis, such as *Clematis recta* var. *recta, C. integrifolia* var. *integrifolia* and their cultivars, divide very easily. The propagation by division can be carried out from mid autumn until late winter, and timing will depend upon your location and how difficult and cold the winter will be. In very cold areas I believe that this should done at the end of winter or in very, very early spring. On the other hand, in mild climates where the springs can be hot, I suggest that propagation by division should be carried out in mid autumn.

Clematis integrifolia var. *integrifolia* can be reproduced by root division in late winter or early spring.

First, remove old top growth down to 2–3 in. (5–7 cm) as with other perennial plants. Then, with a strong garden spade, dig around the clump in a circle to a diameter of at least 24 in. (60 cm) so that all the root area is within the circle. Slide the spade underneath the root crown and lift it from the soil.

To split the root crown, place two normal-sized garden forks back to back, push the forks into the root crown, and then force the root crown apart. (Should the root crown be small, naturally two small hand-forks will be strong enough to do the job.) This should split the root crown in half and, if it is large enough, these two halves may be split again. If the root crown is rather old, it may be necessary to use a large, sharp knife to cut through the thickest part. Do not let the roots dry out, and replant as soon as possible as described on page 221.

I would not recommend that this method of propagation by root division be used on any clematis other than the herbaceous types; it is possible, but the success rate is not high.

Layering

The layering of clematis species and cultivars is a very satisfying method of reproduction. It is time consuming and perhaps should be used only if propagation by cuttings, seed or division is not possible. However, it is an ideal way in which to reproduce an old garden plant that has somewhat woody stems and is possibly not in the best of health.

The only really good time to layer clematis is at the end of winter or in early spring. If the end of winter is chosen, wait until the leaf-axil buds are active so you can be sure the stem you intend to use is alive and in good health. If possible use a stem that is light brown in colour; these are the younger stems and they will root more easily. The stem will need to be long enough to be bent down to soil level and pinned into a soil-filled flowerpot which has been sunk into the soil.

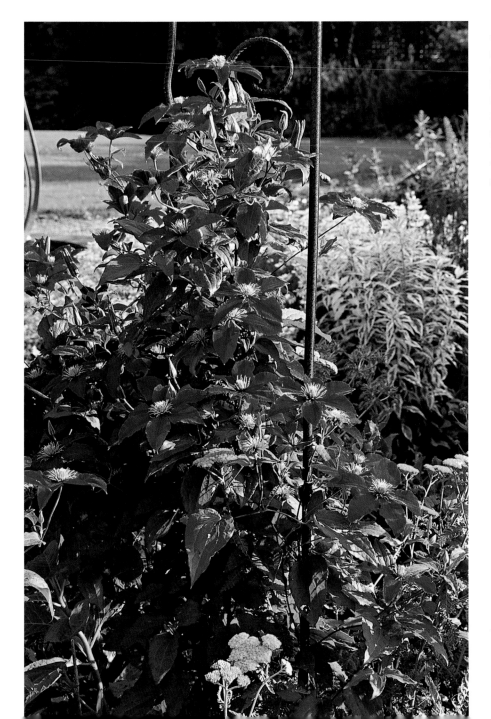

Clematis 'Niobe', seen here on metal supports in a border, can be reproduced by inter-nodal cuttings, or by layering in late winter or early spring.

To reproduce *Clematis tangutica* 'Lambton Park', take inter-nodal cuttings at any point before it flowers in early summer.

You can also choose early spring and use a stem produced that season which will have to be bent to soil level without breaking. Fresh spring growth is more brittle than over-wintered stems, and so new growth is more likely to snap and break, but they may in fact root more quickly.

Having selected the correct stem and made sure that it will reach the soil, the next job is to sink a flowerpot into the soil up to its rim. Use a pot of about 6 in. (15 cm) diameter, which can be either plastic or clay but must have good drainage holes covered with stones or grit, and fill with a good potting soil. Firm the soil to avoid shrinkage.

Take the selected stem, bend it down towards the pot and select a node with a pair of active leaf-axil buds. Using a very sharp knife or a razorblade, cut a slit back into the node and then dip the cut into a rooting hormone powder (to assist with faster rooting) and then peg the stem into the soil with a bent piece of strong wire. Cover this with more potting soil and place a stone over the peg to make sure the layer stays in place. If the location is a windy one, place a bamboo cane in the ground and tie the base of the stem to it, giving the stem more rigidity. The stem above where the cut was made can be reduced to 18 in. (45 cm) and should also be secured to a bamboo cane.

It is essential that the pot should be kept moist during dry weather—the compost must not be allowed to dry out. Rooting will take about two months and any new growth beyond the cut should be a sign that everything is well, but after three months check by gently tugging the layer to see if it has rooted. By late summer or early autumn the new clematis can be cut from its mother plant and the pot lifted from the soil.

If the garden is in a cold location, the new clematis should be placed in some winter protection until the following spring before being planted out. If it is in a mild location, the new clematis can be planted in its permanent position. Use the guidelines for planting clematis given in Chapter 13 (page 217) to make sure the clematis establishes itself successfully.

Inter-nodal Cuttings

Reproduction by inter-nodal cuttings is a very useful way in which to increase clematis in your own garden—and to give away plants as gifts to friends. However, you should be aware that many clematis are protected by plant patents or Plant Breeders' Rights and it is illegal to propagate from these plants without a licence. All protected plants are labelled with this information.

Many of the clematis species and the small-flowered cultivars, along with the large-flowered cultivars, root and grow away easily from cuttings. However, cuttings from some of the evergreen species such as *Clematis armandii*,

the pitcher-shaped American species, and those belonging to the Florida Group such as *C. florida* 'Plena', are extremely difficult to root and develop into plants. Clematis such as the viticella types and *C. tangutica* root quite easily, so perhaps these should be the first ones to be tried out before you move on to the large-flowered cultivars.

Cuttings taken from plants growing in a garden location are much more difficult to root and grow away than cuttings taken from plants grown under greenhouse conditions. The foliage from garden plants is usually larger and coarser, and very often has more damage due to wind and rain. It also seems that outdoor-grown cutting material can succumb to botrytis more easily, which causes the loss of cuttings at an early stage.

Cuttings taken from indoor conditions can be rooted from mid spring until midsummer, while cuttings taken from outdoor plants are not available until late spring and they become generally too woody by the end of early summer. Semi-ripe material should be used; do not use stems which have flower buds as these may root but will not develop into a plant.

When taking cuttings of the winter- to late-spring-flowering evergreen species and the alpina, the macropetala and the montana types, you will need to wait until they have finished flowering and have put on new growth. This new growth will be ideal and will root quite easily. Cuttings from the late spring- to early summer-flowering large-flowered cultivars should, if possible, be taken before they start to flower in late spring. The later-flowering species and their cultivars can be done any time the stems are mature enough, but the earlier in the season the better—cuttings should be taken well before they flower.

The best type of cutting is one where the leaves have developed fully and are neither too hard nor too soft. These, as mentioned earlier, are described as 'semi-ripe' cuttings. Take a stem with several nodes if possible, and if the stem is slightly sticky to the touch this is ideal. Cut the stem 0.5 in. (1 cm) above the node and 1.5 in. (3.5 cm) below the node. Take off one of the leaves, thus reducing the leaf area by fifty per cent. The removal of so much leaf area helps to reduce the loss of moisture from the cutting by transpiration.

It is always a good idea to take cuttings from the mother plant in the early morning before the sun starts to dehydrate the foliage. Once the cuttings are made, I like to put them in a polythene bag and place them in the kitchen fridge for two or three hours; they then rehydrate and are in the best possible condition to be inserted into the rooting tray or flowerpot.

It is sensible to insert only one species or cultivar per container, as this avoids mixing up the different species or cultivars. Obviously, it is important to label them clearly, to record the date of insertion, and to note where the cuttings came from if they are from someone else's garden.

The container that is used to root the cuttings can be chosen based on the number of cuttings available. For small amounts, six to eight cuttings, a 5- to 6-in. (12- to 15-cm) pot is ideal; for larger numbers, a 6-in. (15-cm) deep seed tray is the best. As always, make sure that the container has good drainage.

When rooting cuttings I like to use a 'sandwich mix' of different soils and composts. Above the extra drainage material I place a thin layer of something that has fibre (rough peat, for example). On top of this should be a potting soil or compost which has a small amount of fertilizer, so that when the new roots penetrate into this layer they immediately find some extra feed which helps their development. I then fill up the remainder with a cutting mix, to just below the surface of the container. This mix needs to be fine, so I pass it through a 0.25-in. (6-mm) sieve. This compost can be purchased from a garden centre or made up of one part loam, one part sand (or perlite) and one part peat or peat substitute. The soil or compost then needs to be firmed and flattened, and covered with a thin layer (0.25 in. [6 mm]) of fine sand. The sand helps to prevent botrytis from developing.

The prepared cuttings can now be inserted. I use a rooting hormone suitable for semi-ripe cuttings into which I dip the bottom 0.5 in. (1 cm), and the cuttings can then be pushed into the soil or compost. As the cutting passes through the sand layer the stem may be very slightly lacerated and this assists with faster rooting. Handle the cuttings by the node, rather than the leaf or stem, and if the cutting bends and cannot easily be pushed into the soil or compost, it should be thrown away as it is too weak to produce a good quality rooted cutting. The node can be finally pushed into the soil or compost by using your finger and you should make sure that it is just below the soil or compost surface. If the node is left exposed it may dry out and the leaf-axil buds may not develop after they have rooted.

As soon as is possible, the container with the unrooted cuttings should be placed in a shady location; a shade level of about sixty per cent is best. The container can be placed into a cold frame out in the garden, into a shaded greenhouse or into a propagation unit. If none of these is available, a large polythene bag can be placed over the pot and secured with a rubber band. This will then act as a miniature greenhouse and rooting should take about three to four weeks. As the cuttings root and start into growth, holes should be pierced in the polythene bag to give ventilation. The holes can be slowly increased in size and eventually the bag can be removed completely.

If the container is placed in a cold frame, rooting may take seven to eight weeks, but in a greenhouse with high humidity rooting will take only about three weeks. As well as the extra shading it is a good idea to 'damp over' the cuttings about three times per day—morning, noon and mid afternoon—with a sprayer or with a fine rose on a watering can, using just clear water. This

helps to keep the cuttings from drying out or dehydrating and helps keep the humidity levels up. Make sure that the foliage of the cuttings is dry by night-fall; otherwise, botrytis may start to develop if they go into the night wet.

The exact time for rooting will vary from species to species and from cul-tivar to cultivar. Botrytis is the biggest enemy while the cuttings root, which means that good ventilation during the daytime is essential. Your cuttings may also benefit from a drench with a general fungicide—one with a copper base would be ideal. Use as directed on the package.

Once the cuttings show signs of rooting, the cold frame or greenhouse con-ditions can be changed, with cooler temperatures being introduced so that the cuttings are slowly 'hardened off'. The spraying of water or 'damping over' can also slowly be reduced. Many people have 'mist' propagation units. I do not find these ideal for rooting clematis cuttings, especially those with very hairy leaf-axil nodes, as the water particles tend to become lodged in these hairs and cause the rotting-off of the leaf-axil buds, thus encouraging any botrytis to spread.

Growing Rooted Cuttings

If the cuttings are inserted early in the season, they should root in time to be 'potted on' in the summer months and still be established by autumn. It will take a further three months for the rooted cuttings to become an established plant in a small pot. Therefore, if there is any doubt that the rooted cutting does not have time to become an integrated plant before autumn (in that its roots would supply enough moisture to its foliage), delay the potting on until the following spring. The rooted cuttings in their container can always by pinched back and kept fed (through the use of a general liquid fertilizer) until the following spring, and then potted on.

Once the cuttings are fully rooted and new top growth appears it is helpful to 'soft pinch' this new growth. Once it has reached 3 in. (7 cm) and two nodes are fully developed, pinch out the growing tip with thumb and finger, or use a pair of sharp secateurs (hand pruners). This helps to develop a stronger rooted cutting which will establish much more easily once potted on. If it has been decided to over-winter the rooted cuttings in the rooting container, all leaves should be removed during late autumn or early winter, so that any chance of botrytis setting in is avoided.

However, if summer potting on is planned, then the newly rooted cutting can be transplanted into a 3-in. (7-cm) diameter pot. The rooted cutting should be handled carefully, again by the node, and with the other hand, a dibber or stick can be used to slowly ease the root system from the container. If the roots are at all damaged, they can be cut off with a pair of sharp scissors, and this will, in fact, help with re-establishment and also the development of new rootlets.

Each rooted cutting can be given its own pot and a good potting-on soil or compost should be used. Make sure, as always, that the pot will drain adequately. I believe that the node of the original cutting should be potted 0.5 in. (1 cm) below the compost surface; as with the cutting before it roots, this avoids the chance that it will dry out and, with this extra depth, the node will develop additional growth buds below the soil surface.

The rooted cuttings will require similar growing conditions to those from which they were taken before potting; remember that sixty per cent shade will be required (especially during hot weather). It is also an advantage to 'damp over' the potted cuttings once or twice per day to assist with their re-establishment, creating higher humidity. When potting during the summer, try to avoid air temperatures rising above 80°F (27°C). This can be done by giving extra shade to the cold frame or greenhouse, and the damping down of pathways also helps.

As mentioned earlier, once new growth appears you should take out the growing tip as a soft pinch to help make the plant bushy at its base. When it re-grows, give the young plant a support cane. It can then be potted on into a 1-gallon (2-litre) pot once the root system is fully developed and grown on ready for planting in the garden position the following spring, or autumn in mild areas. (For advice on planting in a garden location, please refer to Chapter 13.)

Breeding New Clematis

I am very much in favour of encouraging amateur gardeners to breed and develop more new clematis. However, in recent years I have become critical of the large numbers of new clematis being raised, named and introduced to gardens, as many lack long-term garden value. It is almost too easy to collect seed from the large-flowered cultivars in gardens, sow them, flower them and then name them. Obviously, only the very best will become really good garden plants that can be grown commercially and still be with us in a century's time. Therefore, while encouraging the development of new clematis by amateur breeders, I do stress that only the very best should be named; those that have better shaped flowers, have good strong colours, have a longer flowering period, flower more profusely and, of course, have a good strong constitution.

The excitement of seeing one's own new cultivar flowering for the first time is marvellous, but it can also be most disappointing. Each year over ninety-eight per cent of our seedlings are thrown away within eighteen months of germination, because they do not meet the early requirements of what we are aiming to produce. Perhaps only ten or twelve become good garden plants out of ten thousand seedlings.

Amateur breeders have the chance to collect what I describe as open-pollinated seed, by going around the garden simply gathering ripened seed and then sowing them. Many, many fine cultivars have been raised and introduced in this way. The other way, of course, is to set a goal: what type of new clematis would you like to develop? Should it be a new *Clematis alpina* for the colder areas, a better-flowering *C. montana* for the smaller garden, the brightest pink double-flowered cultivar, a new Jackmanii type for growing with roses that does not get mildew easily, a new viticella type, or perhaps a cultivar that is wilt-resistant?

Having set the goal, you should list the criteria for the desired new clematis and then set about the task of finding two parents which might meet some of these criteria. The easiest crosses to make are from clematis of similar types, with the same growth habit or the same flowering period. Most species have different chromosome numbers, so they are very unlikely to be compatible and, in theory, cannot be successfully pollinated to produce seed. However, the large-flowered cultivars are now so interbred that they cross-pollinate very easily, so successful cross-pollination is almost guaranteed. But will the seedling be garden-worthy? This is where the fun, frustration and great success can come.

How to Pollinate

Once you have decided which plant will provide the flower that will be the seed-bearing parent (the mother) and the pollen bearing parent (the father), there are a few tools that must be available: a sharp razor blade, a small artist's paint brush, a collection of labels, some small white or brown paper bags, and a few muslin bags.

First, the sepals on the flower which is to be the seed-bearing parent need to be removed with the razor blade and should be carefully cut off at their base. This should be done before the flower opens but when the sepals are nearly fully developed. Then the male parts of this flower, the stamens (the filaments and anthers), must be removed. This leaves just the female parts of the flower, which are the styles and ovaries. It is then important to protect these from any rogue pollen from another flower and this is done by placing a paper bag over the styles and tying it at its base to the flower stem.

The styles may be pollinated when the stigmas are receptive (slightly sticky), probably at midday, by brushing pollen onto them from the pollen donor (the father) with the artist's paint brush. If the pollen is not available, the styles need to be re-covered for a few days until enough pollen is available.

Once the pollination is completed, cover the female flower with a paper bag for about two weeks, and then replace this with a muslin bag. The paper bag will protect the style from any unwanted pollen that might pollinate the female. It is important to be sure about which clematis is the pollen donor and this should be carefully recorded. If the pollination has been successful, the seed will begin to swell and a fluffy seed tail will start to develop. The muslin bag can then be removed and the seed will develop fully. If pollination has been unsuccessful, the seed tails will be very short and stunted, no seed will be visible and the seed tails will eventually drop away. Sometimes there will be only, perhaps, two seeds that develop, but with the most successful pollination some twenty to forty seeds may be produced.

The seeds should be harvested as soon as they are ripe enough. For guidelines, refer to the section on raising clematis from seed at the beginning of this chapter. However, do remember that clematis seeds are designed to be windblown—so after all your effort, do not let them get blown away before you harvest them. Though it may take time, your work will be rewarded. Good luck!

Appendices

US Department of Agriculture Hardiness Zone Map

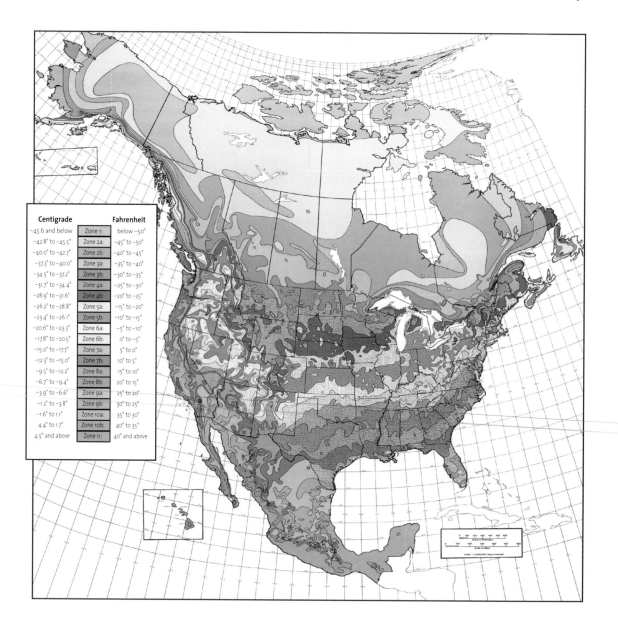

Centigrade		Fahrenheit
−45.6 and below	Zone 1:	below −50°
−42.8° to −45.5°	Zone 2a:	−45° to −50°
−40.0° to −42.7°	Zone 2b:	−40° to −45°
−37.3° to −40.0°	Zone 3a:	−35° to −40°
−34.5° to −37.2°	Zone 3b:	−30° to −35°
−31.7° to −34.4°	Zone 4a:	−25° to −30°
−28.9° to −31.6°	Zone 4b:	−20° to −25°
−26.2° to −28.8°	Zone 5a:	−15° to −20°
−23.4° to −26.1°	Zone 5b:	−10° to −15°
−20.6° to −23.3°	Zone 6a:	−5° to −10°
−17.8° to −20.5°	Zone 6b:	0° to −5°
−15.0° to −17.7°	Zone 7a:	5° to 0°
−12.3° to −15.0°	Zone 7b:	10° to 5°
−9.5° to −12.2°	Zone 8a:	15° to 10°
−6.7° to −9.4°	Zone 8b:	20° to 15°
−3.9° to −6.6°	Zone 9a:	25° to 20°
−1.2° to −3.8°	Zone 9b:	30° to 25°
−1.6° to 1.1°	Zone 10a:	35° to 30°
4.4° to 1.7°	Zone 10b:	40° to 35°
4.5° and above	Zone 11:	40° and above

Sales Names and Collections

The following clematis sales names belong to cultivars that
are protected by Plant Breeders' Rights or plant patents.

Clematis ALABAST
C. ANGELIQUE
C. ANNA LOUISE
C. ARCTIC QUEEN
C. AVANT-GARDE
C. BIJOU
C. BONANZA
C. BOURBON
C. CASSIS
C. CEZANNE
C. CHANTILLY
C. CHINOOK
C. CLAIR DE LUNE
C. CONFETTI

C. CRYSTAL FOUNTAIN
C. EMPRESS
C. FILIGREE
C. FLEURI
C. FRANZISKA MARIA
C. GALORE
C. GAZELLE
C. HARLOW CARR
C. HYDE HALL
C. ICE BLUE
C. JOSEPHINE
C. KINGFISHER
C. MEDLEY
C. OOH LA LA

C. PALETTE
C. PARISIENNE
C. PEPPERMINT
C. PETIT FAUCON
C. PICARDY
C. PISTACHIO
C. REBECCA
C. ROSEMOOR
C. ROYAL VELVET
C. SAVANNAH
C. VERSAILLES
C. VICTOR HUGO
C. VIENNETTA
C. WISLEY

The Evison and Poulsen Clematis Collections described in this
book are as follows.

The Boulevard® Collection
Clematis ANGELIQUE
　'Evipo017'
C. CEZANNE 'Evipo023'
C. CHANTILLY 'Evipo021'
C. FLEURI 'Evipo042'
C. OOH LA LA 'Evipo041'
C. PARISIENNE 'Evipo019'
C. PICARDY 'Evipo024'

The Festoon™ Collection
Clematis AVANT-GARDE
　'Evipo033'
C. BONANZA 'Evipo031'
C. CONFETTI 'Evipo036'
C. GALORE 'Evipo032'
C. PALETTE 'Evipo034'

The Flora™ Collection
Clematis BIJOU 'Evipo030'
C. FILIGREE 'Evipo029'

The Garland® Collection
Clematis CASSIS 'Evipo020'
C. PEPPERMINT 'Evipo005'
C. PISTACHIO 'Evirida'
C. VIENNETTA 'Evipo006'

The Prairie™ Collection
Clematis CHINOOK 'Evipo013'
C. GAZELLE 'Evipo014'
C. MEDLEY 'Evipo012'
C. SAVANNAH 'Evipo015'

The Regal® Collection
Clematis ARCTIC QUEEN
　'Evitwo'
C. CRYSTAL FOUNTAIN
　'Evipo038'
C. EMPRESS 'Evipo011'
C. FRANZISKA MARIA
　'Evipo008'
C. JOSEPHINE 'Evijohill'

Glossary of Plant Classification Terms

Family

Group of one or more genera that share a set of natural characteristics. Family names usually end in "-aceae". The limits of families are often controversial and unclear. Example: Ranunculaceae

Genus (plural form: genera)

Group of one or more plants that share a wide range of characteristics. Names are printed in italic type with an initial capital letter. Hybrid genera are denoted by a multiplication sign before the genus. Example: *Clematis*

Species

Group of plants that are capable of breeding together to produce offspring similar to themselves. Species are given a two-part name (binomial) printed in italic type. The first part, with an initial capital letter, is the genus; the second part is the species epithet, which distinguishes it from other species in the genus. Example: *Clematis alpina*

Subspecies

Naturally occurring distinct variant of a species, often an isolated population. Indicated by "subsp." in roman type, followed by the subspecific epithet in italic type. Example: *Clematis tibetana* subsp. *vernayi*

Varietas (variety) and forma (form)

Minor subdivisions of a species, differing slightly in their botanical structure. Indicated by "var." or "f." in roman type, followed by the variety or form epithets in italic type. Examples: *Clematis* florida var. *sieboldiana*; *C. montana* f. *grandiflora*

Cultivar

Plant raised or selected in cultivation; distinct variant of species, subspecies, varietas, forma, or hybrid, that retains distinct, uniform characteristics when propagated by appropriate means.

Denoted by (a) a vernacular name in roman type within single quotation marks following the binomial, or (b) if the parentage is obscure or complex, the vernacular name directly following the generic name.

Examples: (a) *Clematis montana* 'Freda'; (b) *Clematis* 'Nelly Moser'

Glossary of Horticultural Terms

Annual: plant that completes its life cycle in one growing season

Anther: part of the stamen that releases pollen, usually borne on a filament

Apex: tip or growing point

Axil: upper angle between a part of a plant and the stem that bears it

Axillary: borne in an axil

Basal: at the base of an organ or structure

Bedding plant: annual, biennial or perennial planted to provide a temporary display of foliage and/or flowers

Bell-shaped (campanulate): describes a flower with a broad tube terminating in flared lobes

Bicoloured: having two distinct colours

Biennial: plant that completes its life cycle in two years, growing in the first year before flowering and fruiting in the second

Botrytis (grey mould): fungus that cause patches of rot on stems, leaves, flowers and fruit

Bract: modified leaf at the base of a flower or flowerhead

Campanulate: see Bell-shaped

Climber: plant that clings or climbs by means of modified stems, roots, leaves or leaf-stalks, using other plants or objects as support

Compost: free-draining, moisture-retentive growing medium

Compound: consisting of several parts but still identifiable as a single unit, such as a leaf divided into two or more leaflets

Conservatory: glazed, heated or unheated structure attached to a house

Crocks: broken pieces of clay pot, used to cover drainage holes in containers in order to provide free drainage and improve air circulation to the roots

Cross: to create a hybrid through interbreeding

Cross-pollination: a process whereby the stigma of a flower on one plant is dusted with the pollen from a different plant

Crown: growing point of a plant from which new shoots arise, located at or just below the soil surface, at the junction with the roots

Cup-shaped: describes a flower that is hemispherical with the sides straight or very slightly spreading at the tips

Cutting: section of leaf, stem or root separated from a plant and used for propagation

Damping off: collapse of seedlings and young plants caused by fungi, which rot the bases of stems and roots

Deciduous: shedding leaves annually at the end of the growing season

Dentate: see Toothed

Die-back: death of a shoot, beginning at the tip, due to damage or disease

Dissected: see Divided

Divide: to propagate a plant by splitting it into two or more parts, each with its own section of root system, and one or more shoots or dormant buds

Divided (dissected): deeply cut into segments or lobes (usually referring to leaves)

Dormancy (resting period): suspension of active growth in unfavourable conditions

Double: a flower with several layers of petals or sepals

Dwarf: small or slow-growing variant of a species or cultivar resulting from hybridization or mutation

Evergreen: retaining leaves for more than one growing season

Fertilization: sexual fusion of male and female elements, initiating seed development

Fertilizer: nutrients added to soil or potting compost to promote the vigour of a plant

Filament: stalk of the stamen attached to the anther

Flower-stalk (pedicel): stalk supporting an individual flower singly or in a flowerhead

Frost-hardy (hardy): able to withstand temperatures down to 23°F (−5°C)

Frost-tender (tender): may be damaged by temperatures below 41°F (5°C)

Germination: physical and chemical changes that occur as a seed begins to develop into a young plant

Glabrous: smooth and hairless

Glasshouse: see Greenhouse

Glaucous: with a blue-green, blue-grey, grey, or white coating

Globose/Globular: see Spherical

Grafting: method of propagation by which the stem of one plant and root-stock of another are artificially united so that they eventually function as one plant

Greenhouse (glasshouse): structure glazed with glass or plastic, providing a controlled environment

Grey mould: see Botrytis

Growing point: tip of a shoot from which new extension growth develops

Growing season: part of the year when a plant is in active growth

Grow on: to grow young plants to a stage where they are ready to plant out or flower

Habit: characteristic form, appearance or mode of growth of a mature plant

Habitat: natural environment in which a plant occurs in the wild

Half-hardy: able to withstand temperatures down to 32°F (0°C)

Harden off: to acclimatize young plants reared in a protective environment to cooler conditions outdoors by gradually introducing them to a cooler environment

Hardiness: capacity of a cultivated plant to tolerate low temperatures

Hardy: see Frost-hardy

Herbaceous border: area of land set aside for cultivation of herbaceous plants

Herbaceous plant: non-woody plant that dies back (loses top growth and becomes dormant) at the end of the growing season, over-wintering by means of underground rootstocks

Houseplant: any plant grown for long periods indoors, often frost-tender species

Hybrid (see also Cross): naturally or artificially produced offspring of genetically distinct parents

Internode: section of stem between two nodes

Lanceolate/Lance-shaped: broadest below the centre, tapering to a narrow tip

Layering: method of propagation whereby a stem is pegged into the soil while still attached to the parent plant, to induce rooting

Leaf-axil: angle formed between a leaf or leaf-stalk and the stem of a plant

Leaflet: single division of a compound leaf

Leaf-stalk (petiole): connection between leaf-blade and stem or branch

Liquid feed: water-diluted solution of fertilizers, often used for houseplants or plants growing in containers outdoors

Loam: highly fertile, well-drained but moisture-retentive soil

Mixed border: area in which herbaceous plants, annuals, bulbs and shrubs are grown

Mulch: layer of material spread on the top of the soil around plants

Mutation: see Sport

Native: species that naturally grows wild in a particular area or country

Naturalized: species that apparently grows wild in a particular area, but is introduced and not native

Nodding: describes a flower that hangs down from a curved flower-stalk

Node: point on a stem, sometimes swollen, at which leaves, leaf buds and shoots arise

Nutrients: minerals necessary for healthy metabolism and growth

Ovary: female organ of a flower

Palmate: describes a compound leaf that is fully divided into leaflets arising from a single basal point

Panicle: freely branched flowerhead, with youngest flowers near the tip

Pedicel: see Flower-stalk

Pendulous: hanging downwards

Perennial: plant that lives for more than two growing seasons; in horticulture, usually applied to non-woody plants (herbaceous perennials)

Perlite: light granules of volcanic minerals added to soil, potting or seed compost to improve aeration

Petal: modified leaf that makes up flower, generally brightly coloured

Petaloid: describes a plant part that is similar to a petal in shape, colour and texture

Petiole: see Leaf-stalk

Pinch out (soft pinch, stop): to remove soft growing points to encourage the bushy growth of side-shoots

Pinnate: describes a compound leaf with leaflets arranged alternately or in opposite pairs on a central axis, with or without a terminal leaflet

Pollen: grains released from anthers containing the male element necessary for fertilization

Pollination: transfer of pollen from anthers to stigma of same or different flower

Pompom: describes a roughly spherical flower with tightly packed florets that are often curved inwards

Pot on (repot): to remove a plant from an outgrown container and place it with fresh compost in a larger container, with room for further growth

Pot up: to insert a seedling or rooted cutting into potting compost in a container

Prick out: to transfer seedlings or small cuttings from where they have been propagated into appropriate containers and compost, where they will have room to grow

Propagate: to increase plants by seed or by vegetative means

Prostrate: describes a plant with spreading or trailing stems lying flat on the ground

Prune: to remove unwanted growth from woody and non-woody plants in order to maintain health, control size, train to a desired shape, or stimulate growth or flowers

Recurved: arched backwards

Reflexed: arched or bent sharply back upon itself

Repot: see Pot on

Reproduction: producing new individuals by either sexual or asexual (vegetative) methods

Resting period: see Dormancy

Ripening: maturing of young shoots (wood) on trees and shrubs

Root: 1) Part of plant, usually underground. 2) To insert cuttings into a compost where they will produce roots

Root ball: mass of roots and accompanying soil or compost visible when a plant is lifted

Rootstock: 1) The crown and root system of herbaceous perennial, from which new plants arise. 2) The understock on grafted plants such as fruit trees

Scandent: describes a plant that climbs by means of flexible stems that grow over or through supports, attaching themselves loosely, if at all

Scree: slope of unstable rocky fragments that have slid down a hillside or at bottom of a rockface, retaining little moisture

Scrub: habitat with poor or dry soil, covered with bushes and small trees

Seed: ripened, fertilized ovule containing dormant embryo capable of developing into an adult plant

Seedhead: dry fruit that contains ripe seed

Seedling: young plant raised from seed

Self-coloured: describes a flower with a uniform colour

Semi-double: describes a flower with two or three times the number of petals or sepals of a single flower

Sepal: outer part of the flower, usually green and smaller than petals, sometimes colourful and petal-like, as in clematis

Serrate: describes a fully toothed margin, usually of a leaf

Set: refers to fertilized flowers that have developed fruit

Sharp drainage: very free movement of excess water through the soil

Shoot: first, erect growth of a seedling before it becomes a stem

Shrub: deciduous or evergreen perennial with multiple woody stems or branches

Simple: describes a leaf with a continuous surface, not divided into leaflets

Single: a flower with the normal number of petals or sepals for the species or cultivar

Soft pinch: see Pinch out

Solitary: describes a flower borne singly

Specimen plant: ornamental plant grown in a prominent position

Spherical (globose/globular): describes a round or almost round solid form

Sport (mutation): natural or induced genetic change

Stamen: male part of a flower, composed of an anther, normally borne on a filament

Staminode: sterile, modified stamen that can resemble a narrow sepal

Star-shaped (stellate): describes a flower with widely spaced, narrow sepals that radiate from the centre

Stellate: see Star-shaped

Sterile: describes any flower incapable of producing seeds

Stigma: tip of female reproductive organ that receives pollen to fertilize ovule in ovary

Stop: see Pinch out

Sub-shrub: a plant that is woody-based although the terminal shoots die back in winter

Synonym: name or epithet that is not the accepted one for the plant

Tender: see Frost-tender

Tendril: coiling, thread-like modified leaf, leaflet or shoot used by a climbing plant to attach itself to an adjacent support

Terminal: located at the end of a stem, shoot or other organ

Ternate: arranged in groups of three around a common axis

Toothed (dentate): describes a margin, usually of a leaf, with tooth-like triangular indentations

Tree: woody perennial with a crown of branches developing from the top of a single stem

Trifoliate: describes leaves that arise in groups of three from a single point

True: describes a plant that virtually reproduces the characteristics of the parents when raised from seed

Tubular: describes a flower with sepals fully or partially fused to form a hollow tube

Urn-shaped: describes a cylindrical or tubular flower contracted at or just below the mouth

Variegation: irregular arrangement of pigments

Vegetative propagation: asexual techniques for increasing plants

Woody: describes the fibrous stems of certain perennials, such as trees and shrubs, that persist above ground throughout the year

Bibliography

Evison, R.J. 1997, revised paperback 2005. *The Gardener's Guide to Growing Clematis*. David & Charles/Timber Press.

Grey-Wilson, C. 2000. *Clematis: The Genus: A Comprehensive Guide for Gardeners, Horticulturalists and Botanists*. Batsford Ltd./Timber Press.

The Royal Horticultural Society. 2002. *The International Clematis Register and Checklist*. The Royal Horticultural Society.

The Royal Horticultural Society. 2004. *The International Clematis Register and Checklist: First Supplement*. The Royal Horticultural Society.

The Royal Horticultural Society. 2006. *The International Clematis Register and Checklist: Second Supplement*. The Royal Horticultural Society.

The Royal Horticultural Society. 1998, reprinted with corrections 2003. *A–Z Encyclopedia of Garden Plants*. Dorling Kindersley.

The Royal Horticultural Society. 2006. *Plant Finder 2006–2007*. The Royal Horticultural Society/Dorling Kindersley.

Plant Index

Page numbers in **bold face** point to plant directory entries, while page numbers in *italics* indicate illustrations.